Original Sin

Also by Jake Tapper

All the Demons Are Here

The Devil May Dance

The Hellfire Club

The Outpost: An Untold Story of American Valor

Down and Dirty: The Plot to Steal the Presidency

Body Slam: The Jesse Ventura Story

ORIGINAL SIN

President Biden's Decline, Its Cover-Up, and
His Disastrous Choice to Run Again

JAKE TAPPER AND ALEX THOMPSON

HUTCHINSON
HEINEMANN

HUTCHINSON HEINEMANN

UK | USA | Canada | Ireland | Australia
India | New Zealand | South Africa

Hutchinson Heinemann is part of the Penguin Random House group of companies
whose addresses can be found at global.penguinrandomhouse.com

Penguin Random House UK, One Embassy Gardens,
8 Viaduct Gardens, London SW11 7BW

penguin.co.uk
global.penguinrandomhouse.com

First published in the US by Penguin Press 2025
First published in the UK by Hutchinson Heinemann 2025
001

DESIGNED BY MEIGHAN CAVANAUGH

Printed and bound in Great Britain by Clays Ltd, Elcograf S.p.A.

The authorised representative in the EEA is Penguin Random House Ireland,
Morrison Chambers, 32 Nassau Street, Dublin D02 YH68

A CIP catalogue record for this book is available from the British Library

ISBN: 978–1–529–15548–8 (hardback)
ISBN: 978–1–529–15549–5 (trade paperback)

Penguin Random House is committed to a sustainable future
for our business, our readers and our planet. This book is made
from Forest Stewardship Council® certified paper.

To Jennifer, Alice, and Jack
You are my everything.

—Jᴀᴋᴇ

To Mom and Dad
Thanks for putting up with me.

—Aʟᴇx

Tho' much is taken, much abides; and tho'
We are not now that strength which in old days
Moved earth and heaven, that which we are, we are;
One equal temper of heroic hearts,
Made weak by time and fate, but strong in will
To strive, to seek, to find, and not to yield.

—*"Ulysses," Alfred Lord Tennyson*

They told me I was everything; 'tis a lie,
I am not ague-proof.

—King Lear, *William Shakespeare*

CONTENTS

AUTHORS' NOTE

Our only agenda is to present the disturbing reality of what happened in the White House and the Democratic presidential campaign in 2023–2024, as told to us by approximately two hundred people, including lawmakers and White House and campaign insiders, some of whom may never acknowledge speaking to us but all of whom know the truth within these pages. Most of the information laid out in this book was shared with us *after* the election of 2024, when officials and aides felt considerably freer to talk. There are very few people named herein with whom we didn't speak.

Our most important sources were Democrats inside and outside the White House who were grappling with how so many of them had been so focused on convincing voters that Donald Trump was a true existential threat to the nation that they put blinders on, participating in a charade that delivered the election directly into Trump's hands.

Some spoke to us with regret that they hadn't done more, or that they had waited so long to talk to the press about what was going on behind the scenes. Many were angry and felt deeply betrayed, not just by Biden but by his inner circle of advisers, his allies, and his family. They had seen bad moments behind the scenes but had been assured all was well. And then came the debate.

Readers who are convinced that Joe Biden was little more than a husk from the very beginning of his presidency, barely capable of stringing two sentences together, will not find support for that view here. Nor will this book satisfy those seeking comfort that he was, through to the end, unaddled and perfectly capable of being president twenty-four seven; that his rumored deterioration was all right-wing propaganda. This is also false. As Biden's presidency ended, it was difficult to find many top Democrats outside his immediate circle of family and closest aides who thought he could ably serve a second four-year term.

This book is not an exoneration of the candidacy or presidencies of Biden's opponent, Donald Trump. Journalism about Biden does not excuse or normalize any actions and statements by anyone else, including the forty-fifth and now forty-seventh president. Indeed, for those who tried to justify the behavior described here because of the threat of a second Trump term, those fears should have shocked them into reality, not away from it.

The lessons from this book go beyond one man and one political party. They speak to more universal questions about cognitive dissonance, groupthink, courage, cowardice, and patriotism.

George Orwell once wrote that "we are all capable of believing things which we *know* to be untrue, and then, when we are finally proved wrong, impudently twisting the facts so as to show that we were right. Intellectually, it is possible to carry on this process for an indefinite time: the only check on it is that sooner or later a false belief bumps up against solid reality, usually on a battlefield."

He was writing about World War II, but he could have been writing about any time, any era. "The Germans and the Japanese lost the war quite largely because their rulers were unable to see facts which were plain to any dispassionate eye," Orwell went on. "To see what is in front of one's nose needs a constant struggle."

Here is what was in front of our noses.

—Jake and Alex

Original Sin

"He Totally Fucked Us"

President Joe Biden got out of bed the day after the 2024 election convinced that he had been wronged.

The elites, the Democratic officials, the media, Nancy Pelosi, Barack Obama—they shouldn't have pushed him out of the race. If he had stayed in, he would have beaten Donald Trump. That's what the polls suggested, he would say again and again.

His pollsters told us that no such polls existed.

There was no credible data, they said, to support the notion that he would have won. All unspun information suggested it would have been a loss, likely a spectacular one, far worse than that suffered by his replacement as Democratic nominee, Vice President Kamala Harris.

The disconnect between Biden's optimism and the unhappy reality of poll results was a constant throughout his administration. Many insiders sensed that his inner circle shielded him from bad news.

It's also true that for Biden to absorb those poll results, he would have had to face the biggest issue driving them: The public had concluded—long before most Democratic officials, media, and other "elites" had—that he was far too old to do the job. In truth, before that consequential June 27, 2024, presidential debate, many insiders—people with a much better window into Biden's condition than the wider public had—saw things that shocked them. Most of them said nothing.

President Biden awoke the morning after the election sure that he was not to blame.

Two and a half miles away, north on Connecticut Avenue Northwest, then west on Massachusetts, Harris walked solemnly into the dining room of the vice president's residence at the US Naval Observatory.

She was joined that morning by her husband, Doug Emhoff; her sister, Maya; and her brother-in-law Tony West. They were incredulous. It was real. It wasn't a nightmare. It had really happened.

They knew that they'd been running from behind, that their challenge had been considerable: They'd had only 107 days to convince America that the vice president to a historically unpopular president would be a change agent. They had hoped that the margin of error in the polls they saw would break their way. The enthusiasm they felt on the trail was tangible. They were hopeful.

But overnight, the TV networks had called the race for Trump.

Sitting at the breakfast table, Harris knew she would have to call the president-elect and concede. And then she would have to finish the speech she never wanted to give.

Victory has a hundred fathers and defeat is an orphan, so goes an old saying President John F. Kennedy invoked after the Bay of Pigs fiasco. Few Democrats were running around claiming paternity of the political wipeout that was the 2024 campaign.

No one thought that the Harris campaign had been without error.

But for the most knowledgeable Democratic officials and donors, and for top members of the Harris campaign, there was no question about the father of this election calamity: It was Joe Biden.

Harris, loyal to Biden to a fault, might never say such a thing. But plenty of people around her would.

"We got so screwed by Biden as a party," David Plouffe, who helped run the Harris campaign, told us.

Plouffe had served as Senator Barack Obama's presidential campaign manager in 2008 and as a senior adviser to President Obama before largely retiring from politics in 2013. After Biden dropped out of the race on July 21, 2024, Plouffe was drafted to help Harris in what he saw as a "rescue mission." Harris, he said, was a "great soldier," but the compressed 107-day race was "a fucking nightmare."

"And it's all Biden," Plouffe said. Referring to Biden's decision to run for reelection, then wait more than three weeks to bow out, Plouffe added: "He totally fucked us."

This isn't the typical finger-pointing of a losing campaign.

Before the 2020 primaries, in December 2019, four Biden advisers—in what *Politico* reporter Ryan Lizza read as a strategic leak to get the idea out into the open—told Lizza that it would be "virtually inconceivable that he will run for reelection in 2024, when he would be the first octogenarian president."

"Look, I view myself as a bridge, not as anything else," Biden reiterated in March 2020 as he was on the verge of capturing the Democratic nomination.

Instead, supported by his senior advisers and his wife and family, the oldest president in American history announced in April 2023 that he would run again. This meant potentially being president until he was eighty-six.

The real issue wasn't his age per se. It was the clear limitations of his abilities, which got worse throughout his presidency. What the public saw of the realities of his functioning was concerning. What was going on in private was worse.

While Biden on a day-in, day-out basis could certainly make decisions and assert wisdom and act as president, there were several significant issues that complicated his presidency: a limit to the hours in which he could reliably function and an increasing number of moments where he seemed to freeze up, lose his train of thought, forget the names of top aides, or momentarily not remember friends he'd known for decades. Not to mention impairments to his ability to communicate—ones unrelated to his lifelong stutter.

It wasn't a straight line of decline; he had good days and bad. But until the last day of his presidency, Joe Biden and those in his innermost circle refused to admit the reality that his energy, cognitive skills, and communication capacity had faltered significantly. Even worse, through various means, they tried to hide it.

The original sin of Election 2024 was Biden's decision to run for reelection—followed by aggressive efforts to hide his cognitive diminishment.

And then came the June 27 debate against Trump, when Biden's decline was laid bare before the world.

It was not just one bad night, as Biden and his team claimed in the aftermath. Millions were shocked by Biden's unintelligible, slack-jawed performance at the debate, but some Democrats weren't surprised at all. Though they had seen him like this behind closed doors, they didn't say anything. For a variety of reasons, they rationalized their silence.

As a result, Democrats stumbled into the fall of 2024 with an untested nominee and growing public mistrust of a White House that had been gaslighting the American people. With only three and a half months to run a campaign against a candidate and machine that had been going pretty much full speed since 2015, Harris was fearful of distancing herself from her boss and publicly unable to acknowledge what the world continued to witness of his decline.

Harris made plenty of mistakes, both before Biden became a candidate and afterward, but no decision that she and her campaign made was anywhere near as consequential as his decision to run for reelection and pretend he wasn't mentally melting before our eyes.

"It was an abomination," one prominent Democratic strategist— who publicly defended Biden—told us. "He stole an election from the Democratic Party; he stole it from the American people."

Biden had framed his entire presidency as a pitched battle to prevent Trump from returning to the Oval Office. By not relinquishing power and being honest with himself and the country about his decline, he guaranteed it.

ANOTHER TOP DEMOCRAT, one who spent much of 2023 and early 2024 publicly and privately defending the president and his acuity, spoke with White House and campaign officials regularly and received constant reassurance. "He's fine, he's fine, he's fine," they all said.

This was the experience of dozens of officials, from politicians to donors to left-leaning pundits.

In the spring of 2024, this Democrat called top White House officials. "Every day I'm defending this guy," the top Democrat told them. "Someone tell me he's okay. Like, it doesn't look great. The press conferences don't look great." He was reassured every time, the top Democrat told us. "Anita [Dunn] told me he was fine; [Jeff] Zients told me he was fine. [Mike] Donilon goes, 'I promise he's okay.'"

In 2024, after Biden withdrew from the race, this Democrat privately met with the First Couple and saw the reality with their own eyes.

"He was not fine. She [the First Lady] had to complete some of his thoughts. It was not fine. I got emotional leaving the White House because he was clearly not fucking fine."

The Democrat says they want to believe that Biden's top aides "weren't intentionally deceitful. I think sometimes people think the best. I think the theory was always 'He's a gamer; he's going to deliver.' And I think they believed that. But when you're with him every day, they had to have moments like I had with him, where you were like, 'Whoa, this is not okay.' And at some point, you shut the door and say, 'Hey, you're not up to this.'"

Trump ended up winning the Electoral College by 312 to 226 electoral votes, and he secured the popular vote by more than 2.2 million. But the race was closer than those numbers suggest. Harris lost the three key "Blue Wall" states by a total of roughly 230,000 votes. If she had beat the margins of 1.44 percent in Michigan, 1.73 percent in Pennsylvania, and 0.87 percent in Wisconsin, she would be president today.

Ponder the question that Democrats such as Harris and others who might have run in 2024—Secretary of Transportation Pete Buttigieg, Senator Amy Klobuchar of Minnesota, Governor Gavin Newsom of California, Governor JB Pritzker of Illinois, Governor Gretchen Whitmer of Michigan—replay in their minds: If Biden had not run for reelection, or if he had acknowledged his decay and changed his mind about it in 2023, what would have happened?

If history is any guide, a competitive primary and caucus process would have produced a stronger Democratic nominee, one who had more experience with debates and taking questions from reporters, one with a more cogent and precise answer as to why they were running, one with time to introduce themselves to the American people. Past flip-flops on issues would have been addressed, policy proposals would have been fleshed out, winning messages would have been formed. The nominee would have figured out a way to respectfully but forcefully distance themselves from the unpopular incumbent president and forge a new path, representing change.

Would that candidate have been able to do 1.5 percentage points better in Michigan, 1.8 points better in Pennsylvania, and 0.9 points better in Wisconsin?

To the Plouffes of the world, it's hard to argue no.

"If Biden had decided in 2023 to drop out, we would have had a robust primary," Plouffe said. "Whitmer, Pritzker, Newsom, Buttigieg, Harris, and Klobuchar would have run. Warnock and Shapiro would have kicked the tires of it. Maybe Mark Cuban or a businessperson of some sort. Twenty percent of governors and thirty percent of senators would have thought about it. We would have been eminently stronger."

Once it became clear to the world that Biden needed to drop out, Obama, former House Speaker Pelosi, and others pushed for some sort of open process in July and August. Biden's refusal to budge until July 21 and then his immediate endorsement of Harris meant that this, too, fell by the wayside.

THIS ISN'T HINDSIGHT. Everyone saw it happening.

Throughout 2023 and into 2024, Biden's gait grew stiffer, his voice softer. People would call Plouffe—the president looked frail and sounded weak. He would often do small fundraising events with the aid of a teleprompter and leave early. People ponying up big bucks would call Plouffe to ask if everything was okay. This wasn't normal.

Plouffe asked folks at the White House and in the party if they were sure he could win. Yes, they said, noting that Biden had beaten

Trump in 2020, that the election cycle of 2022 wasn't as bad as it could have been for Democrats, and that he was achieving FDR-level accomplishments. The Biden team also argued that if he didn't run, Vice President Harris would likely be the nominee, and they had little confidence in her abilities.

Plouffe found that theory bizarre. No one had any idea who might win a contested round of Democratic primaries and caucuses. If—*if*—Harris emerged victorious, that would be because of those political abilities they were doubting. The most enraging part of their anti-Harris argument? Biden was the one who had picked her to be his vice president.

It was 2023. Plouffe had retired from politics and his former boss, Barack Obama, was staying out of it. Biden was still pissed at Obama for not backing his possible presidential run in 2016, implicitly backing former Secretary of State Hillary Clinton.

Obama had never directly told Biden not to run, but he had encouraged his VP—still deeply grieving the loss of his son Beau—to focus on himself as a person. Plouffe had cautioned against a run—Clinton and Senator Bernie Sanders were way too popular—and Obama political director David Simas had presented Biden with polling that showed the improbability of a victory.

"The president was not encouraging" is how Biden had put it.

Folks in the Obama camp felt that they had spared Biden from a third presidential primary disaster following his 1988 and 2008 failures.

Then they rallied the party around him in 2020 because he had the best chance of beating Trump. He did, and many felt his was a presidency of accomplishment. Reviving the economy after COVID, getting vaccines into arms. A historic infrastructure bill. Boosting semiconductor manufacturing in the US. A bipartisan gun safety package.

In June 2023, Obama popped in on Biden for a visit. He wanted to kick the tires, make sure the old guy was still up to it. Biden seemed fine—old, still Biden, but fine. Obama cautioned that Trump would be a formidable foe because of the increasingly polarized nation, Trump's entrenched base, and the fractured media landscape.

"Just make sure you can win the race" is all Obama told Biden this time, notwithstanding any doubts.

What could Obama do? This was Biden's decision.

He was, after all, the president.

THESE ARE THE POLITICS, the what-ifs, of the original sin.

More concrete are the facts we uncovered about Biden's health and abilities; the silence of witnesses; the complicity of enablers; and the scheming of those who endeavored to hide it from others and from the public.

As of early 2025, Biden can still, of course, engage in a coherent conversation if he is prepared and rested. Former top aides insist his decision-making is sound.

But the hours during which he can perform are limited. Since at least 2022, he has had moments where he cannot recall the names of top aides whom he sees every day. He can sometimes seem incoherent. He is increasingly prone to losing his train of thought, occasionally speaking so softly that he cannot be understood, even if he's talking directly into a microphone.

The presidency requires someone who can perform at 2:00 a.m. during an emergency. Cabinet secretaries in his own administration told us that by 2024, he could not be relied upon for this.

What the world saw at his one and only 2024 debate was not an anomaly. It was not a cold; it was not someone who was underprepared or overprepared. It was not someone who was just a little tired. It was the natural result of an eighty-one-year-old man whose capabilities had been diminishing for years. Biden, his family, and his team let their self-interest and fear of another Trump term justify an attempt to put an at times addled old man in the Oval Office for four more years.

What was the extent of it? Who knew about it? Was it a conspiracy? We will let the facts speak for themselves.

"Get Up!"

To grasp how Joe Biden could have decided to run for reelection at his historically advanced age, one must understand Biden's own mythology. Even before one gets to his belief that he, and only he, was capable of defeating Donald Trump, consider the legend of Joe Biden and its grounding in exceeding expectations, defying odds, and surviving.

"Get up!" he wrote in his first memoir, *Promises to Keep*. "To me this is the first principle of life, the foundational principle, and a lesson you can't learn at the feet of any wise man: Get up! The art of living is simply getting up after you've been knocked down."

A lesson from his father, Joseph Robinette Biden Sr., who'd been knocked down hard but had "no time for self-pity." His dad struggled. Biden Sr.'s crop-dusting business on Long Island went bust, and he moved the family back to Scranton to live with his wife's parents. Destitute, Biden Sr. couldn't find work, so he started commuting to Delaware where he cleaned boilers and sold trinkets at the farmers' market, eventually moving the rest of the family to join him.

"Champ, it's not how many times you get knocked down," Biden Sr. would tell his son. "It's how quickly you get up."

"Get up!" Biden wrote, "has echoed throughout my life."

Get up!

The other kids in Scranton mocked Biden's stutter. In high school, they dubbed him Joe Impedimenta or Dash—not because of his speed on the gridiron but because he spoke like Morse code, dot-dot-dash-dash. Kids can be cruel; that's why Biden took time out on the campaign trail to talk to children who also had stutters. They needed to know that they shouldn't let the bullies define them by it.

Get up!

A little-known first-term New Castle county councilman in 1972, Biden took on Delaware's popular GOP Senator James Caleb "Cale" Boggs. He attacked Boggs for being old (sixty-three) and out of touch. No one thought he could win. And then he did.

Only about a month later came that horrible day when his brother Jimmy, in Wilmington, Delaware, called his sister, Val, who was with Senator-elect Biden in a Hill office that Senator Robert Byrd had lent him. "There's been a slight accident," Val told him. "Nothing to be worried about. But we ought to go home."

Biden's wife, Neilia, and thirteen-month-old baby girl, Naomi, had been killed in a car crash. "I'm sorry, Joe, there was nothing we could do to save them," he was told. Sons Beau and Hunter were banged up and in the hospital. It is hard to imagine the pain, the grief, the black hole in which Biden found himself.

Get up!

His 1988 presidential run ended in a plagiarism scandal before 1987 even ended.

A few months later, in February 1988, the headaches he'd been ignoring the previous year resulted in his being rushed to Saint Francis Hospital in Wilmington. His second wife, Jill, was told not to go into his hospital room because he was being given last rites. He had blood in his spinal fluid and a leaking aneurysm below the base of his brain. He was warned that the necessary brain surgery might cause him to lose his ability to speak. Jill pointed out that if he hadn't withdrawn from the presidential race, he would have been campaigning in New Hampshire at the time his aneurysm began bleeding and he wouldn't have stopped. "You wouldn't be alive," she said. "Things happen for a reason."

Get up!

His 2008 presidential run also ended in an embarrassing flop—fifth place in Iowa with less than 1 percent of the vote.

But the winner and eventual nominee, Senator Barack Obama, picked him as his running mate, and Biden became one of the most consequential vice presidents in modern history, at times more popular than Obama.

Get up!

In May 2015, Biden's son Beau died of brain cancer.

It crushed him.

His forty-five-year-old son, Hunter, spiraled into addiction and broke up his family. For the first time in decades, Biden said, he didn't know his purpose.

Get up!

Biden ran again in 2020. Obama didn't endorse him in the primaries and many in the media doubted him. But he won the nomination and beat Trump.

He saw himself as a man of historic achievements, akin to FDR and LBJ. America was flat on its back, and he saved the economy, he would say. Fifteen million new jobs! Eight hundred thousand in manufacturing! Unemployment under 4 percent for a record two years in a row! Infrastructure projects that would be felt for decades! The critics said it couldn't be done, Biden would say. The press, the doubters, the elites— none of them ever thought he could do any of it.

Get up!

So to think that aging or ailment would make Biden reconsider his run is to not understand Joe Biden and the true believers with whom he surrounded himself. Fate had spent the better part of the last half century throwing everything it could at him, the worst tragedies imaginable.

And every goddamn time, he got up. Every. Goddamn. Time.

To family and close aides, the mythology became almost a theology, a near-religious faith in Biden's ability to rise again.

And as with any theology, skepticism was forbidden.

As one reporter who has closely covered Biden told us, "Biden literally says, 'Keep the faith.' Which means to say, don't allow yourself to even question it. And it created a strange circle of groupthink where none of them would permit the other ones to demonstrate any doubt."

Part of that theology is made up of narratives of questionable accuracy. The image of Joe—aviators, ice cream, 1967 Corvette—as avuncular and Jill as warm. These are not universally held impressions among those who know them well.

The president was fond of using the formal family motto, of giving "my word as a Biden," but they had another, more private saying:

"Never call a fat person fat." It wasn't just about politesse; it was about ignoring ugly facts.

"Don't say mean truths" is how someone close to the family put it.

"The Bidens' greatest strength is living in their own reality," this person told us. "And Biden himself is gifted at creating it: *Beau isn't going to die. Hunter's sobriety is stable. Joe always tells the truth. Joe cares more about his family than his own ambition.* They stick to the narrative and repeat it."

From 2020 until 2024, all of this resulted in an almost spiritual refusal to admit that Biden was declining.

There were some aides who appreciated the president but did not share their colleagues' religious zeal. The Bidens' closest aides, they told us, essentially hid his deterioration from the public and from others in the administration.

One senior White House aide who left because they didn't think Biden should run again confessed to us that "we attempted to shield him from his own staff so many people didn't realize the extent of the decline beginning in 2023."

"I love Joe Biden," the aide said. "When it comes to decency, there are few in politics like him. Still, it was a disservice to the country and to the party for his family and advisers to allow him to run again."

THREE

The Politburo

2020

During an eight-day, grueling bus tour in Iowa in December 2019, Biden gave his aides pause. While doing prep, he struggled to remember the name of longtime aide Mike Donilon. "You know, you know," he said, groping for it. His aides side-eyed one another—Donilon had worked with Biden since 1981.

It wasn't the only time aides worried during the 2020 presidential primary. Biden's campaign team saw that he was not always the guy he'd been as VP. His debate performances had never been commanding, but aides now found themselves white-knuckling their way through them. And his team often shied away from tough interviews, even though Biden had spent his career being one of the most press-friendly senators. He struggled to communicate the way he once had.

In the office, campaign aides would whisper about how he was not always 100 percent, but there was no way to have that conversation with him or his most senior aides. It was almost taboo.

It was as if there were two Bidens. He'd have high-energy rallies and then events where his own staff winced at his meandering and subdued performance.

Still, Good Biden was far more present than Old Biden.

Some aides became alarmed, though, after that bus tour through Iowa in December. With the caucuses just weeks away, Biden hit the trail hard but had trouble bouncing back.

At events in Iowa in January 2020, aides privately noted that voters were seeing a diminished man who was not as he had been just two months earlier. Voters were coming out of Biden's events less likely to support him. Precinct captains disappeared or said no thanks after attending a Biden rally.

His team knew he wasn't the best speaker, but they believed that his decision-making remained sharp, and that he was the best candidate to defeat Trump. That's what mattered most in the end.

THOSE CLOSE TO HIM say that the first signs he was deteriorating emerged after the death of his beloved son Beau in 2015. Biden often referred to Beau—Joseph Robinette Biden III—as an upgraded version of himself. He was the heir apparent, groomed to be the Biden who would finally become president. An army officer and veteran of the Iraq war, a husband and father, Beau lived a mere mile away from his parents. He had twice been elected Delaware's attorney general, in 2006 and 2010, and planned to run for governor in 2016. By the end of 2012, Beau had already begun organizing for a potential White House run, hiring a national fundraiser and crisscrossing the country.

When Beau died from glioblastoma in May 2015 at age forty-six, Biden was devastated.

It was the rare funeral where he did not give a eulogy. He couldn't.

His grief seemed to break something inside him. A senior White House official at the time told us that "parts of Biden's brain and mental capacity seemed to dissolve like someone poured hot water on [them]. Anyone who spent ten minutes with him when it was clear Beau was going to die in those last six to nine months could see it."

Others close to Biden noticed it too. "Beau's death aged him significantly," said a longtime Biden confidant. "His shoulders looked smaller. His face looked more gaunt. In his eyes, you could just see it."

Biden's torment was compounded by his younger son, Hunter, spiraling into crack cocaine addiction. His and Jill's daughter, Ashley, also battled addiction.

Biden was intensely private about what was going on with his family, but aides could hear Hunter yelling at his dad on the other end of the line during phone calls between the two. When bad news about Hunter came—and it was usually bad—Biden would grow unusually quiet. He seemed to be losing both of his sons at the same time.

BEAU'S CANCER TREATMENT also demonstrated the Bidens' capacity for denial and the lengths they would go to avoid transparency about health issues, even when the person in question is an elected official, in this case the sitting attorney general of Delaware.

In the summer of 2013, Beau collapsed during a family vacation and underwent brain surgery to remove a tumor. "Beau's tumor was definitely glioblastoma. Stage IV," Biden later wrote about the postoperative findings. "It was a death sentence," Hunter wrote. Beau began limiting his public appearances that fall. He stopped doing extended media interviews. He appeared gaunt. He had a fresh surgical scar on his head and a new haircut with it.

In September, Biden and Beau's team internally debated how much to disclose about Beau—the vice president's son and a state's top law enforcement officer—but ultimately said nothing. In November, Beau told a local reporter that he had been given a "clean bill of health."

In February, Dr. Wai-Kwan Alfred Yung released a statement to *The News Journal* that echoed Beau. The attorney general, Yung wrote, had a "clean bill of health" after an exam.

The neurologist told the public that they had removed a "small lesion" from Beau's brain. In fact, it was a "tumor slightly larger than a golf ball," Biden later revealed.

Beau would remain the sitting attorney general of Delaware for the entirety of 2014, even as his family secretly flew him all over the country for a variety of experimental treatments. In April 2014, he began having difficulties with his speech. He would often enter hospitals under an alias: George Lincoln.

Beau's wife, Hallie, told people she didn't understand why they had to keep his illness a secret. Making it public likely would have led people to rally around the family. He was an elected official. But both Biden and Beau opposed disclosure.

At times, Biden also instructed his team to mislead the media about his whereabouts. They would publicly say that the vice president was going to Delaware for the weekend, then returning to DC the next week. That was technically true, but Biden sometimes flew to Houston, where Beau was receiving treatment, to be with his eldest son over the weekend.

Publicly acknowledging Beau's illness would make it a reality. It was them against the world.

THE POLITBURO

Every president arrives at the White House with a team of loyalists, but by any historical standard, Biden's inner circle was particularly insular. Not a lot of unwelcome light got through the cracks. The team solidified in 2015 amid Biden's grief.

In the 2020 campaign, titles meant little. There was technically a campaign manager, a communications director, and deputy campaign managers, but the ultimate decision-makers were a group of seasoned political veterans known internally by any number of nicknames, including "the Politburo": Mike Donilon, Steve Ricchetti, and the policy wonk Bruce Reed. They'd worked with Biden for many years, if not decades.

There were other close aides. Anita Dunn and her husband, Bob Bauer, joined the team in 2015 to help Biden prepare for a presidential bid, even as most of their colleagues from the Obama administration backed Clinton.

Donilon had been in the center of Democratic politics for decades, shaping dozens of campaigns, beginning in the late 1980s when he worked on the campaign of Douglas Wilder, the first African American ever elected as governor. Something of a loner, he was a man of few words and could be immovable when he had a theory of the case. A former pollster, he now often went with his gut. He had crafted Biden's messaging for 2020—"a fight for the soul of the nation"—even as the data supporting that approach was fuzzy at best. Donilon's brothers were also in the national spotlight; one had been a national security adviser for Obama, and the other was the spokesperson for the Archdiocese of Boston. They shared Biden's Irish Catholic working-class self-image. The president valued Mike Donilon's advice so much that aides would later joke that if he wanted, he could get Biden to start a war.

He was protective and admiring of Biden. When some expressed doubts about Biden running in 2016, Donilon would snap, "Don't take this away from him."

Ricchetti, an affable former lobbyist and an alum of the Clinton White House, had been Biden's chief of staff through Beau's illness. Ricchetti was also a friend, and all four of his children would end up working in the Biden administration. He'd often watch MSNBC's Biden-friendly *Morning Joe* and then talk about segments throughout the day—drawing eye rolls from others. He had good relationships with Capitol Hill, and was a talker.

Reed had grown up in Idaho, the son of a politician, and had been a Rhodes Scholar studying English literature and a speechwriter for Al Gore. He also had been a top policy aide to Bill Clinton and tried to stay in his lane. Aides described him as Biden's security blanket who tried to stay out of palace intrigue and not rock the boat.

In 2019 and 2020, the Politburo mostly approached concerns about Biden's age as simply a political vulnerability, not a serious limitation on his abilities. Ricchetti floated the idea that Biden commit to serving only one term.

Outside the Politburo but in that next concentric circle were Dunn, an expert in communications, and Bauer, a respected lawyer, who had both worked for the most powerful Democrats in Washington. They didn't have the almost familial ties that Donilon, Ricchetti, and Reed did, but Dunn and Bauer had more credibility with the Democratic establishment, including Obama.

Obama thought that too many leaders of Biden's 2020 campaign team were hangers-on and not world-class political consultants. In 2019, he expressed worry about their steering Biden's campaign. "He's my friend," Obama said at the time. "I love him; I don't want him to be humiliated."

In 2020 Biden was running to be the oldest president ever elected, and rival Democratic campaigns were not shy about trying to exploit that, peddling opposition research to reporters that made Biden look feeble.

And he struggled to campaign, coming in fourth in the Iowa caucuses, then fifth in New Hampshire. Some on the campaign believed it was over after Bernie Sanders came in second in Iowa and then first in New Hampshire and Nevada.

"I've got news for the Democratic establishment. They can't stop us," Sanders proclaimed before the Democratic establishment successfully rallied to stop him.

Many top Democrats, including Obama, believed that Sanders, a democratic socialist, could not beat Trump and would hurt Democrats downballot.

After the fading of more moderate candidates, such as former New York Mayor Michael Bloomberg, South Bend Mayor Pete Buttigieg, and Minnesota Senator Amy Klobuchar, Biden became the candidate of last resort for the establishment. At root, politics is a numbers game— Biden could get Black voters in big numbers, and the others couldn't. Party leaders such as South Carolina Congressman James "Jim" Clyburn threw their support behind Biden just before that state's primary and propelled him to a commanding win.

He romped on Super Tuesday, including in many states where he had barely campaigned.

Biden and much of his team saw their victory as an affirmation of themselves. Their theory of the case had been right, and the doubters had been wrong. They bristled when anyone suggested that they had also gotten a little lucky. The sweep created a new level of self-confidence that tuned out their critics.

BIDEN WAS CLINCHING the nomination, but his communications struggles continued. On March 2, he forgot the words of the Declaration of Independence: "We hold these truths to be self-evident. All men and women are created, by the, you know, you know the thing."

In April, he struggled to explain his plan for the coronavirus outbreak. "You know, there's a, uh, during World War II, uh, you know, where Roosevelt came up with a thing, uh, that, uh, you know, was totally different than a, than the, it's called, he called it the, you know, the World War II, he had the war, the-the war production board," he said, faltering.

Democrats remained publicly mum; Biden at any age was better than Trump.

THE COVID COCOON

It was terrible to admit, but Biden's own aides would say that while the COVID-19 pandemic was one of the worst things to happen to the world, it was one of the best things to happen to Biden's presidential hopes. They doubted Biden could have otherwise kept up the pace of campaigning through November.

As pandemic lockdowns became widespread in March 2020, Biden could avoid that grueling travel and campaign remotely from Wilmington. He could rest. Close aides pushed for events to start in the afternoon, if possible.

The isolation also changed the power dynamics of Biden's inner circle. Longtime aide Annie Tomasini and Jill's top aide, Anthony Bernal, moved to Wilmington. For the next several months, they were some of the only people to have consistent access to the nominee and were often the last people the Bidens talked to at night.

The duo, who had been with the Bidens off and on since the mid-2000s, had an older-brother-and-little-sister vibe. They worked around the clock and were intensely loyal. Their life was the Bidens, and the Bidens found them indispensable. They could quickly cut through the sometimes slow-moving Politburo to get things done. They were like family. Kind of.

Their instinct was to protect. During the COVID lockdown, they loaded a written Q&A into a prompter ahead of a local interview—a document that the campaign had used in prep with Biden. Campaign leadership confronted them to end the practice.

It put the campaign press team in an awkward position that fall, when they were forced to dodge questions about whether Biden had ever used a teleprompter during interviews.

Bernal and Tomasini's protective impulses were understandable; even in tightly choreographed Zoom calls with friendly audiences, Biden could step on a rake. The team was constantly trying to change the Zoom configurations and production designs to adapt to him. Aides privately noted that they couldn't rely on him to stay on message, and he often had a very short attention span.

THE 2020 CONVENTION

Meanwhile, the Democratic National Convention in Milwaukee was looming, and the team in charge of creating the content was grappling with not only how to do it during a once-in-a-century pandemic but also how to do it with an aged president whose communication skills were starting to founder. Programmers knew that one of Biden's great selling points, particularly in contrast to Trump, was his perceived empathy and ability to relate to regular folks in an authentic and compassionate way. It would be tough to do that during COVID, so a creative team worked up a plan. Biden would sit in a room with several monitors beaming the faces of real Americans in front of him so that they could discuss issues of importance.

The videos came back, hours of footage. Some on the team couldn't believe their eyes.

"The videos were horrible," one top Democrat said. "He couldn't follow the conversation at all."

"I couldn't believe it," said a second Democrat, who hadn't seen Biden in a few years. "It was like a different person. It was incredible. This was like watching Grandpa who shouldn't be driving."

A special team was brought in and told to edit the videos down to make them airable, if only a few minutes' worth. They had to get creative.

The racial-justice conversation aired the first night for less than five minutes, the health-care exchange on the second night for under four.

Edited, the videos likely appeared fine to viewers, Biden no worse than any other senior on Zoom. But two of the Democrats who were involved in the films' production together were dumbfounded.

"I didn't think he could be president," the second Democrat said. After what they'd seen, they couldn't understand how Biden could be capable of doing the job. "This was when some top Democrats entered an angry phase. I became disillusioned with the entire apparatus. Because what I was seeing on this video in 2020—that means people working for him every day see this."

From a distance of four years, the second Democrat reached a harsh conclusion about the team around Biden: "They've been gaslighting us."

Two other top Democrats thought the first two overstated the case, that the footage was lousy because the Zoom experience was awkward.

VIRAL CLIPS

Rob Flaherty, who served as digital director for the presidential campaign of former Texas Congressman Beto O'Rourke, joined the Biden campaign in December 2019. By then already aware of Biden's occasional verbal stumbles, he observed how quickly Republicans clipped any such moment—real or imagined, fair or unfair.

It is always tough to push back on misinformation, Flaherty knew. He also understood that for every unfair and bogus clip, there were real ones. The campaign convened a focus group to determine the best way to fight those videos. By blasting a targeted audience with images of Biden looking stronger and assertive, the campaign quelled doubts about his age, sowing new ones about the validity of the viral clips.

But the bogus videos were tough to counter because the underlying preexisting belief they reaffirmed—that Biden seemed old and prone to misspeaking—was true.

TRUMP WAS CHAOTICALLY managing the worst public health crisis in a century, but the election results were closer than the Biden team expected.

Biden earned seven million more votes but only won the Electoral College due to a margin of about forty-three thousand votes across

Arizona, Georgia, and Wisconsin—fewer than Trump had secured in his Electoral College victory in 2016. In the House of Representatives, Democrats lost seats, and the Senate majority was still undecided.

Despite those thin margins and mixed results for Democrats, Biden and the Politburo took the outcome as more reason to have faith in the Biden theology. Biden's age had been a top concern among voters, and he won anyway.

FOUR

The Bidenness

A complication for anyone struggling to discern the president's acuity as he aged was the Bidenness of it all. Since the 1970s, he'd had a reputation for being hot-tempered to staff and not remembering their names. He was known on the Hill for being congenitally prone to long stories, gaffes, and inappropriate comments.

"You cannot go to a 7-Eleven or a Dunkin' Donuts unless you have a slight Indian accent," he told an Indian American during his 2008 run.

In 2007, he called his primary opponent, Barack Obama, "the first mainstream African American who is articulate and bright and clean and a nice-looking guy. I mean, that's a storybook, man."

"I didn't take it personally, and I don't think he intended to offend," Obama told *The New York Times*. "But the way he constructed the statement was probably a little unfortunate."

When eventual nominee Obama tapped Biden to be his running mate, the campaign well knew what they were getting themselves into.

In 2021, this gaffe-prone reputation meant it was harder for people to figure out if Biden was having senior moments—not just for staffers and reporters but for world leaders. One former leader of a European country met with Biden during a UN General Assembly meeting and recalled the "meeting going on for an incredibly long time, maybe an hour and a half. We pretty much had to end the meeting; he just went on and on. It was like talking to your grandpa—he was slightly rambling." But, the former leader said, nodding to Biden's reputation, "he's always been a bit like that, hasn't he?"

This leader recalled meeting with the president again maybe a year later. He seemed even more rambling. "[Secretary of State] Tony Blinken had to remind him to talk about the crucial issue the meeting was meant to be about."

"I didn't think he should run for reelection; he was clearly not at the top of his game," the leader said.

Being close to the president on a daily basis made it even more difficult to recognize the extent of his dotage. White House and campaign officials referred to "boiling frog syndrome," an allegory about a frog placed in tepid water brought ever so slowly to a boil so that the frog doesn't perceive the change until it's too late.

The president's deterioration, the argument goes, was less discernible to those who saw him consistently and up close than to those who saw him only occasionally. Reporters, donors, and Democratic lawmakers who met with him only intermittently were increasingly alarmed, while top aides dismissively tossed out a "He's fine."

After the 2024 debate, one top adviser was stunned when he viewed side-by-side clips of Biden during a 2020 debate and Biden during the calamity of June 27, 2024.

But many of these same aides and advisers made accommodations to help the aging president appear at his best, becoming accomplices—knowingly or not—in what would be, by 2024, a cover-up.

It's worth noting that boiling frog syndrome is apocryphal. When scientists tried to replicate the parable in real life, their research subjects leaped out of the pot.

Confronted with unfortunate realities, people with proximity to the president had much more complicated decisions to make than did the frogs.

FIVE

"I, Joseph Robinette Biden Jr., Do Solemnly Swear"

2021

On the afternoon of January 20, 2021, the Politburo sat in the Oval Office, waiting for the president to descend from the Executive Residence. He walked in, sat down at the Resolute Desk, and opened the drawer to see the letter Trump had written him, as is tradition. Biden didn't share the contents but called it "shockingly gracious." Then he turned to the stack of executive orders that the Politburo had amassed for him to sign, many of them dealing with the pandemic. The country was in a bad place, and there was much to do.

Ron Klain was the newest addition to the Politburo—or rather a returning member. Biden's first vice presidential chief of staff, who had first worked for Biden in the 1980s, Klain was regarded as a turncoat by many in Biden's inner circle after working for Clinton's 2016 campaign when Biden was still thinking of running. He had done what was needed to return to Biden's good graces, and had a reputation for hard work, policy chops, and Hill relationships.

The rest of the Politburo also filled the top rungs of the White House along with their immediate family members. Reed's daughter started as Biden's day scheduler, Donilon's niece worked at the National Security Council, and Ricchetti's children would find jobs in the White House social office, the State Department, the Treasury Department, and the Department of Transportation.

But Biden showed a particular deference to Klain even though his chief of staff was often more progressive. Biden had deep respect for Klain's intellect. "Only one person here is smarter than me and it's Ron," aides heard him say.

Eager to deliver on the president's progressive promises made to unite the party after the primary, Klain steered the ship of state to the left of where Biden had been for most of his career.

Nine months later, Biden's $1.2 trillion bipartisan infrastructure package had passed the Senate and was finally approaching a vote with a narrowly divided and brutally partisan House. As far as House Speaker Nancy Pelosi was concerned, President Biden had one task on Friday, October 1, 2021, when she invited him to Capitol Hill to speak before the House Democratic Caucus: Ask them to vote for the bill—on its own.

Progressives in the caucus were pushing back. They wanted to tie the infrastructure deal to a larger package, a wish list called Build Back Better. They didn't want their ambitions for more far-reaching legislation to vanish.

The chair of the Congressional Progressive Caucus, Washington Congresswoman Pramila Jayapal, was skeptical that moderates would vote for the Build Back Better Act if they weren't forced to do so. The night before Biden came to the Hill, she told Klain that they didn't have the progressive votes for infrastructure without the two bills directly linked.

Those who disagreed with this strategy thought that the progressives were essentially hostage-taking and snatching defeat from the jaws of victory. Pelosi supported the Build Back Better Act, but she was also open-eyed about the fact that there wasn't enough support for it in the Senate to become law. She needed Biden to call for the entire House Democratic Caucus to unite behind the infrastructure bill, take the win, and then work on Build Back Better.

Biden spoke for roughly thirty minutes. It was a long, digressive speech. He quoted legendary Black Negro League then–Major League pitcher Satchel Paige, who had played into his fifties: "How old would you be if you did not know how old you were?" One House Democrat called Biden's remarks "incomprehensible."

And he left without making the ask.

Many House Democrats were confused. Progressives took it as a sign that Biden was with them. Years later, other House Democrats would see in the president's flawed presentation evidence of perhaps some communicative, if not cognitive, slippage.

Pelosi saw it as strategy—Klain's strategy. She admired Klain but knew he also liked being considered a hero by the Progressive Caucus. She didn't like to be surprised, and she had been surprised.

Negotiations continued, and continued to go nowhere. Democrats running for office that November—New Jersey Governor Phil Murphy, former Virginia Governor Terry McAuliffe, seeking to reclaim his old job—were intensely frustrated. Democrats needed to demonstrate what control of the House, Senate, and White House could mean. And here they were, dithering.

Pelosi beckoned Biden back to Capitol Hill the morning of Thursday, October 28. She hoped that this time he understood the job at hand.

He didn't. Biden praised the progressives in the audience and thanked them for pushing to raise the federal minimum wage. It was a curious thing to single them out for, given that almost all members of the House Democratic Caucus had been making the same push for years. Indeed, it was one of the first pieces of legislation that Pelosi had passed as the new House Speaker in 2007 and, while it was certainly in need of an update, it was hardly a controversial topic for the Democrats. She thought it a strange speech. "He was meandering and incoherent," a second House Democrat recalled.

"That's all I gotta say," the president concluded. "Let's get this done!"

"Everyone looked around," the second Democrat recalled. "Get what done? He hadn't asked us to do anything. He never made an ask. Then he starts walking away, and Pelosi gets out of her chair." She stood at the front of the room.

Thank you for that speech, Pelosi said. *The president is leaving now, and he is going overseas, and when he lands, I want the message to be that we have passed the infrastructure bill!*

House Democrats laughed knowingly.

A Pelosi staffer who was standing next to two aides to Klain saw one of them write to the other, "That's exactly the message Ron did not want said."

"Wow, that was stunningly ineffective," Congressman Dean Phillips of Minnesota said to colleagues at the time.

"He was bad at the caucus meetings," recalled a member of House Democratic leadership. "We wondered: *Did he forget to make the ask, or is this just him being a super-safe politician?* Between his stutter and aging, we were never clear what, exactly, was going on."

In 2024, after Biden's communication difficulties became impossible to ignore, House Democrats would disagree about whether these

October 2021 meetings reflected his confusion and decline. Many recalled meetings where he was on top of facts and figures, mucking about in the weeds of legislation. He was never a great orator, they would say.

Pelosi saw these events as evidence that Biden was doing what his chief of staff had advised him to do.

Klain had become one of the most powerful chiefs of staff in modern history. Republicans taunted Biden by calling Klain "the prime minister," but people inside the White House sometimes quietly called him that too. He steered and staffed the White House in a way that seemed contrary to Biden's centrist reputation. Klain would say he was merely trying to enact the bold progressive agenda that the president had campaigned on.

Either way, Biden and his team accomplished many significant legislative goals in the first year. The infrastructure bill passed the House on November 5, three days after the election, which McAuliffe lost and Murphy almost lost. President Biden signed it into law on November 15. Trump had repeatedly promised such a package but never came close.

Some pundits had mocked Biden for promising to govern in a bipartisan way, and yet nineteen Senate Republicans, including Senate GOP Leader Mitch McConnell, voted for the bill. To offset the progressive nos, Pelosi got the bill passed in the House with thirteen Republicans.

"Monday was an unambiguous victory for the central promise of Biden's presidential campaign: to lower the temperature in Washington and find places of common ground," Alex wrote at the time.

As he noted in an article for *Politico*, after the win, Biden indulged himself by reading a dossier of twenty-seven articles and cable news tickers that said his agenda was in trouble. DEMS STRUGGLE ON WAY

FORWARD AS BIDEN AGENDA STALLS, blared one chyron. BIDEN'S AGENDA STALLED AS HE BEGINS 8-DAY FOREIGN TRIP, proclaimed another.

Fools. They always counted Biden out.

TO MILLIONS OF AMERICANS, however, the most lasting memory of Biden's first year in office was the calamitous US withdrawal from Afghanistan in August.

The president ended the war, as promised, but thirteen US service-members and hundreds of Afghans were killed in the chaos as the Taliban recaptured power. He never communicated adequate regret, never fired anyone, and would react defensively when the issue was brought up. The topic could easily trigger his temper at his own aides.

His approval ratings sank into the low forties, then by the following summer the thirties, and never recovered.

"WHY DIDN'T ANYONE stop that?" the First Lady asked, chastising senior White House staff.

On the eve of Biden's first full year in office—January 19, 2022—the president had given a press conference.

It lasted nearly two hours. And long after he had crossed off every reporter on the list provided by his communications office, he went rogue, calling on James Rosen from the conservative TV channel Newsmax.

"Why do you suppose such large segments of the American electorate have come to harbor such profound concerns about your cognitive fitness?" Rosen asked.

"I have no idea," Biden said.

Staffers slipped him a piece of paper telling him to wrap it up, but he kept going.

Afterward, Biden, Klain, Communications Director Kate Bedingfield, and Press Secretary Jen Psaki went with the president into the Treaty Room to chat.

That was when the First Lady appeared at the door and blasted the staff for letting that go on for so long. The truth was, it was all Biden—some of his aides suspected he had done it precisely to show the American electorate whom Rosen had asked about that they were wrong.

"Where were you guys?" the First Lady asked, as if the president wasn't sitting right there.

The confrontation exemplified part of a larger change that aides had noticed in Jill Biden since 2016, when she was Second Lady.

In the past, she had been a reluctant political spouse. When Biden was considering running for president in 2003, she walked through a planning meeting in a bathing suit with NO scrawled on her stomach. As Biden weighed a run in 2015 after Beau's death, she was overwhelmed by grief and couldn't muster any enthusiasm for the idea.

After Trump won in 2016, aides noticed that she began saying yes to political events more often. By 2019, she was on board with Biden's bid for the presidency. She became a political partner in addition to a spouse. She saw herself first and foremost as his defender.

It was a reversal of roles for the two most influential women in Biden's life.

Jill and Biden's sister, Valerie "Val" Biden Owens, had always had a tense dynamic, each feeling that she held Biden's best interests at heart. Val had been campaign manager for all her brother's campaigns since 1972. She never had doubts about any of them until 2020. She wrote that she "didn't want the family to go through it. I was worried the family *couldn't* go through it. I worried about Hunter. The grandkids. And Joe."

But Hunter Biden was already going through it, and his troubles weighed Biden down. To understand Joe Biden's deterioration, top aides told us, one has to know Hunter's struggles.

As a three-year-old in the car accident that killed his mother and sister, Hunter had suffered a fractured skull—an injury that could have lifelong effects. He had emerged as a bottomless source of disappointment, gossip, and shame but still beloved by his family.

Beau and Hunter were tight, but there was an heir-and-the-spare dynamic at play. Beau was the chosen one while Hunter struggled to figure out his place and could not keep his addictions at bay. After Beau died in 2015, Hunter tried to fill the void. He told others he would run for mayor of Wilmington. He would pick up the family mantle; Biden supported him. It could help soothe the pain from the loss of Beau.

Instead, Hunter spiraled more wildly than ever before. In the four years after Beau's death, Hunter had gone through a bitter divorce, fathered a child he didn't want to acknowledge, shuffled in and out of rehab facilities, experimented with sobriety methods including yoga retreats and ingesting toad secretions, and carried on a made-for-tabloids affair with his recently deceased brother's widow in which he introduced her to crack cocaine.

In the winter of 2019–2020, Hunter was not okay and his family knew it. In desperation, Biden and much of the family staged an intervention in Wilmington.

"Not a chance," Hunter said when he realized what was happening.

"I'm so scared," Biden said. "Tell me what to do."

"Not fucking this," Hunter snapped, and ran out of the house in Wilmington. Biden ran after him and hugged him tight on the driveway in front of the family. Hunter said he would go to rehab—only to bolt from the facility.

As the Biden campaign got off the ground, Biden often didn't know where Hunter was. In the weeks after Biden announced his run, Hunter pulled himself out of his nosedive, got sober, and married someone he'd known for only a few days. They soon had a child they named Beau. Hunter had left a long trail of collateral damage in his wake.

Biden's other adult child, Ashley, had also been struggling with addiction for years. In early 2019 she was in an outpatient rehab facility and she relapsed days after learning that Biden was going to run. In July, she relapsed again. Hunter and Ashley stayed away from the campaign, but other members of the family picked up the slack, particularly Jill.

She weighed in on potential hires and reviewed many of the campaign ads before they were aired. She campaigned hard and peppered aides with questions about how many reporters would be at her events.

Anthony Bernal, Jill's top aide, had the title of deputy campaign manager—unusual for a staffer to a spouse. He had started out as an advance man for the Clinton-Gore campaign, orchestrating events for how the candidates would look on camera, and had worked in scheduling for Gore after he became vice president. Since joining her team in 2008, he had become her closest confidant and strategist.

With a sharp eye, he had worked over time to elevate her profile and glamour. He was the only staffer who called her Jill. He felt free to criticize her looks and outfits in front of others, and she appeared to want his approval, aides noted.

As Jill's power rose, so did Bernal's. Biden aides would say that she was one of the most powerful First Ladies in history, and as a result, he became one of the most influential people in the White House.

If Bernal made a request, the West Wing usually worked to make it happen. It wasn't worth fighting or second-guessing, Klain counseled people. "You don't fight city hall," he'd say.

He was a constant source of gossip about Biden's aides, which he passed along to the First Lady. He considered loyalty to be the defining virtue and would wield that word to elevate some and oust others—at times fairly and at times not. "Are you a Biden person?" he would ask West Wing aides. "Is so-and-so a Biden person?" The regular interrogations led some colleagues to dub him the leader of the "loyalty police."

The significance of Bernal and Tomasini is the degree to which their rise in the Biden White House signaled the success of people whose allegiance was to the Biden family—not to the presidency, not to the American people, not to the country, but to the Biden theology. They were the Bidens' eyes and ears, the keepers of the flame, the protectors of the myth. That included casting out potential heretics. Bernal, in particular, took on this role.

As we researched this book, it was difficult to find many Bernal defenders among those who have known him longest. He had allies among aides he had mentored but more detractors who resented his internal machinations. He freely trash-talked senior, mid-level, and junior aides. They thought Bernal was confiding in them, only to discover that he was insulting them to others. Some even described him as the worst person they had ever met.

Bernal knew he could be unkind. He would even acknowledge acts he wasn't proud of. But he loved the Bidens. Everything he did, seemingly every waking moment, was about them. He got the job done—that's all that mattered. "He would not be welcome at my funeral," one longtime Biden aide said.

On day one of his administration, Biden warned, "If you're ever working with me and I hear you treat another colleague with disrespect, talk down to someone, I promise you I will fire you on the spot. On the spot. No ifs, ands, or buts."

If the disrespectful behavior was on their behalf, though, the Bidens didn't seem to mind it so much.

BEAUTIFUL THINGS

Many Democrats and journalists averted their gaze from Hunter's tabloidy mess. Starting in 2021, his father no longer could.

In April, Hunter—eager to recast himself by shedding the perception that he was a ne'er-do-well junkie influence peddler—published *Beautiful Things: A Memoir*. Biden's senior team was unhappy about it. In their view, any day spent discussing Hunter and his antics was a bad day for Joe Biden.

The president's son thought he was politically sharper than most of his dad's advisers and often told Biden when he thought particular aides weren't serving the president well.

Aides had to pick their battles with Hunter.

Following the publication of his memoir, he planned to do a book tour through South Carolina, stopping at famed Black churches to talk about his crack addiction, but Biden's advisers pushed back. Though Hunter believed that he could provide some hope to those with loved ones battling addiction, Biden's advisers argued it would turn into a circus and come across as tone-deaf. Hunter relented.

Hunter's book is "organized around two parallel narratives: pervasive grief over Beau's absence and the unvarnished confessional of an addict," a *Washington Post* review observed. "Page after page features assertions of the brothers' closeness juxtaposed with gallons of vodka, bowls of crack, dissolute characters parading in and out of trashed hotel rooms—both five-star and no-star—and repeated failed treatment efforts."

Biden was shocked at some of the revelations, which were still only partial confessions.

"I didn't know the extent of any of it until now," the president told a top adviser.

Beyond the headlines Hunter's memoir generated, Biden's team had other sensible reasons to be worried. The president wasn't the only one learning new information. So was US Attorney David C. Weiss and his team. Weiss's team had been investigating Hunter's business activities since 2018—including seizing a laptop that Hunter had left behind at a repair shop in 2019. Biden had decided to keep Weiss, who was appointed by Trump, so as to avoid an appearance of covering up his son's malfeasance. The prosecutors pored over Hunter's memoir with interest.

HUNTER HAD ALSO caused a rift between the Bidens and the Obamas.

Barack Obama and Joe Biden's White House relationship began with typical tensions between a president and vice president, with slights both real and perceived. At Obama's first press conference as president, he was asked to respond to an errant comment that Biden had made. "I don't remember exactly what Joe was referring to—not surprisingly," he quipped, drawing laughter from reporters.

The relationship grew warmer over time. Obama's daughters and Biden's granddaughters went to school together. Obama delivered a moving eulogy for Beau and draped a Presidential Medal of Freedom around the vice president's neck. Their respective aides sniped at one another, but Obama and Biden had developed a bond.

The relationship took a more dysfunctional turn in 2015. Michelle Obama had become close with Hunter's then-wife, Kathleen Buhle. As Hunter began to spiral into addiction and infidelity, Michelle stood in solidarity with her friend, while the Bidens reflexively rallied around Hunter. When salacious details about Kathleen's divorce filing hit *Page Six* in early 2017, Biden was angrier at Kathleen for the details becoming public than he was at Hunter for his sleazy behavior. The Bidens slowly began exiling Hunter's estranged wife. And Michelle privately resented them for doing so.

That put Obama in an awkward position.

When he went to Biden-related events, he would usually go solo. In the fall of 2017, he attended a fundraiser in Wilmington for the Beau Biden Foundation, a children's advocacy group founded after Beau's death. Hunter also attended this event and appeared high or inebriated. He got into an argument with Biden's sister, Val, backstage and then left the fundraiser early. "Weird shit," Obama told someone soon after. (His office later denied it.)

In 2020, Obama began coordinating with the Biden team early on, while Michelle resisted campaigning. She didn't like politicking, but her feelings toward the Bidens were also a factor. Democrats had to privately argue that the stakes were too high for her to sit things out. She compromised by focusing on the nonpartisan voter registration group she'd formed in 2018 to avoid partisan politics. Her relatively light campaigning schedule didn't attract much notice, given the ongoing pandemic, but the Bidens noticed. On the staff level, the resentment ran even deeper.

DURING THAT FIRST YEAR, the pandemic made it easy to justify some of the barriers around Biden. He'd turned seventy-eight after the 2020 election and protecting him from COVID was a priority. The travel schedule was lighter. Meetings with Biden were often limited to small groups. He spent a lot of time in the White House residence.

Some on the Executive Residence staff—the small cadre of caretakers who look after the living quarters—felt that the barriers weren't just COVID-related.

Residence aides usually staffed the president's elevator. Biden's team told them that this would no longer be necessary. Many days, residence staffers would sit around twiddling their thumbs. They were often sent home early and informed that their services weren't needed. The official explanation was that the Bidens didn't like to be waited on, but the intense privacy was unusual, even for a First Family.

Bernal and Tomasini took on some of these roles. They had all-time access to the living quarters, with their White House badges reading "Res"—uncommon for such aides.

Residence staffers saw age taking a toll on the president, who often seemed tired. The famously garrulous politician could be quiet and didn't make small talk. At one point, Biden mistook a badge-wearing residence aide for one of his granddaughter's friends before the president's body man intervened.

"It was strange. In my head, I was like, *I see you all the time.* But he sometimes would look at you like he'd never seen you before," the aide recalled. White House staff "treated him as very delicate."

MANY OF BIDEN'S own aides were also kept at arm's length from the president.

Alumni of the Obama administration noticed the difference. Obama would hash it out with deputies and mid-level aides. Biden, by contrast, mostly met with the Politburo and his top national security aides.

Some of this was Biden's temperament. "Speaking Biden" was a particular skill, and some people just set Biden off. A meeting could easily get derailed, and then aides would have to reconvene without the person who had triggered the president. They noted that they sometimes spent more time on strategizing how to present the decision to Biden than on the substance of the decision itself.

Some tried to find workarounds to speed up the process. They would make the decision binary or sneak smaller items into the daily presidential brief in hopes that Biden would just say yes.

In practice, Bruce Reed was the real domestic policy adviser, Mike Donilon was the actual political director, Steve Ricchetti controlled Legislative Affairs, and Klain controlled a bit of everything.

He's nearly eighty, he knows what he wants, and we know how to handle him—that was the message sent internally.

All of these factors led to a uniquely small and loyal inner circle. Some felt that the insularity was the Politburo's way of protecting its influence. "Five people were running the country, and Joe Biden was at best a senior member of the board," said one person familiar with the internal dynamic. A cabinet secretary expressed a similar sentiment about the Politburo. "I've never seen a situation like this before, with so few people having so much power. They would make huge economic decisions without calling [Treasury] Secretary Yellen."

DOC O'CONNOR

On November 19—the day before the president's seventy-ninth birthday—the White House released the results of Biden's health examination by White House physician Dr. Kevin O'Connor.

The assessment was perhaps more notable for what it didn't include than for what it did: There was no mention of a cognitive exam. That seemed odd to physicians who were paying attention.

Many consider it standard practice to begin performing such tests when a patient turns sixty-five, even if they aren't showing symptoms. Several of the tests can be done in about ten to fifteen minutes. They do not provide conclusive diagnoses; rather, they are a tool for early detection.

It seemed appropriate to perform a cognitive test on a seventy-eight-year-old man—especially one who was starting to show flashes of memory loss, especially one who was president of the United States.

In 2017, when then-President Trump was seventy-one, Democrats in Congress introduced resolutions and legislation essentially pushing Trump to undergo a psychiatric evaluation, given his erratic behavior.

In early 2018, the White House physician gave Trump a short cognitive test called the Montreal Cognitive Assessment (MoCA), which can be used to detect early signs of dementia. Trump and his doctor—now a Republican member of Congress since 2021—claimed he aced it. The same Democrats who had earnestly voiced concerns about Trump were conspicuously silent about Biden's not taking a cognitive exam in 2021 despite obvious moments of mental slippage.

O'Connor told people that the ten-minute test was for physicians who saw their patients only occasionally, and he constantly saw the president. When others suggested doing the test to make sure that Biden was capable of being president, O'Connor would sometimes point to the Oval Office and say, "Biden's already being president." He'd add that people may not like how Biden was doing the job, but that was different than being incapable.

O'Connor's overall prognosis was bullish. "President Biden remains a healthy, vigorous 78-year-old male, who is fit to successfully execute the duties of the Presidency," he wrote.

Still, O'Connor detailed Biden's physical deterioration.

The president's "ambulatory gait is perceptibly stiffer and less fluid than it was a year or so ago," and he has "experienced increasing frequency and severity of 'throat clearing' and coughing during speaking engagements," he wrote.

Biden was old and had a shuffle, so O'Connor arranged for a neurological exam to see if his physical movements signaled a deeper disorder, such as Parkinson's. (Cognitive tests, by contrast, are about testing memory, language skills, and other functions.)

"There were no findings which would be consistent with any cerebellar or other central neurological disorder, such as stroke, multiple sclerosis, Parkinson's or ascending lateral sclerosis," O'Connor wrote.

Still, some doctors speculated that the only reason to perform a neurological test but not a cognitive one was if you feared the results.

People around Biden worried that O'Connor, whom almost everyone called Doc, might be too close to his patient. Doc O'Connor had been Biden's primary-care physician for thirteen years, since the beginning of his vice presidency, and had helped with Beau's treatment. A former army surgeon, he was a blunt, quirky presence.

He thought closeness to a patient—even the president—was an asset rather than a liability. He had gotten in Biden's face plenty of times and had the scars to prove it. He once counseled then–Vice President Biden not to make an international trip because "right now, you look like shit. I can't make you not look like shit."

He wasn't naive to the stresses of the presidency, and he privately expressed worry about the toll it was taking. He fought other Biden officials on scheduling to try to get Biden more rest.

O'Connor quipped that Biden's staff were trying to kill him, while O'Connor was trying to keep him alive. And no one had to look too hard around Washington in 2021 to see political figures whose decline was much more noticeable than Biden's.

SIX

"The Most Privileged Nursing Home in the Country"

In July 2024, Congresswoman Kay Granger, the first Republican woman to represent Texas in the House, cast her last vote in Congress at eighty-one years old and was then secretly placed in an assisted-living facility for patients with dementia. She (or her family) continued to collect her congressional paycheck; her constituents were not officially informed, and members of Congress who knew about it kept quiet.

Covering for an aging politician is commonplace in modern Washington, a town that has a long, gruesome record of powerful seniors trying to obscure their obvious infirmities—with the complicity of their colleagues, families, and staffs, who have turned a blind eye to these crises.

This context is not excusable, but it is part of the background of the Biden story.

After Senate Republican Leader Mitch McConnell suffered his second moment of seeming to freeze up, or glitch, while speaking publicly in August 2023, former GOP Governor Nikki Haley said: "The Senate is the most privileged nursing home in the country.... You have to know when to leave."

A life of power, fame, and relevance is not easy to give up. As four-time California Governor Jerry Brown bluntly put it to a Los Angeles TV newsman when reflecting on Biden's decision to not drop out sooner: "Politics is addictive. It's exciting. It's a kind of psychic cocaine.... People don't want to just go back to their former boring lives." Unlike athletics or entertainment or business, there are no coaches or producers or boards of directors to intervene—politicians are truly accountable only to their voters, who can be snookered.

There may be no world in which this toxic dysfunction is as tolerated—and consequential—as politics. South Carolina Republican Senator Strom Thurmond was perhaps the most notorious example. Thurmond served in the Senate from 1954 until retiring a few months before his death, in 2003—at age one hundred. The senior-most Republican senator since 1989, Thurmond was for many years the GOP's president pro tempore of the Senate—typically the senior member of the majority party, third in line to the presidency after only the vice president and the Speaker of the House. Beginning in the 1990s, it was a blatant lie, perpetuated by Senators from both major parties, that Thurmond was up to the task at hand.

In 1996, seven years before his death, Thurmond was, at ninety-three, referring to the Mexicans who attacked the Alamo as "Russians." Many who met him questioned his basic competence and cognition.

Progress in Washington, DC, on this front came when women senators were able to age into protected incoherence as well.

In November 2020, Senator Dianne Feinstein, an eighty-seven-year-old California Democrat, asked Twitter CEO Jack Dorsey the same question twice in a row at a public hearing. During that period, Senate Minority Leader Chuck Schumer, a New York Democrat, tried several times to encourage Feinstein to retire on her own terms, but she never did. She even seemed to forget that the conversations had happened.

Michigan Congressman John Conyers, Mississippi Senator Thad Cochran, West Virginia Senator Robert Byrd—the list of addled lawmakers, former and current, goes on and on. Why? Welcome to a system where power is distributed by seniority. And where spouses, children, staffers, and lobbyists invest deeply in the life and success of an individual politician, then grow reluctant to give it all up.

Presidents have been trying to hide or downplay politically problematic health challenges since the beginning of America. In George Washington's first years in office, he became so sick that it affected his eyesight and hearing. After Woodrow Wilson suffered a stroke in September 1919, his doctor, wife, and secretary maneuvered for over a year to conceal the damage from everyone, including his own cabinet.

Even in the glare of the television age, Republican and Democratic presidents alike have hidden the truth, and there's no law or oversight forcing them to be transparent. Newly elected president, John F. Kennedy in 1960 told a reporter that he did not suffer from Addison's disease—a lie. As the Cuban Missile Crisis unfolded, Kennedy was taking many drugs to help manage his various ailments. We still don't know when Ronald Reagan's Alzheimer's truly began.

The Biden cover-up may not be unique, but it is arguably the most consequential.

SEVEN

"Who Else Is Going to Do This?"

2022

Russia invaded Ukraine at dawn on Thursday, February 24, 2022. The Biden team had been publicly warning Ukrainian President Volodymyr Zelensky of the pending attack for weeks.

On March 26, in the midst of rallying allied nations to support Ukraine in its defensive war against Vladimir Putin's Russia, Biden spoke at the Royal Castle in Warsaw, Poland. "For God's sake, this man cannot remain in power," he said, speaking of Putin. After talking to Ron Klain, senior White House aides rushed to walk back the comment, which seemed a clear call for regime change.

Two months later, on a swing through Asia, Biden said something that appeared at odds with a long-standing US policy known as "strategic ambiguity"—essentially, trying to keep the government of China confused as to whether the US commitment to Taiwan, which China considers part of its territory, includes US military intervention.

Speaking alongside Japanese Prime Minister Fumio Kishida at the Akasaka Palace in Tokyo, Biden was asked: "You didn't want to get involved in the Ukraine conflict militarily for obvious reasons. Are you willing to get involved militarily to defend Taiwan if it comes to that?"

"Yes," Biden said.

"You are?" the reporter responded, surprised.

"That's the commitment we made," Biden said. His top advisers tried hard to hold their poker faces, as if he hadn't said anything newsworthy.

Aides fell back on the Bidenness to explain it.

"He just struggles to communicate nuance," one senior White House official told us. "First, he's not a great communicator, and second, when he feels something, he has a hard time pretending otherwise."

Travel is grueling on a president, of course. All the more so when that president is pushing eighty. The next month, White House aides intervened when they saw on the schedule a ten-day overseas trip, first through Europe and then the Middle East, including a stop in Saudi Arabia that was fraught with potential problems. It was too much, they ruled. The president went to Europe in June. He would do the Middle East in July.

Peter Baker of *The New York Times* reported that an aide thought the original ten-day schedule was "crazy."

Senior White House officials admitted that the president's age was obviously part of the considerations, but there weren't discussions of "he's too old to do this trip; it's more that the Saudi piece was complicated."

As Baker noted in his story, this was just one of many accommodations that the White House made for the aging president. Biden had given only 38 interviews at that point in his presidency, compared with 116 for Trump, 198 for Obama, 71 for Bush, and 75 for Clinton. By July, Biden had held only 16 press conferences—fewer than half as many as Bush, Obama, and Trump each held at the same point in their presidencies, and fewer than a third as many as Clinton held. Biden had once been one of the easiest quotes for Beltway reporters, and now he was being hidden away.

As Senior White House officials acknowledged to us, the first reason for this was that, yes, the president had lost a step in his communication abilities since his vice presidency. "Before Beau died, he was one hundred percent sharper," said one senior Biden White House official. "Beau's death wrecked him. Part of him died that never came back after Beau died. Was he the same guy he was in 2009? Of course not."

The second reason, of course, was the Bidenness.

The third was the president's obsessive need to prep for either interviews or press conferences, a demand for data and time and details. "He would demand hours and hours and hours of prep for one interview," a second senior White House official said. "You had to blow up the schedule for half a day. . . . Often, the feeling was 'We don't have time for this.'"

The fourth, said the first official, was "a strategic sense that the media landscape was dramatically different, and there was a lot of discussion about whether there was enough benefit to a long sit-down." Newspapers and TV news shows simply didn't reach the same massive audiences they had a decade before. So when it came to press conferences or interviews with legacy media outlets, "we were not going to get what we needed out of it, and so we weren't going to do it."

As the second official explained, "We saw press conferences as an outdated mechanism, and he wasn't good at communicating in those forums."

But foremost among the reasons was Biden's dwindling capacity to communicate. And this was only 2022.

"The presidency is about two things: making decisions and communicating those decisions to the American people," one senior administration official who worked closely with Biden told us. "The president's decisions were always solid and deeply considered. But the second part of that—communicating those decisions—that was never easy for him throughout his presidency, and in fact it got worse."

Someone else close to Biden, a senior White House official, conceded that a quick fifteen-minute interview Jake had done with the president in October 2022 would've been impossible for the president to pull off just one year later.

The accommodations that were in place by 2022—and the further isolating of the president—would continue as his decline accelerated the following year. Biden's staff and advisers had begun his presidency by helping to make it as positive an experience as they could for someone pushing eighty, and as they continued to do so, they also began grading him on a curve compared to his former self, something many of them acknowledged they did far more often in 2023 and 2024, when matters deteriorated to an alarming degree.

SPEECHIFYING

The White House's speechwriting team sensed Biden's limitations early on.

He flubbed lines more often. Longer speeches became more difficult.

Certain complex ideas just didn't quite land. It sounded like he was simply reading the words rather than selling the concepts behind them.

Everything got shorter: speeches, paragraphs, even sentences. The vocabulary shrank.

When Biden was struggling, he often reverted to his go-to lines, like wanting to "build the economy from the middle out and the bottom up, not the top down."

His speechwriters then tried to graft versions of Biden's catalog onto whatever issue they were talking about.

White House officials didn't order them to do it; rather, the speechwriters noticed what worked better. Their job was to make Biden successful. But they were also slowly adapting to Biden's diminished capabilities.

Though Biden had long overestimated his rhetorical gifts, he had at times been a rousing orator. When aides went back and looked at his old speeches, they realized he just couldn't do that any longer. He didn't have the booming voice. He didn't have the energy.

In Iowa, at an April 2022 event about ethanol, Biden plodded through a list of policy priorities but eventually admitted: "I'm starting to bore myself here. But this is important stuff, I think." Aides watching the speech knew how much effort Biden had put into prep but noted that even he seemed to sense he wasn't landing the argument.

It was hard to have explicit conversations about such issues because Biden was defensive about them. In 2020, when *The Atlantic*'s John Hendrickson, who has a stutter, wrote a compassionate piece that framed the president's verbal stumbles as the result of his lifelong stutter, Biden clearly hated doing the interview. He often talked about his stutter as something he had overcome. It was in the past.

Others in his administration were noticing it, however. As he struggled to communicate, his aides and allies noted that he began to increasingly rely on teleprompters and note cards. This even held true for private discussions, such as cabinet meetings.

Before these meetings, White House staff called the various departments and agencies to figure out what they were going to ask the president so that answers could be prepared. The conversations were largely scripted, even after the press had left the room.

Some cabinet secretaries felt that, in fact, Biden relied on the cards more heavily when reporters were absent.

Four cabinet secretaries spoke to us on the condition of anonymity so that they could be candid without fearing retribution.

"The cabinet meetings were terrible and at times uncomfortable— and they were from the beginning," Cabinet Secretary Number One told us. "I don't recall a great cabinet meeting in terms of his presence. They were so scripted."

In 2022 on a trip with the president when the idea of a reelection campaign came up, the official privately expressed bewilderment. "There's just no way. He's too old," the cabinet secretary told another member of the cabinet.

Cabinet Secretary Number Two said they hated "the scripts" for the cabinet meetings. "You want people to tell you the truth and have a real dialogue, and those meetings were not that."

But some Biden aides argued that cabinet meetings were always stilted affairs and a time suck. Biden was more probing in smaller meetings. They didn't sweat the occasional bad speech or his more frequent use of note cards. One speechwriter equated it to watching an actor adopt a bad fake accent for a movie role; over time, they just got used to it.

DAVID AXELROD, PART ONE

David Axelrod, a former White House adviser to President Obama, was not getting used to it. On the contrary, he was growing increasingly worried about what he was seeing from afar.

He and the president had a history. Axelrod and David Plouffe were the last two Obama campaign advisers to meet with Biden before then-Senator Obama picked him as running mate. On a private plane, they hopped from state to state to meet with the final three possibles: Indiana Senator Evan Bayh, Virginia Governor Tim Kaine, and Biden, who had run for president against Obama and dropped out after Iowa.

One of the campaign discussions about picking Biden went like this, Axelrod recalled: "Well, he's sixty-five years old, so he's certainly not going to run for president at seventy-three. So he'll be focused on the business at hand."

"I guess we were right," Axelrod would later joke, "because he didn't run until he was seventy-seven."

Biden seemed mad at both Axelrod and Plouffe after they advised him in the summer of 2015 not to run, but after Axelrod made some nice comments about Biden to a reporter in 2018, Biden reached out and asked him to swing by the house he was renting in Virginia. Axelrod agreed.

He was stunned by how much Biden had aged.

Back in the Obama years, Axelrod would often see Biden running on a treadmill at the gym on the White House grounds. He had been very athletic. And now here he was just two or so years later looking as if he'd aged ten years. His gait was stiff and slow, and he was speaking more softly.

"They're going to say, 'Well, what about your age?'" Biden told Axelrod that day. "What should I say?"

"I think it will be an issue," Axelrod said. "If you do run, I think the only thing you can say is the truth, which is, 'Look, I am old, but I hope that with age comes some experience and wisdom. And I think we need some of that right now.'"

When Biden's campaign began, Axelrod's concerns grew. The other candidates looked like they were in Technicolor, while Biden appeared as if in faded black-and-white. He was not particularly good on the stump.

Except for one thing—his empathy.

During one of the low points of Biden's campaign, Axelrod attended a New Hampshire town hall. Biden's remarks were not particularly stirring, but a line of voters formed afterward. Each one wanted to talk to him, most with sad stories, seeking a kind ear. And Biden stood and greeted every single one of them.

Like the pilgrimages to Lourdes, Axelrod later said.

And, ultimately, he pulled it off. He won the nomination, then the presidency.

But by 2022, Axelrod had come to fear that Biden was going to discard his previous pledge to be a bridge and a transitional president. He shouldn't run for reelection, Axelrod thought, and he should make the decision with enough time for the bench of potential Democratic all-stars to suit up and get in the game.

Primaries are important. Primaries are how parties sort things out. How voters learn who candidates really are and see how they perform under pressure. Obama would not have become president if he hadn't had two years to run and prove his mettle.

After all, it was ridiculous to assume that Biden—who would be eighty-six at the end of his second term—was seriously asking the American people to vote for him again. Wasn't it?

When a *New York Times* reporter called Axelrod in June 2022, he gave an honest answer: "The presidency is a monstrously taxing job and the stark reality is the president would be closer to ninety than eighty at the end of a second term, and that would be a major issue."

After the story ran, Axelrod got a call from White House Chief of Staff Ron Klain.

"Who else is going to do this, Axe?" Klain asked angrily. "Who's going to beat Trump? President Biden is the only one who has done it. You better have a lot of certainty about a different candidate before you say the president should step aside. The future of the country depends on it!"

Klain thought that too many strategists underestimated how difficult it was to beat Trump. The GOP had run a stellar field against him in 2016, and all of them had gotten their asses kicked. Same with Hillary Clinton. The idea that beating Trump was easy, that if you took away Joe Biden, anyone else could win, was sloppy thinking.

But for Axelrod, this wasn't political; it was actuarial. Biden was old—he looked it, seemed it. And the problem was only getting worse.

THE FALL

In 2017, the Bidens bought a luxurious, contemporary six-bedroom, five-and-a-half-bath beach home with four fireplaces, an elevator, and ocean views in Rehoboth Beach, Delaware.

On June 18, 2022, Biden was riding his bike on a trail near the home when he spotted some reporters. He hollered, "Good morning!" Then, while stopping to greet a crowd that had gathered to wish him a happy Father's Day, he fell off the bike in front of the cameras. Apparently, he'd been unable to dislodge one of his feet from the pedals' toe cages.

The images were blasted around the world and went viral on social media.

Some inside the White House pushed for there to be recognition that this bike fall was going to impact how the world saw Biden, but senior aides dismissed these concerns.

On a regular basis, the White House would internally distribute a progressive pollster's "word cloud analytics" illustration of the specific words that voters used when answering open-ended poll questions about the president.

Two weeks after the fall, the bike incident filled the balloon like an ad for Schwinn.

NOVEMBER 2022

For more than a year, Biden had been privately telling allies he intended to run for reelection, but before the midterms, in conversation with other staff, Ron Klain raised the question of whether the president should—because of his age and high disapproval ratings—announce he wasn't. His ratings would go up and buoy Democrats on the ballot. They were just brainstorming messages, but it was on the table.

But the 2022 midterms ended up being not as bad for Democrats as many had predicted. The "red wave" was more of a splash. Democrats even picked up a Senate seat, and though they lost the House, the GOP only saw a net gain of ten seats. Klain was now 100 percent on board with Biden 2024.

At the White House on election eve, staff had gathered for a party in the Roosevelt Room to watch the results and dine on pizza and salad. As the results became more promising, Biden himself walked into the room with a blue sweater and a ball cap on. He sat down and watched the TV with some staff. To people in the room, he didn't look surprised—he looked vindicated. *Told ya so.* Biden and his aides felt he had a special relationship with the everyday people that elites just didn't get.

The Politburo reminded everyone of the historical context. In 2010, during Obama's first midterms, Republicans picked up six seats in the Senate and sixty-four in the House. In 1994, during Clinton's first midterms, Republicans picked up eight seats in the Senate and fifty-two in the House.

Under Biden, Democrats came through the midterms better than ever before in the twenty-first century.

Why wouldn't he run for reelection? the Politburo asked. He deserved it.

The 2022 midterms results further convinced Biden and the Politburo that he had a rationale, even a right, to run again.

The truth, of course, was more complicated than the Biden view. Most vulnerable Democrats had run away from the president rather than run on his record. To them, the Republicans' shortfall at the ballot box seemed wrapped up in the failures of Trump-backed fringe House and Senate nominees, as well as a backlash against the *Dobbs* decision overturning *Roe v. Wade.* The general election would draw a larger pool of less engaged voters, more attuned to pocketbook issues.

But no Democrats in the White House or leaders on Capitol Hill raised any doubts, either privately with the president or publicly, about Biden's second run. The week after the midterms, House Speaker Nancy Pelosi encouraged him to do so on ABC News. "He has accomplished so much," she said.

Other Democrats knew that the White House watched closely for any signs of dissent. They kept quiet and went along.

A week after the midterms, Trump announced he was going to run for president in a meandering and subdued speech. That made Biden and his team even more confident. Trump was an existential threat, but he looked politically weak. The court cases against him were brewing. Throughout 2023, Biden and Mike Donilon expressed confidence that Trump would wind up in prison.

But the warning signs were there. An early November 2022 Ipsos poll had the president's approval rating at a low 39 percent, with 57 percent disapproving. Two-thirds of the public surveyed, or 66 percent, thought the country was on the wrong track. When Ipsos ran a poll after the election, a full 68 percent of those surveyed said Biden might not be up for the challenge of running in 2024, and almost half of Democrats, 46 percent, agreed.

Biden was aware of the public's doubts about his age, but he always believed that he could address them by governing.

Klain would tell detractors that they were clear-eyed about the vulnerability: They couldn't change the fact that he was old, that he looked old, that he sounded old. There was no step they could take to make him seem young again. It had been his number one liability in the 2020 campaign; they expected it would continue to be a big concern of the electorate. All candidates had pluses and minuses, Klain argued. This was going to be Biden's minus, and they had to overcome it to get him reelected.

THE MIDTERM ELECTIONS did result in the stepping down of some powerful octogenarians.

House Speaker Nancy Pelosi, eighty-two, opted to relinquish her leadership role, handing over her gavel to New York Congressman Hakeem Jeffries, forty-two. Others in House Democratic leadership followed her lead. Majority Leader Steny Hoyer, eighty-three, and Majority

Whip Jim Clyburn, eighty-two, gave the reins to Massachusetts Congresswoman Katherine Clark, fifty-nine, and California Congressman Pete Aguilar, forty-three.

It's never fun for leaders to cede power, and it cannot be claimed that the publicly seamless transition was entirely joyful or without mixed emotions behind the scenes. That said, the prospect of these three willingly transferring power they had worked decades to accrue—for the sake of what was considered best for their party and the country—was remarkable because of how sadly rare it is in Washington, DC.

STEVE

On December 9, 2022, WNBA star Brittney Griner, who had been sentenced to nine years in a Russian penal colony for possession of cannabis oil, arrived back in the United States after the president's team successfully secured her release in exchange for Russian arms dealer Viktor Bout.

"These past few months have been hell for Brittney and for Charlee and her entire family and all her teammates back home," the president said at eight forty that morning, botching the name of Griner's wife, Cherelle.

The president had just turned eighty.

Later that day, behind the scenes, the president had trouble with two names that were much more familiar to him. Standing in the Outer Oval with National Security Adviser Jake Sullivan and Kate Bedingfield, his communications director, he couldn't come up with either of their names, according to one witness.

"Steve . . ." he said to Sullivan. "Steve . . ." he continued, obviously struggling to recall Jake's name.

He turned to Bedingfield. "Press," he called her, as he beckoned them into the Oval Office.

THERE WERE OTHER signs that the presidency was wearing on him in serious ways.

During a six-day, three-country trip to Asia in mid-November, Biden skipped the gala dinner with world leaders from the Group of 20 and went back to his hotel instead. Biden aides later told CNN that he had done so to help prepare for his granddaughter's upcoming White House wedding. But the truth was they'd decided that the dinner was not a top priority after a packed day that had exhausted the president and people on his team. (That rest came in handy; aides woke the president up hours later to tell him about a missile that had landed in Poland, killing two people. Biden rallied world leaders to coordinate a response.)

Over the next two years, Biden would be absent from other such dinners abroad, and Secretary Antony Blinken would become a go-to seat filler. Blinken would usually not find out if he was replacing the president until the day of—it depended on how the president was feeling or if other policy priorities came up.

National security officials rationalized the absences. Biden was fatigued, but that was because American presidents had more to do than their peers on such trips. The dinners were mostly theater without much substance, they said. It wasn't a big deal.

NO PROCESS

What was notable about the reelection decision-making process is how little of a process there actually was. There were limited conversations about pros and cons among the staffers—the Politburo, Anita Dunn, and Jen O'Malley Dillon, who had served as Biden's 2020 campaign manager and now worked as a deputy chief of staff for the White House.

But to the surprise of some senior staff, there was no formal meeting between them and the president to hash it out, no real discussion about the risks of running for reelection at eighty-one or whether he could do the job at eighty-six.

Although aging can be unpredictable for anyone, it was especially so for a president who in 1988 had undergone two separate surgeries for brain aneurysms, including one that had ruptured.

Staffers didn't interrogate whether he could robustly campaign in 2024, whether he'd be prepared to resign if he began struggling during a second term, or whether he was confident that the vice president could take over in such a scenario.

Instead, Donilon made it clear that he had talked to Biden and the president was running. And that was that.

"The president of the United States gets to choose if he wants to run again," Donilon would say. Biden had both the record and the vision that merited reelection. He got a record number of votes in 2020. By all credible accounts, he was having a very successful presidency. End of story. Some of Biden's senior aides had concerns, but no one directly confronted the president about his decision.

Outside Biden allies who voiced fears were flicked away like lint.

In early 2023, John Anzalone, a longtime Biden pollster, arranged a call with Dunn and O'Malley Dillon to talk about whether the president would run for reelection. To him, it was not a foregone conclusion. Biden was the oldest president in the history of the republic.

"We don't need polling," Dunn told him. "The decision has been made. He's running."

Anzalone was stunned. They weren't going to assess his strengths versus his vulnerabilities? His polling numbers, after all, were atrocious. The pollster, who had been with Biden since the 1980s and was willing to raise uncomfortable questions, increasingly found himself ostracized by the White House.

"You don't run for four years—you run for eight," Anthony Bernal would tell others, giving voice to the First Lady. He'd often bring up different trips or projects they would do "in the second term." He had already begun planning the First Lady's 2025 international travel schedule.

Whenever the idea of Kamala Harris running came up, Bernal and others senior staffers reacted dismissively. *Please. She can't win.*

THE KAMALA EXCUSE

During the 2020 campaign, Biden's team was divided on his pick for running mate. What started out as a list of eleven "equal finalists" behind the scenes came down to two: Harris and Gretchen Whitmer, the governor of Michigan.

Biden thought Whitmer had a "Scranton Joe" vibe and cared about making sure that the Democrats remained the party of working people. She prided herself on bringing people together and not holding grudges. Like Biden, she often quoted her dad's bits of homespun wisdom. Biden's heart was with Whitmer—she represented the next generation of Biden Democrats.

But Harris made the most sense on paper. Her 2020 campaign had been a train wreck—she dropped out in 2019—but she'd already been vetted on the national stage. Whitmer had only been elected governor in 2018.

Biden had long seen Harris as the likeliest pick. She had been friends with Beau when they both served as state attorneys general, and she had experience.

Biden had already pledged to pick a woman, but by the summer, many of Biden's top aides and confidants, including Ron Klain, Louisiana Congressman Cedric Richmond, and South Carolina Congressman Jim Clyburn, were pushing Biden to pick a Black woman. The murder of George Floyd and the Black Lives Matter movement influenced the politics of the decision. Black Americans, particularly Black women, were the beating heart of the Democratic Party, and they had been key to Biden's clinching of the nomination.

Richmond joked to Biden that he could pick whomever he wanted, but if he didn't pick a Black woman, Richmond was going to have to go into the federal witness protection program. Public speculation had the three finalists as Harris, California Congresswoman Karen Bass, and Florida Congresswoman Val Demings.

But, in truth, it came down to Harris or Whitmer.

Klain pushed for Harris, a senator from the most populous state in the country and a former attorney general. He also thought it would demonstrate grace because Harris had hit him hard in the first primary debate in June 2019 when she went after him for working, in the 1970s, with segregationist senators and opposing Department of Education–mandated busing to integrate public schools. "There was a little girl in California who was part of the second class to integrate her public schools," Harris had said. "And she was bused to school every day. And that little girl was me."

Jill particularly resented the attack. But Harris was the politically pragmatic pick, and beating Trump was too important to let feelings get in the way.

Still, Biden's advisers did not fully trust her. Harris and her advisers felt it. Her aides got the impression that doing more than the bare minimum to help her was considered an act of disloyalty to Biden. Some of that culture carried over into the White House.

Given Biden's age, Harris's team thought that building the vice president up should have been a priority, but many on the Biden team didn't agree.

Harris aides began dividing Biden advisers between the helpful and what one called "the cabal of the unhelpful." Bernal, the First Lady's office, and O'Malley Dillon, along with many in the political and communications shops, were often in the latter group.

Harris sensed the Biden team's distrust and wanted to avoid giving them any reason to question her loyalty. She even tried to deploy her husband, Doug Emhoff, to try some rapprochement with Jill that later included going to a spinning class at SoulCycle together, but the chill never fully thawed.

To the Biden team, Harris was a regular headache. She often shied away from politically tough assignments when Biden had accepted such assignments as vice president. She even turned down seemingly simple asks, such as headlining DC's Gridiron Club dinner.

She had considerable turnover, as her aides tired of what they called her "prosecuting the staff" style. And her cautious nature could reach the point of parody.

In April 2022 Harris attended a salon-style dinner with journalists and other socialites at the home of David Bradley—an influential DC news mogul. Harris aides were always anxious about an event going poorly, and before this dinner they held a mock soiree with staff acting the part of guests. Aides weighed having wine served so Harris could practice with a glass or two but ultimately decided not to.

Biden aides noted that the politically safe ground of the National

Space Council appeared difficult for Harris. The vice president's aides internally mixed up astrology and astronomy, then drew mocking public headlines by using child actors for a video about space.

Many on the Biden team felt that Harris didn't put in the work and was also just not a very nice person. Several quietly expressed buyer's remorse: They should have picked Whitmer.

In the eyes of Harris's team, the Biden White House was setting her up to fail. They gave her assignments her team considered politically toxic, such as dealing with the migration crisis, rarely offered to help, and knifed her to reporters along the way. Harris's camp didn't understand the hostility and the reluctance to offer her opportunities to shine.

But Biden was not likely to back any other candidate as his successor. He had fumed for years about how Obama hadn't backed him in 2016; he wouldn't do the same thing to his vice president.

Still, he had beaten Trump, and he wasn't confident that she could. He privately called her a "work in progress."

It became an additional rationalization for his reelection run: There was no plan B.

THE LAPTOP

In the final weeks of the 2020 election, Biden and his campaign had enlisted national security experts who risked their own credibility to discredit Hunter's laptop as Russian disinformation.

It was not.

Biden aides realized they wouldn't be able to do that in 2024; prosecutors from Biden's Justice Department were using the very real, very scandalous evidence in their investigations.

While the White House refused to acknowledge the authenticity of

Hunter's laptop, Biden's team quietly had the DNC obtain a copy of the hard drive. The campaign needed to be politically prepared, and Biden needed to be personally prepared.

In early 2023, Bob Bauer privately met with the president and the First Lady for an hour to go through all the sordid details. Having recaptured the House, congressional Republicans seemed likely to broadcast some of the most embarrassing pictures, text messages, and emails involving not just Hunter but the entire Biden family. Biden's brother Jimmy would get dragged into it, given his business dealings with Hunter that capitalized on the family name.

The reelection effort would likely take a toll on the family. Hunter, however, was on board. The Republicans would overplay their hand, he believed, and he would finally get a chance to fight back after lying low. Biden aides sensed that Hunter saw an opportunity to redeem his reputation.

The delusion that this would be good for him or for his father was of a piece. "Don't say mean truths."

The hideousness of Hunter's personal life was another unacknowledged ugliness.

He seemingly brushed it all off—the influence peddling, the infidelities, the drug use, the child he had denied. He was doing so much better now. He was clean and in a new relationship; that's all that mattered.

For the Biden family, the 2020 campaign and the presidency had been a glue that brought them together. Biden's political aspirations formed a shared purpose.

"I think it's understandable from the outside to see it as a tragedy, but from the inside, it's a love story," Hunter told Alex in early 2024. "And that is the story of being able to withstand tragedy and not lose yourself or your family."

Hunter and the rest of the Biden clan weren't exactly eager to go through Republican investigations into their family and friends. But they were united in the mission to stop Trump, and they believed that Biden was the only one who could do it.

The family also had anxiety about the threats Trump had been making to seek retribution against them and anyone in their orbit. His own criminal charges and conflicts of interest notwithstanding, Trump repeatedly referred to the Bidens as an "organized crime family" that ought to be investigated. In 2023, he pledged to "appoint a real special prosecutor to go after the most corrupt president in the history of the United States of America, Joe Biden, and the entire Biden crime family."

It was a situation unique in the history of the republic: Two candidates who both claimed to be running again for the sake of protecting the country from the other also had very real reason to run for the purpose of protecting themselves.

EIGHT

Dr. Biden

During a summer 2022 swing through the Northeast, Democratic donors gathered in Boston for a dinner with First Lady Jill Biden.

Joshua Bekenstein, the co-chairman of Bain Capital, found the nerve to speak up about the president's potential reelection. His remarks were meant to delicately convince rather than confront. He talked about how much the Biden family had sacrificed and how they had restored faith in institutions.

He urged them to bolster that legacy by turning to a new generation.

If there was any doubt about what Bekenstein meant, he added that he didn't want an eighty-six-year-old doctor operating on him or an eighty-six-year-old pilot flying him, and he didn't want an eighty-six-year-old president running the country either.

Before the First Lady could respond, Anthony Bernal jumped in to ask if Trump's third run would change the donor's position, given that Trump was only a few years younger than Biden.

Bekenstein said no. Biden's age mattered regardless of who was running against him.

It was awkward. The dinner went on, but the confrontation lingered in Jill's mind. Later that evening, talking to aides, hand on her head with a glass of wine, she kicked herself for how she had responded. "I can't believe I didn't defend Joe," she said. It wouldn't happen again.

First Lady Jill Biden had earned a doctor of education (EdD) in educational leadership from the University of Delaware, and she told the White House to call her Dr. Jill Biden, or Dr. B for short.

Dr. B was a strong, protective force in the White House. She was also, without question, one of the chief supporters of the president's decision to run for reelection, and one of the chief deniers of his deterioration. All she ever wanted to do was love Joe. He was a great president. If he wanted to run, she would be there.

Her influential role during the 2020 campaign continued into the White House. She sat in on job interviews with White House aide candidates, while Bernal helped place people throughout the administration. They both kept score of who was with them and against them. "I remember every slight committed against the people I love," she wrote. "I can forgive, sure—but I don't believe in rewarding bad behavior." Though she continued teaching community college classes in Virginia, through Bernal she had constant influence over the West Wing. Bernal would sometimes refer to himself as the Biden marriage counselor and he inserted himself in the president's day-to-day business. He had a lot of control over the president's schedule and the manifests on trips— often keeping the traveling group tight. Bernal would loop himself in to several meetings at once across the White House—listening in on one and talking in another—and often invoked the First Lady's name. "Jill isn't going to like this" was a conversation-ender and a threat about going forward. No one knew if he had talked to Jill about the issue, but they didn't question it. "Anthony approved" became an internal signifier that an event could go forward. He was so abrasive with colleagues in the West Wing that senior White House aides reminded their staffs of the mechanisms to report unprofessional conduct.

On foreign trips, Bernal and other aides began requesting events just for Jill—"spousal programming," it was called internally. Before State visits from foreign leaders, her team asked for talking points, which some national security officials found unusual. She frequently asked White House personnel like retired Rear Admiral John Kirby, a national security spokesman, to attend her briefings about state dinners.

When the issue was Biden's age and ability, you'd better not bring it up in front of Dr. B or Bernal, her prized pupil.

AS SOME DEMOCRATS wondered about Biden's future plans, Jill appeared to have little doubt that her husband was going to run again.

On December 1, 2022, the president hosted French President Emmanuel Macron for a state dinner. Speaker Nancy Pelosi was seated next to Biden with Macron across from them. The French president was flanked by Pelosi's daughter Alexandra on his right and the First Lady on his left.

Later in the evening, Alexandra overheard the First Lady tell Macron about her rigorous exercise routine. Campaigns are so tough and she needed to be in shape, she explained.

Alexandra looked surprised. Campaign? What campaign? Everyone seemed happy with the four-year, "I'm a bridge" situation.

Alexandra then turned to the president and asked if they should toast to another campaign. He looked back at her like he didn't understand. Alexandra thought her mom looked shocked.

Everyone quickly gathered themselves. With Macron, they toasted to four more years.

NINE

"Are We Sure This Is a Good Idea?"

2023

The year 2023 began with the transfer of power from outgoing Chief of Staff Ron Klain to his successor, Jeff Zients.

Klain had been a twenty-four-seven blur who had sacrificed his body for the job. By the end of 2022, he did not look well. In early 2023, he had a health episode in his office. He was also traveling back to Indiana on weekends to visit his ailing mother. As he scanned for the exit, Klain started preparing for a replacement. He looked at COVID czar Zients, Steve Ricchetti, Anita Dunn, and Secretary of Energy Jennifer Granholm, who quickly took herself out of contention.

Ricchetti was gifted at fostering relationships and dealing with Capitol Hill, but others felt that his skill set didn't necessarily meet the needs of the gig: being able to triage problems, to hold people accountable, and to drive the team to outcomes. He was also seen as too close to, and admiring of, Biden to tell the president hard truths.

Klain was more political and had a longer relationship with Biden, but he thought Zients met the requirements of the job in a way Ricchetti didn't. Zients would be there to implement what had been set on course in 2021 and 2022, to keep morale up, and to make sure no one got ethically shady. Biden respected Zients and had gone to him in 2016 for counsel on his post–vice presidency moves, but their relationship wasn't as tight. He was perceived as an Obama guy, which didn't help.

When Zients interviewed for the job, Biden had told him that he was running for reelection—even though it hadn't yet been announced—so the chief of staff job would be even more complicated. Zients was the kind of guy who sought out rigorous analytics and intense discussions of options. He would have liked to pressure-test the decision, to talk about the pros and cons. But the decision had already been made.

He wasn't the only one wondering if the plan made sense.

Dunn would privately ask other White House officials, "Are we sure this is a good idea?"

She believed that Biden's cognitive and decision-making abilities were fine, but she did worry about his ability to perform as a candidate. She didn't want him to be embarrassed.

Others on staff wondered whether they should at least hold a meeting to discuss it. But any conversations about this continued to get shot down by the two men who had the ears of the First Couple: Mike Donilon and Anthony Bernal.

So they bit their tongues and didn't confront the president with their concerns.

DOC O'CONNOR'S 2023 EXAM

The president was about to embark on a reelection campaign, and on February 16, 2023, Doc O'Connor released the results of Biden's latest medical exam.

Once again, the doctor did not conduct a cognitive exam.

Other than that, O'Connor's report was much the same as the one from November 2021. "The President's gait remains stiff, but has not worsened since last year," O'Connor noted, though some of Biden's own aides thought his stride appeared worse.

EXUBERANCE

In early 2023, Biden was feeling more confident and necessary than ever.

On January 4, he made a rare joint appearance with the Senate Republican leader, Mitch McConnell, to tout a $1.385 billion federal grant to improve and expand the Brent Spence Bridge Corridor, which connects McConnell's home state of Kentucky to Ohio.

The investment was part of the bipartisan infrastructure bill that Biden had signed. The president said the bill and the event sent "an important message to the entire country: We can work together. We can get things done. We can move the nation forward if we just drop a little bit of our egos and focus on what is needed for the country."

McConnell added that the bill had been "literally a legislative miracle."

The next month, Biden embarked on a dangerous and grueling trip to Kyiv in a splashy show of solidarity with Ukraine to mark the first anniversary of Russia's invasion. Biden had secretly taken off on a VIP government plane at 4:15 a.m., ultimately landing in Poland, where National Security Adviser Jake Sullivan disembarked from the front of the plane and walked out onto the tarmac as a decoy, while Biden, wearing a hat, scarf, and COVID mask, snuck out the back. Then came a ten-hour overnight train from Poland to Kyiv.

The Secret Service had cautioned against the trip. The US had no control over the air, unlike even in Iraq and Afghanistan during previous surreptitious visits, and most alarmingly, there was a four-hour block of the rail ride where if something happened to their train, they would have to evacuate on foot—not a small consideration for an eighty-year-old with an ailing spine and a stiff gait.

But Biden was determined to go—after all, Nancy Pelosi, two years his senior, had done it—and soon the world saw compelling images of Biden standing side by side with Ukrainian President Volodymyr Zelensky while air-raid sirens were blaring, and declaring that Russian President Vladimir Putin's "war of conquest is failing."

"Putin thought Ukraine was weak and the West was divided," Biden said. "He thought he could outlast us. I don't think he's thinking that right now."

The daring trip had demonstrated stamina and grit. Biden, a former chairman of the Senate Foreign Relations Committee, believed he was uniquely prepared for this moment. He was working to expand NATO and contain an authoritarian Russia. He was bringing the temperature down in Washington with bipartisan accomplishments.

Though Biden's approval rating still hovered at about 40 percent, he and his team increasingly saw fate and providence in his being in charge at this moment. He was not just the right man but perhaps the only man for the job.

"How many thirty-year-olds could travel to Poland, get on the train, go nine more hours, go to Ukraine, meet with President Zelensky?" the First Lady asked CNN about a month later in response to concerns about the president's age. "So, look at the man. Look what he's doing. Look what he continues to do each and every day."

In retrospect, the Ukraine trip would end up being a peak presentation of the president's verve and physical abilities. In the images beamed around the world, they appeared impressive, but they would decline significantly over the final two years of his presidency—at a rate far exceeding that of the first two years, according to top aides.

MARCH 2023

Antony Blinken had spent more than twenty years working for Biden, having been hired as his staff director on the Senate Foreign Relations Committee in 2002. Now Blinken was the secretary of state, working closely with the president on the issues that he cared more about, and knew more about, than perhaps any other.

In early 2023, Blinken had no concerns about Biden's ability to do the job, but as he'd seen with past bosses Clinton and Obama, the presidency ages a person exponentially. Biden was eighty and showing every day of it, and they were only halfway through one term.

"I'm with you one hundred and ten percent, whatever you want to do," Blinken said to him before the reelection was announced. "But I want to make sure you want to take this on."

It wasn't just about how he felt in 2023. How would he feel four, five, six years from now?

The president said he felt good and confident. He had the legislative record, and the midterms had reaffirmed to him that the American people were with him. And he was the only one who had ever beaten Trump. He had this.

Truth was, to others the president was having behind-the-scenes moments where he seemed completely out of it, spent, exhausted, almost gone.

IRELAND

It was during Biden's four-day trip to Ireland in April 2023 that Democratic Illinois Congressman Mike Quigley realized who the president reminded him of and why.

The trip had been incredible, with the president in such great spirits, energized by the crowds. He delivered a prime-time speech to an audience of roughly twenty-seven thousand—one of the biggest of his political career. He had brought with him his sister, Val, and son Hunter.

He hadn't yet officially announced that he was running for reelection, though it was expected. Moments of the trip were emotional, especially as the family looked down on a Beau Biden memorial plaque at the Mayo Roscommon Hospice in Castlebar, County Mayo. One of the priests at the Knock Shrine turned out to be the same one who had given Beau last rites in 2015, which brought the president to tears.

In a speech to the joint houses of the Irish Parliament, the president said it was Beau who "should be the one standing here giving this speech to you."

In Dublin on Thursday, April 13, Biden was welcomed to Áras an Uachtaráin, the official residence of the president of Ireland, Michael

D. Higgins. There had been a tree-planting ceremony, a ringing of the Peace Bell, an honor guard presenting arms, and on and on.

At one point in the busy schedule, as the room emptied out and there were fewer than a dozen of them left—including Quigley and his friend Brian Higgins, then a New York congressman—Hunter began impressing upon his father the need to rest.

"You promised you wouldn't do this," Hunter said. "You promised you'd take a nap. You know you can't handle all this."

The president waved off his son and walked over to the bar in the back of the room, where a lone woman was working. She served him a soft drink. He seemed utterly sapped and not quite there.

And that was when Quigley realized why this all felt so familiar to him. This was how his father, Bill, had been before he died. He would seem weak, but then, like Biden gaining strength from the Irish crowds, he would get an adrenaline boost when everyone showed up at family functions.

When the high wore off, though, it was akin to witnessing all the air empty from a balloon. Bill, like Biden at that moment in the ballroom, would appear deflated and drained.

Biden, Quigley thought, needed to go to bed for the rest of the day and night. He wasn't merely physically frail; he had lost almost all of his energy. His speech was breathless, soft, weak. Quigley's father had died of Parkinson's disease in February 2019. There was so much about the president on this trip that reminded Quigley of his dad.

He shared this observation with Congressman Higgins, who had lost his father to Alzheimer's and was also noticing a familiarity in the president's shuffling. "A diagnosis is nothing more than pattern recognition," Higgins would later say. "When people see that stuff, it conjures up a view that there's something going on neurologically."

He and Quigley were discussing their dads and the president because, quietly, Democratic officials were beginning to question if the president was possibly in cognitive decline, "which was evident to most people that watched him," Higgins said. He was also mindful of the fact that the president's medical history included not only a debilitating childhood stutter but also two near-fatal aneurysms.

"We were commiserating," Higgins said, "because it was top of mind" as the president prepared to announce his reelection bid.

"BETWEEN 10:00 A.M. AND 4:00 P.M."

Some Biden aides didn't want him to run for reelection. They thought he had been a good president but didn't believe he could competently serve another four years. Democrats were asking the country to choose between Trump and a man who likely couldn't finish the job he was running for.

As it became clear that Biden was going to run anyway, some of those aides began talking to Alex about the president's limitations.

His body was wearing down. Everything was slower: the way he moved, talked, and ran meetings. The White House was increasingly trying to organize around his limited energy. Biden was good "for his age," they said, but they were worried.

Biden officially announced his candidacy on April 25. Days later, Alex reported that some White House officials said it was "difficult to schedule public or private events with the president in the morning, in the evening, or on weekends: The vast majority of Biden's public events happen on weekdays, between 10:00 a.m. and 4:00 p.m."

The numbers were undeniable. From January 1, 2023, to April 27, Biden had only four public events before 10:00 a.m., twelve full weekends with no public events, and only twelve public events after 6:00 p.m., most of which were off camera.

"The White House is basically hiding Biden as he auditions for another term," Alex wrote.

The White House denied the story. Jen O'Malley Dillon gave a one-word statement: "False."

The White House press team publicly labeled Alex a peddler of fake news.

Most White Houses deny damaging but true stories and try to undermine reporters they don't like. Many reporters took the White House denials at face value. Few other outlets outside conservative media followed the story.

In June, *The New York Times* built on *Axios*'s analysis of how age had limited Biden's schedule. Noting that neither Obama nor Biden were early birds, the paper observed that "Mr. Obama was twice as likely to do public events after 6 p.m. compared with Mr. Biden."

The White House responded to any question about Biden's age by pointing to Trump's wild and seemingly unhinged behavior on the campaign trail. But Trump's limitations didn't mean that Biden's deserved less scrutiny. Biden was the sitting president, and he was struggling to not only keep a robust schedule but also articulate his thoughts in public and private.

Some Biden aides were in denial, but others knew that the president might not last through another four years and made peace with it. Beating Trump mattered more.

"He just had to win, and then he could disappear for four years—he'd only have to show proof of life every once in a while," said one longtime Biden aide. His aides could pick up the slack. "When you vote for somebody, you are voting for the people around them too," the aide argued.

THE LOST CAMPAIGN YEAR OF 2023

The Biden team chose Julie Chávez Rodríguez as campaign manager, but she had never run a campaign before. It was largely an honorary title, as she lacked real authority to make decisions. The campaign was controlled by the Politburo and other senior aides that often made decisions slowly by committee.

This meant that 2023 would end up a stagnant year for the reelection. The campaign raised significant funds, and Mike Donilon was running ads, but hiring was slow, and the internal culture was fractious. With every passing month, pressure mounted to send O'Malley Dillon to Wilmington to run things again like she had in 2020.

But the campaign had another problem: the candidate.

Biden had trouble taping even mundane video remarks without flubbing lines.

Aides helped manage that challenge in subtle ways. When a group wanted Biden to tape a five-minute video address to keynote an event, the White House usually responded by saying the video would be one to two minutes.

However, even with the time limitation, Biden often couldn't make it through one or two minutes without botching a line or two.

To compensate for that, aides filmed Biden with two cameras instead of one. If Biden messed up, the edit was less obvious with a jump cut. Other politicians use jump-cuts, but Biden aides noted to themselves how much more often they had to use them for the president.

When they recorded videos, much of the footage was unusable. "The man could not speak," said one person involved. It wasn't his stutter; it was his inability to find words, to remember what he was saying, to stay on one train of thought. Aides would sometimes make the videos in slow motion to blur the reality of how slowly he actually walked. Every shoot was anxiety-inducing for Biden's team. If he was off, editing footage in a way that cast him in the best light would require hours of work.

Doing the videos without the extra camera would have been impossible, they concluded. At times, the president had such trouble communicating that the videos were unsalvageable, and the Biden team just opted not to release them. At other times, they released videos whose heavy editing was so obvious that they immediately regretted putting them out.

In April 2024, the campaign held a staged town hall in a high school gym to film a campaign commercial. The campaign was trying to make it look like the president was out there taking off-the-cuff questions from voters in public. But the event was closed to reporters, and the campaign had the full list of questions that people would ask.

Biden took these prepared questions for about ninety minutes while the campaign cameras rolled.

Other campaigns have staged such events for ads, but even in such a controlled and scripted setting, Biden had trouble. The campaign ultimately decided that the footage wasn't usable.

Some said the problem was that the advance team had failed and the gym's lighting was terrible. Others admitted that there was a deeper, far less fixable problem: Biden.

THERE WERE many seemingly normal steps taken by the White House that many Biden aides now see retrospectively as crutches.

One was internally called "the news card."

It began in late 2021 as a presidential cue card with news of the day on it. If reporters asked Biden something, he'd have responses prepared. By 2023, the news card had morphed into several cards a day, each bearing information that Biden's own aides sometimes felt was elementary.

For months, Biden's cards told him that if he was asked about Hunter, he should respond, "I love my son." Around Thanksgiving, the cards offered simplistic answers if Biden was asked what he was thankful for.

Biden had trouble pronouncing the names of world leaders, so staff began writing "President / Prime Minister of X country" rather than writing out the names of the leaders.

THE DONORS

After Biden launched his reelection campaign in April, he began hitting the road to raise money. Fundraisers were one of the few settings where people outside the White House got to see Biden up close. And some donors noticed that something had changed about the president since they'd last seen him in 2019 or 2020, before the COVID pandemic. He had always been old and had curious miscues, but this seemed different. Biden was no longer Biden, they whispered to each other.

The way his eyes moved across the room was atypical. The garrulous pol no longer seemed to have the gift of gab with any consistency. Small talk was stilted. People working on the events noted that aides like Annie Tomasini and Ashley Williams were directing his every step to a degree they hadn't before.

Sometimes Biden would stop speaking and start shaking hands, as if the event were over, only to then start speaking again.

On June 20, 2023, Biden attended a fundraiser with Governor Gavin Newsom in Kentfield, California, that went awry. He casually called Chinese President Xi Jinping a dictator, sparking outrage in China just after Secretary of State Blinken had flown to Beijing to cool down tensions. And attendees were shaken by Biden's meandering remarks. The contrast with the younger, agile Newsom didn't help.

"I remember leaving that fundraiser thinking, *Fuck*," one attendee said. "We got so desensitized to how bad it had gotten."

To help hide this, over the course of 2023, Biden's top aides made changes so that fundraisers would be even more scripted and tightly controlled.

Usually, there wouldn't be an open Q&A. Three questions would be provided to Biden's team in advance. If he had traveled that day to a place with a time change, aides pushed back on having events late in the evening. They tried not to schedule multiple fundraisers in a single day after such travel, and if they did, they aimed not to have any the next day.

Even the photo lines became hypercontrolled. Instead of taking pictures with fifty or one hundred donors, Biden, at the insistence of his aides, usually took only twenty or twenty-five photos. The campaign had to constantly fight with the White House to get a few extra photos in to help raise money. His photo lines had once regularly gone over schedule because he liked to spend time chatting people up, but now they were quick and efficient.

At an August fundraiser, a former longtime aide who was helping to work the event reacted with surprise when Biden didn't recognize them. A Biden aide quickly jumped in to remind the president: "You remember [so-and-so], right?" Minutes later, Biden seemed to snap back and recall who they were.

But no one went public. One donor who witnessed it all explained their tortured calculus: "We weren't going to change that he was running, and no one wanted to be on the outside in case he did win. So no one said anything. No one wanted to hear it, and if you said anything, you got your head chopped off."

EARLIER IN JUNE 2023, Biden had tripped on a sandbag onstage at the US Air Force Academy in Colorado.

He quickly got up and later joked that he got "sandbagged." But internally, the incident prompted panic. Given voter concerns about Biden's age, White House officials began changing protocols to avoid another fall.

Aides tried to figure out shorter walking paths to the stage and the mic. The less walking, the better. They became more insistent that any steps to the stage have handrails. The visual briefings became more detailed so that Biden knew every step.

He started wearing tennis shoes more often, including a pair of all-black HOKAs. He began taking the shorter stairs onto Air Force One, as he had stumbled on the longer ones.

Aides put more pressure on speechwriters to make his speeches shorter and reduce the amount of time he had to spend standing at the podium. Some speeches were scrapped altogether. For a period he stopped delivering regular remarks in response to the monthly jobs report. Aides were told that a written statement would now suffice.

Accommodations such as teleprompters and note cards became lifelines. When he tried to ad-lib, it sometimes looked as if it took him a minute to form a cogent thought.

Biden resisted and bristled at some of these cognitive aids. He thought he didn't need them.

SPECIAL COUNSEL ROBERT HUR,
PART ONE

Playwrights sometimes refer to the principle of Chekhov's gun, attributed to Russian dramatist Anton Chekhov: "One must never place a loaded rifle on the stage if it isn't going to go off. It's wrong to make promises you don't mean to keep." In the narrative of Joe Biden and his decline, Chekhov's gun is Special Counsel Robert Hur, appointed in 2023.

The gun goes off in 2024.

Hur's part of the story actually began decades before, in one of the best books about American politicians and presidential campaigns: Richard Ben Cramer's *What It Takes: The Way to the White House*. Published in 1992, it chronicles six of the men who ran for president in 1988, including Joe Biden. Mark Zwonitzer was Cramer's researcher and worked on the book with him for five years.

In the run-up to his second ill-fated presidential campaign of 2008, then-Senator Joe Biden hired Zwonitzer to write his first memoir, *Promises to Keep*, published in 2007. And as early as 2010 Biden began making notes for a second memoir, in which he would defend his record as vice president, keeping his options open for a run for president, perhaps in 2016. He saw himself as a historical figure, and wanted his career presented that way.

In late 2015, shortly after Beau's tragic death, Biden began meetings to hash out his next memoir, *Promise Me, Dad*. He and Zwonitzer decided to focus the book on the window between late 2014 and early 2016, when he was a vice president dealing with his son's tragic illness. Zwonitzer interviewed Biden more than a dozen times, recording their conversations.

Years later, these recordings would become key evidence in Hur's investigation into Biden's mishandling of classified information—an investigation that would, perhaps more than anything else, bring to light Biden's deterioration and the degree to which his team attempted to hide it from the public.

Hur's path to those recordings began on November 2, 2022, a few days before the midterms, when one of Biden's personal attorneys, Patrick Moore, found classified documents improperly stored in boxes that Biden had taken with him after serving as vice president. Classified documents were on the minds of Biden's attorneys; Trump was in the middle of a standoff with the Justice Department about his possession of such materials, leading to an FBI raid on Mar-a-Lago in August 2022.

Moore alerted Bauer, who contacted White House Counsel Stuart Delery, who discussed it with Richard Sauber—a seasoned Democratic lawyer brought to the White House Counsel's Office in anticipation of Republicans taking over the House and launching investigations. At eight that evening, Delery and Sauber phoned the general counsel for the National Archives and Records Administration to let him know what had happened and to ask for archivists who could handle the documents that night.

The next morning, archivists were shown the documents and the three boxes where they were found: nine classified documents up to the Top Secret level, with some considered "Sensitive Compartmented Information." Forty-four pages.

The public knew nothing about this, but on Wednesday, November 9, the day after the midterm elections, the FBI began investigating. On November 10, Jay Bratt, the chief of the Justice Department's Counterintelligence and Export Control Section, wrote to Bauer to tell him what steps they needed to take, and warning that "the prospect that classified material may have been stored in an unsecure location over a prolonged period may have national security implications."

Trump's situation would explode because there was an audio recording of him in which he seemed to inappropriately show off to an author what he called "highly confidential" information in his possession. Trump had also refused to return the documents, and there was evidence that he and his team had engaged in a conspiracy to hide the documents from the FBI. (Trump and his co-defendants later pleaded not guilty to the charges brought against them, which were ultimately dropped after he won reelection.)

In the wake of the dramatic August search of Mar-a-Lago, Biden inserted himself into the charged investigation. In a *60 Minutes* interview, he initially demurred from weighing in on the case before chiding Trump's conduct, wondering "how one—anyone—could be that irresponsible."

ATTORNEY GENERAL MERRICK GARLAND saw himself as trying to be fair, despite any number of probes that were politically fraught, including those focused on Hunter. The Justice Department had ongoing investigations into not only Trump's handling of classified documents but also his efforts to overturn the 2020 election. Once Trump became a second-time candidate for president in November 2022, Garland appointed Special Counsel Jack Smith to handle the Trump investigations so as to avoid any real or perceived conflicts of interest.

When Biden had announced Garland's nomination, he had told him publicly: "You won't work for me. . . . Your loyalty is not to me. It's to the law, the Constitution, the people of this nation." Garland wouldn't have accepted the position under any other circumstances; he reminded his aides of that quite often. Public trust was a key part of his job. He was the attorney general for the United States of America, not for Joe Biden.

Biden's team had come to view the AG differently. They saw him as endlessly trying to appease right-wingers who acted in bad faith, hurting the president in the process. Garland drove the Politburo nuts. Long before the fall of 2022, Biden aides had soured on him. They would vent their buyer's remorse to reporters and allies: Should've picked former Alabama Senator Doug Jones, they huffed. Anyone but the guy they had picked.

Garland's team felt that the Biden folks were in denial—it was the president and the president's reckless son who kept putting them in impossible situations.

He was running a Justice Department that was investigating the president for some of the very same crimes he was building a case against Biden's predecessor for committing. He was once again saddled with upholding legal standards and trying to keep the public's trust despite the Bidens' sloppiness and lack of discipline.

BAUER AND MOORE thought about other places where Biden might have stowed classified documents. The attorneys became concerned about what might be stored in the garage at Biden's 6,850-foot residence in Greenville, Delaware, a suburb of Wilmington.

Biden kept his 1967 Corvette Stingray in that garage. Also there, it proved, was a binder containing documents with classified markings and an unsealed box containing classified documents from 2009 regarding US policy in Afghanistan.

Bauer and Moore stopped their rummaging. This was bad. Bauer called in the FBI to finish the search of Biden's garage.

More searches resulted in the discovery of other classified documents.

On January 11, 2023, Bauer and attorney Jennifer Miller found documents in the basement den of Biden's Greenville home, all within the pages of a notebook labeled "1/6/12 #2 Foreign Policy." When FBI agents came to the home and were shown the notebook, they found two documents with classified markings—one about Afghanistan, the other about Iraq.

It was during this period that Robert Hur got a phone call from Principal Associate Deputy Attorney General Marshall Miller.

Hur had worked for years in the public sector including as a US attorney for Maryland and was now comfortably ensconced as a partner at Gibson Dunn, a white-shoe firm where he represented big clients—such as Meta and the NFL—and was finally making some money to support his wife and three kids.

Hur was an American success story. He was the son of refugees from the Korean War, and his father remembered American soldiers sharing their food with him when he was a boy. Born in New York City, Hur had been taught to appreciate the greatness of America. His parents didn't talk politics, but they told Hur and his sister to work as hard as they could. And they told him that he would go to Harvard, which he did, followed by Stanford Law School, then a clerkship for US Supreme Court Justice William Rehnquist.

Hur's phone rang one Friday in January 2023. It was Miller, who wanted to know if Hur would consider serving as a special counsel.

"Can you tell me anything else about it?" Hur asked.

"Not really."

"There isn't anything else you can tell me about the investigation? Who's being investigated?"

"A senior government official," Miller said.

Hur asked for the weekend. He discussed it with his wife, Cara. They speculated that it was some undersecretary of the Interior in trouble for an improper flight or something. A quick and easy matter.

On Monday, he called Miller back. "I'm inclined to do it," he told him. "But it would be helpful if you told me more about it."

"It's a *very* senior government official," Miller said.

In addition to a sense of patriotic obligation, Hur felt a sense of duty toward the Justice Department, which had been caught up in some very difficult cases with politically charged dynamics. Hur had worked under Christopher Wray when Wray, now the FBI director, had been head of the DOJ's Criminal Division, and had been the top deputy for Deputy Attorney General Rod Rosenstein, serving as chief liaison between the Justice Department leadership and Robert Mueller's investigation into Russian attempts to intervene in the 2016 election. Difficult stuff.

But did he really have to resign from his job? Ken Starr had remained active with his law firm while serving as an independent counsel, and Special Prosecutor Robert Fiske had taken a leave of absence from his firm without resigning. But in 2023, the Justice Department took the position that Hur had to resign from his firm unless he secured a written waiver from every single client of the firm who had business before the Justice Department, which would be impossible.

Hur made the rounds at work to give everyone the news.

"Wow, that's the completely wrong decision," one colleague told him.

"You need to get out of it," another said. "That's a mistake."

On January 12, Garland appointed Hur to serve as special counsel in the investigation of the president's mishandling of classified material.

FOR THOSE WORKING on the case throughout 2023, the hours would be long and grinding. They had to be thorough in their task. Hur and his team—seven other lawyers, three paralegals, and an administrator—began their investigation in earnest.

Mark Zwonitzer became one of their key witnesses. After reaching out to him and obtaining transcripts and audio files of his interviews with Biden from after the vice presidency, Hur's team noticed that they had transcripts for which they didn't have corresponding audio files. Zwonitzer's attorneys told them that the ghostwriter had deleted some of those files for fear of being hacked, after he learned that a special counsel had been appointed.

The FBI told him to hand over all his devices—anything he had used to write the book or record Biden. He did. FBI technicians recovered a trove of files and sent them to Hur's team, who went to their office's SCIF—the sensitive compartmented information facility—to listen to them.

The first tape Hur listened to featured Biden talking to Zwonitzer and his sister Val, saying, "I just found all the classified stuff downstairs."

It was recorded in McLean, Virginia, in 2017. When Biden was no longer vice president.

To Hur, Biden was clearly acknowledging that he knowingly possessed classified materials. Discussing them with others.

On tape.

The moment was something like the twitching gauge of *The New York Times*'s Needle, that infamous digital prognosticator that displays real-time estimates of election outcomes. The needle had been hovering on one side—any prosecutor would have been unlikely to bring criminal charges against Biden based solely on finding classified documents in his possession.

Then the prosecutors heard the tape: "I just found all the classified stuff downstairs."

Suddenly, the needle shot in the other direction.

HUR AND HIS TEAM listened to every one of the Zwonitzer tapes. Repeatedly, Biden referred to classified materials that he seemed to share with his ghostwriter.

Beyond how damning they were, the tapes revealed something else important to the case.

Biden sounded very old and quite diminished.

In 2017.

He grasped to remember things, he sometimes had difficulty speaking, and he frequently lost his train of thought.

Hur and his team wondered: *What would a jury make of this man?*

Biden was really struggling in 2017. How would he seem to twelve random citizens in, say, 2025 or 2026, when this case might theoretically come before a jury if Hur were to recommend filing charges?

Would there be one juror unconvinced that this elderly man knew exactly what he was doing? After all, his cognitive capacity seemed to have been failing him in 2017. State of mind—mens rea—would be crucial. However much political operatives tried to hide this enfeeblement from the public, any defense attorney would want a jury to see as much of it as possible.

Given how Biden presented on these tapes, Hur and his team thought it would be tough to get a unanimous jury to conclude that he knew what he was doing was illegal and that he intended to break the law.

Hur raised the issue with his team, encouraging everyone to discuss the matter openly and forcefully. Dissent was welcome.

THE PLEA DEAL

Top aides point to Hunter Biden's plea deal falling apart—and the very real fears that he would go to prison—as an inflection point, like the months following Beau's death, where the president suddenly and steeply declined.

On June 20, Hunter entered a tentative plea deal with US Attorney David C. Weiss, pleading guilty to having avoided paying on time more than $200,000 in taxes on $3 million in income. Two misdemeanors. He also agreed to a diversion program for one count of possessing a firearm at a time when—as he seemed to admit in his book—he was an unlawful user of or addicted to a controlled substance.

Republicans on Capitol Hill and IRS whistleblowers complained that the investigation had been stymied by powerful forces. They criticized the agreement as a slap on the wrist.

In July, US District Judge Maryellen Noreika, a Trump appointee, told the prosecution and the defense that she would not be a rubber stamp on what they'd agreed to. "I know you want to get this over with, and I'm sorry," she told Hunter.

As she picked apart their agreement, Weiss's team and Hunter's lawyers began pointing fingers at each other. At one point, Hunter's lawyer Chris Clark confronted Weiss's team and said to hell with their deal. "Just rip it up," he fumed. The defense felt that Weiss was moving the goalposts in response to Republican political pressure. Hunter halfway threw up his hands in frustration before catching himself. He and his family had thought it was over and that the hearing would just be a formality.

House Republicans would continue their investigation of him and his past business deals, but that was a political fight Hunter welcomed.

He had the dubious distinction of being at the center of impeachment inquiries into two different presidents.

Hunter left the courthouse on July 26 with his plea deal in limbo. He pushed aside Clark, whom Bob Bauer had convinced to work on the case, in favor of a more combative attorney, Abbe Lowell.

Weiss responded by asking Garland to be made a special counsel so that he could continue his investigation into Hunter. On August 11, Garland announced he had granted that request. Biden aides cursed Garland—there were now two special counsels investigating Biden and his family.

The Bidens went into panic mode. Hunter was now likely headed for two trials. And possibly prison time. As someone close to the family noted, Hunter could have told the family that he was going to face this all as an adult, and the family should not worry about him. That wasn't his approach. He would talk about how his opponents were after him, how it was a grand conspiracy. He was angry that the White House wasn't doing more to protect him. Why weren't they?

They're trying to kill me, Hunter would say, *they're pushing me to relapse, knowing it will inflict devastating pain on my father. They're only doing this to me to go after him!*

It wore on the president's soul. He lived in fear that he would lose a third child.

SHOOTING THE MESSENGERS

The Biden campaign and White House operatives now had a modus operandi for attacking any journalists who covered any questions about the president's age, enlisting a corps of social media influencers, progressive reporters, and Democratic operatives to besmirch as unprofessional and biased those in the news media investigating this line of inquiry.

One tame example: a text from Biden campaign operative Brooke Goren to Democratic operatives: "Wanted to flag this story we'd love your help doing some pushback on, if you're up for it," she wrote, highlighting a relatively straightforward *New York Times* story by Michael D. Shear, who had more than fifteen years of experience writing about the health of presidential candidates and presidents.

Goren also asked recipients to amplify a tweet from Eric Schultz, Obama's onetime deputy press secretary, who criticized the editors at *The Times*, saying that they "cannot help themselves."

The goal was to shame journalists and create a disincentive structure for those curious about the president's condition.

These texts from Goren were mild, Democrat operatives told us, with the more aggressive ones sent on the encrypted messaging app Signal by Andrew Bates from the White House and TJ Ducklo from the campaign.

"When there were negative news stories about Biden's age, both the campaign and White House reached out repeatedly and insistently urging me and others to go negative on the news outlets and reporters," one Democratic operative explained to us. "They wanted us to shame them on social media—point out how they got the facts wrong, how their takes were biased, and how they weren't holding Trump to the same standards. It was a full-blown freak-out whenever these stories dropped."

To Shear, the intense pushback seemed clearly designed to dissuade reporters from writing about the matter, to undermine the credibility of the news media on the topic of the president's acuity, and to argue that none of this was even a valid subject for discussion and examination.

Even mentioning Biden's age in the lead of a brief story on his COVID infection resulted in a White House official screaming at Shear, demanding that *The Times* remove his age because it wasn't "relevant."

For Shear, the Biden team's handling of that story, and all the others the paper wrote about the president's age and health, basically amounted to one thing: a complete denial that the issue even existed. Every conversation with a Biden official went like this: "He's exactly the same person he always was. Age is not an issue. He's incredibly sharp in meetings. There are no accommodations being made for him because of his age."

Those answers were not true.

Shortly after 4:00 p.m. on Wednesday, September 20, 2023, for example, Shear was among the small "pool" of White House reporters permitted to attend a Biden fundraiser at the Manhattan home of Cary Fowler and Amy Goldman Fowler. Before a crowd of roughly two dozen donors, Biden stumbled through remarks, reading from note cards.

He referred to the January 6 insurrection as happening on January 8 and had some trouble making basic arguments. But the biggest shock came when he told his campaign origin story.

He wasn't planning on running for president after the Obama administration, he said, "but then along came, in August of 2017, Charlottesville, Virginia. You remember those folks walking out of the fields literally carrying torches, with Nazi swastikas, holding them forward, singing the same vicious, antisemitic bile—the same exact bile—bile that was sung in—in Germany in the early '30s. And a young woman was killed. A young woman was killed."

Then, Biden said, he heard Trump's response: "You also had people that were very fine people, on both sides." Biden told the donors, "And I mean this sincerely, from the bottom of my heart, that's when I decided I—I was going to run again." Next, Biden went through a story about his family meeting to discuss whether he should run. And after describing some of that conversation, he said, "You know, you may remember that, you know, those folks from Charlottesville, as they came out of the fields and carrying those swastikas, and remember the ones with the torches and the Ku—accompanied by the Ku Klux Klan. And in addition to that, they had—there were white supremacists. Anyway, they were making the big case about how terrible this was. And a young woman was killed in the process."

Biden then noted, "My predecessor, as I said, was asked what he thought. He said, 'There are some very fine people on both sides.' Well, that kept ringing in my head. And so I couldn't, quite frankly, remain silent any longer. So I decided I would run."

The president had just told the exact same story three minutes earlier.

The room, Shear noticed, was stone-cold silent.

Two days later, when the White House press secretary was asked about the president repeating the same story mere minutes apart, Karine Jean-Pierre said, "The president was making very clear why he decided to run." She added that "he was speaking from his heart" and doing so "in an incredibly passionate way."

BY LATE 2023, Biden's staff was pushing as much of his schedule as possible to midday, when Biden was at his best.

Months of Biden's internal schedule in late 2023 and 2024—also known as "the Block"—show how Biden's staff would try to lighten the president's day.

On October 3, 2023, for instance, Biden had prep and meetings with officials from 9:00 a.m. to noon, then lunch from 12:15 to 1:15 p.m. The rest of his day was "Desk Time" from 1:30 to 2:15 p.m., then "POTUS

Time" from 2:15 to 4:15 p.m. And then he ended his day with dinner at 4:30 p.m. "POTUS Time" could mean many different things. At times, it was a stand-in for something that Biden's aides wanted only a few to know about. Other times, it was just to carve out a chunk of the schedule for the president.

When Biden was in Washington, many of his days would end with his going to the residence by around 5:15 p.m. He would take calls, but he rarely came back down.

NAVY JOAN ROBERTS

In July 2023, shamed into action by *New York Times* columnist Maureen Dowd, President and First Lady Biden finally acknowledged one of their grandchildren existed. She was already four years old. A DNA test in 2019 had proven Hunter was the father of Lunden Roberts's baby girl.

Hunter denied this reality. Even after the DNA test, he told people that he believed it could have been tampered with by the Republican-dominated state of Arkansas where Roberts was living. He wrote in his 2021 book that he didn't recall his "encounter" with Roberts, even though he put her on the payroll for months. He tried to prevent her from giving their daughter, Navy, the last name Biden and claimed he couldn't afford to pay child support, even as he was selling paintings—he was an artist now—for hundreds of thousands of dollars to buyers whose names were not disclosed.

The situation was tabloid fodder but relevant because of how much it suggests a family dynamic built around rejection of reality, one steered at times by Hunter, whose judgment and motivations were hardly solid.

He told his parents not to acknowledge her. When the First Lady wrote a children's book in 2020 about her husband, she dedicated it to six grandchildren, naming each one and excluding Navy. During Christmas season in 2021 and 2022, Jill hung six stockings for every grandchild—except Navy.

SPECIAL COUNSEL ROBERT HUR, PART TWO

Long before summer turned to fall in 2023, it had become clear to Hur and his team that they would need to interview Biden. There was substantial evidence that he had willfully and knowingly kept both marked classified documents and unmarked classified handwritten notes, recklessly stored. He had done so as a private citizen, when he had no legal authority to possess those materials.

Hur informed Garland of his intent to interview the president. Garland, as always, granted the special counsel what he felt he needed.

There were negotiations. Bauer and Ed Siskel, the new White House counsel, did not want the interview to be recorded on video. Hur wanted there to be audio, at least, so that no disagreements would arise about content based on notes or even a real-time transcript.

They agreed on audio and five hours total over two days.

Hur and his team were willing to do it anywhere—Wilmington or Camp David, for instance—but they were invited to the White House.

The first interview began early in the afternoon on October 8, 2023.

The day before, the terrorist group Hamas had invaded Israel, slaughtering more than 1,100 Israelis and other foreign nationals, including Americans, and taking more than 250 others hostage. The attack had deeply upset the president. Hur and his team offered to reschedule, but the White House said the president wanted to proceed.

Hur brought his deputy, Marc Krickbaum; two FBI agents; and one other person from the special counsel's office. They entered the China Room, with its collection of china from various presidencies, and took COVID tests. Then they were beckoned into the Map Room, where the team was surprised to find Biden already seated, Bauer to his right, Siskel to his left. Others from the White House Counsel's Office were there—Richard Sauber and Rachel Cotton—as well as David Laufman, one of Biden's attorneys.

It took Hur a couple of minutes to set up, with his binder and exhibits to show the president.

"I know there's a lot of other things in the world going on that demand your attention," Hur acknowledged.

"I just got off the phone with Bibi Netanyahu," Biden noted.

"Yes, sir," Hur said. "So I also wanted to say that we know that you have provided significant cooperation with our investigation, and I wanted to personally recognize that and thank you for it."

"The FBI knows my house better than I do," Biden quipped, drawing laughter.

His voice was so quiet throughout the interview that the FBI agents kept moving the microphones closer and closer to him. Biden was just shy of eighty-one and seemed every day of it.

The interview was alarming. Biden forgot words, trailed off in the middle of thoughts. His answers would jump around. Tales would ramble, then end abruptly, and he would rely on "anyway" and "all kidding aside" to try to end the stories when he lost his train of thought.

Asked if he had brought classified material from the West Wing or the Naval Observatory to the Greenville home, the president pointedly joked about the FBI spending ninety-nine hours there with 375 people searching the place, then noted, "I'm teasing you."

"You left everything in place," Biden said. "I just hope you didn't find any risqué pictures of my wife in a bathing suit. Which you probably did. She's beautiful. But all kidding aside, I have a library, and the library has a—two filing cabinets in it, and it has built into the walls— when I built that home, built into the walls, a space for a copy machine, for a—what do you call it when they send these—"

"Fax machine," Siskel broke in, quickly supplying the term that Biden couldn't find.

"Fax machine," the president echoed.

Some of his files, he said, contained speeches. "I just warn you all, never make one great eulogy, because you get asked to do everybody's eulogy," he added, to laughter. "You think I'm kidding? I'm not. How many people you know did—eulogize Teddy and Strom Thurmond? You know. Anyway, all kidding aside."

Departing senators could purchase their chairs, Biden noted—his was in that library. Then he was describing the house he had purchased in Delaware. Then he was detailing the rental in Virginia and "the desk I had as a lawyer. The first big case I won, I went out and bought a beautiful desk and credenza. You guys may have done something similar. And I have that in there, a couch and book shelving and a television in there. And there is a file cabinet in there, plus the file cabinets on the credenza behind that open with two big file drawers."

Nominally still on the topic of classified documents, Biden then returned to other furniture, a television, and a drafting board. "I also had, because I'm a frustrated architect, my gift was a drafting board that I got for Christmas a long time—"

"I'm sorry," Hur interrupted. "Drafting what, sir?"

"A drafting board, you know" Biden said. "You sit and draft designs. And so I have more stuff stacked up there now. And what happens is, as vice president and as president, a photographer takes hundreds of pictures of you. And if you—on the way out, just so you know what we're talking about, you got to walk them by just so they know what I'm talking about—is—there are pictures that are put on—what kind of board is that called? Anyway—"

"Poster board," Siskel said.

"A poster board or a sticker," Biden said.

The poster board had "great pictures of all kinds of different things," Biden said. "And so I have them hanging on the walls all over the downstairs, the television room, and some in the library, because they—you know, they tell stories like I—

"You know, I went to Mongolia and, and great pictures. I, unfortunately, embarrassed the hell out of the leader of Mongolia. They were showing—they were doing a—what they would do at the time of the invasion of the Mongols into Europe in the 14—in the 800s."

Was Biden running out the clock? The White House had only agreed to give Hur five hours. Was he being wily? Or was this something else?

"And they—and then show what a normal day was, or how they, how they bivouac," Biden continued. "And so we're out in the middle of nowhere and they're looking up on the hill and we see this tiny line. You know, it's a twenty-mile horse race with all these kids under the age of sixteen on bareback racing to come down. And you know, there are sumo wrestlers doin' everything they do. And so they walked over and they had a target with bales of hay a hundred yards away, and these guerrillas were, you know, taking shots. And I think—I don't know if it was to embarrass me or to make a point, but I get handed the bow and arrow. I'm not a bad archer." Biden mimicked firing an arrow. "So I—and pure luck, I hit the goddamn target."

People in the room laughed. (Reviewing the interview recording afterward, Hur and his team would consider how a jury might respond to this kind of testimony. Many might be overcome with sympathy. And even those who were impatient would be reluctant to convict this man of a federal crime and send him to prison.)

"No, I really did," Biden insisted. "Bales of hay that were, like, twenty bales of hay with a big target in the middle of the bale of hay. And so I didn't mean anything by it. I turned to the prime minister and handed it to him and the poor son-of-a-bitch couldn't pull it back. I was, I was like, 'Oh God.'"

There was laughter again.

"Anyway, so I have pictures like, like that, you know, that are up against the wall, and down here they're all over in my—in the, in the West Wing. Anyway, a lot of those pictures that you remember seeing them piled up—I know there must be fifty of them. I don't know what to do with them, you know. So there's a lot of stuff in that attic that is material that—and some of it is, you know—I think some of it is note-books of mine. I'm not sure, but anyway, that's the totality of where things would be."

They were close to the one-hour mark already.

An hour later, Hur was showing Biden images from the Delaware home.

"I just wanted you to know I picked out the walnut tree that got cut down," Biden said. "I found the guy who did [Winterthur] Museum Library, I picked out the craftsman to come do this—this room cost one-third of the entirety of my entire home. Swear to God."

Hur tried to refocus the president on the set of drawers where some of the classified materials had been found.

"So there's—the top opens to shelving, and the bottom opens to filing," Biden said. "So the bottom—so when you open this up, the first—the door on the—the first door there on the left, you see where there's a printer and there's a—what do they call it, the machine that—"

"Fax machine," Siskel said wearily, reminding the president of the term *fax machine* for the second time.

"A fax machine," Biden said.

"Yes, sir," Hur said.

At another point, Hur was asking Biden about the time he lived in McLean, Virginia, on Chain Bridge Road.

"Well, um . . ." Biden said. "I don't know. This is, what, 2017, 2018, that area?"

"Yes, sir," Hur said.

"Remember, in this time frame, my son is—either been deployed or is dying," Biden said.

That wasn't accurate. Beau had been deployed in Iraq from October 2008 to September 2009. He had died in May 2015.

"And by the way," Biden went on, "there were still a lot of people at the time when I got out of the Senate that were encouraging me to run in this period, except the president. I'm not—and not a mean thing to say. He just thought that she had a better shot of winning the presidency than I did. And so I hadn't, I hadn't, at this point—even though I'm at Penn, I hadn't walked away from the idea that I may run for office again. But if I ran again, I'd be running for president. And, and so what was happening, though—what month did Beau die? Oh, God, May thirtieth."

"2015," Cotton clarified for him.

"Was it 2015 he had died?" Biden asked.

"It was May of 2015," Biden was reminded.

"It was 2015," Biden said.

"Or I'm not sure the month, sir, but I think that was the year," Bauer said.

"And Trump gets elected in November of 2017?" Biden asked.

"2016," he was reminded.

Though Hur had not even remotely raised it, Biden was now on the topic of Beau's tragic death, and he was off and running.

"Beau was like my right arm and Hunt was my left," he said. "These guys were a year and a day apart, and they could finish each other's sentences, and Beau—I used to go home on the train, and in the period that I was still in the Senate—anyway." After an indiscernible utterance, he continued: "There was pressure—not pressure. Beau knew how much I adored him, and I know this sounds—maybe this sounds so—everybody knew how close we were. There was not anybody in the world who wondered whether or not—anyway."

Hur was growing concerned for the president, who seemed confused and had landed on an emotional topic. He felt bad for him.

"Sir, I'm wondering if this is a good time to take a break briefly," Hur suggested. "Would that be—"

"No, I—let me just keep going to get it done," Biden said. "Anyway, here's the deal. Beau—I used to go home when Beau was at—from Penn, I used to go home on the train on Fridays, and always Jill and I would go—as the crow flies, Beau and his family lived a mile from where we lived in Delaware."

And then he was off on a six-minute story about the promise that Beau, as he was dying, insisted his father make to him, and the horrific white supremacist rally in Charlottesville, and a Biden family meeting, and on and on.

None of it had anything to do with the question about the house on Chain Bridge Road.

ARI EMANUEL AND THE WEEKEND

For months now, Ari Emanuel—CEO of Endeavor, a talent and entertainment company, and a major Democratic donor—hadn't been able to believe what he was watching.

President Joe Biden was quite obviously deteriorating before the nation's eyes, and Democrats seemed to be in complete denial about it. Emanuel would call governors and encourage them to run. He would talk to his brother Rahm, a former Obama chief of staff and then an ambassador to Japan. He would discuss it with anyone who would listen.

In late September 2023, at his annual power-player retreat, known as "The Weekend," Emanuel sensed an opportunity to directly challenge the Biden team. Among the figures in attendance were Ron Klain, participating in a panel discussion about the upcoming election with former New Jersey Governor Chris Christie; former George W. Bush adviser Karl Rove; and ABC News' Jonathan Karl.

From the back of the room, Emanuel began yelling at Klain.

Joe Biden cannot run for reelection! He needs to drop out! He can't win! What's the plan B? Emanuel was flat-out shouting at Klain.

There is no plan B, Klain responded. *He's the sitting president of the United States. He's the only one who can—who has—defeated Donald Trump.*

Emanuel was incensed. *What the fuck are we doing?* he asked. *The first party to put a younger candidate before the voters, if we give him enough time, we can win.* Emanuel knew Trump well, having been his agent for almost a decade.

"It was wild," attendee Michael Kives later recalled. "A public yelling match between them." Obviously, it was Emanuel's conference, but up until then, it had been a pretty civilized affair, Kives remembered.

Eventually, Emanuel came to believe they were all lying about Biden's health. "We're seeing it!" he would shout. "It's called age! It happens!"

Everyone around the president—worst of all, Jill—was lying, Emanuel would say. Jill and Hunter and Jeffrey Katzenberg and Ron fucking Klain. And the president had lied, too, when he said he would be a bridge. Then, all of a sudden, he wasn't a bridge. And no one around Biden was telling him the obvious—he wasn't capable of running anymore.

Katzenberg, a Hollywood power broker and major Democratic fundraiser, would call Emanuel to solicit donations, but Emanuel wasn't interested. He didn't want to be anywhere near the Biden campaign. He was stomping his feet in the town square. And no one was taking it seriously.

BILL DALEY, PART ONE

Throughout 2022, William "Bill" Daley, a former chief of staff to Obama and Clinton Commerce Secretary, watched Biden on TV and got a sinking feeling. He'd known Biden for forty years—he had been the political director of Biden's 1988 campaign—and was stunned by how much his old friend and colleague seemed to be deteriorating. He knew Biden as a feisty, energetic senator, then vice president, full of piss and vinegar. He hardly recognized the guy on TV. There was no way this was going to work, he would tell friends.

In 2023, he made some calls to see if any heavy hitters were thinking about running against Biden in the Democratic primaries. Having been around politics forever, Daley felt strongly that the notion that Biden would be up to the task the following year was unsustainable. If they waited too long, the inevitable moment when Biden bowed out would saddle the Democratic Party with Vice President Harris as the nominee, and she was even less popular than Biden.

Neither California Governor Gavin Newsom nor Kentucky Governor Andy Beshear was willing to take the plunge. Daley also reached out through an emissary to his own governor, JB Pritzker.

They all said no. Others had advised them that doing so would make them pariahs; when and if Biden lost, they would be blamed.

By THAT FALL, it was worse behind the scenes for senior Democrats, who were having disquieting experiences with Biden.

Jaime Harrison, whom Biden had picked to chair the Democratic National Committee, met the president at an event with the Congressional Black Caucus in the fall of 2023.

Biden took his hand and just seemed to keep shaking it without saying anything. It didn't appear as though he recognized him.

Afterward, Harrison confessed what had just happened to another Democrat. "Uh, that wasn't good, right?"

Around the same time, Senator Mark Warner took a call from the president. The chairman of the Senate Select Committee on Intelligence had been concerned about a potential presidential action. When the call ended, he had a brand-new worry.

The Senate Intel Committee had been informed that eleven detainees currently housed at Guantánamo Bay—ones who were Yemeni—were going to be sent to Oman.

Warner and other colleagues worried that some of them would end up right back in the terrorist fight—attacking Israel or the West by joining Hamas in Gaza, Hezbollah in Lebanon, the Houthis in Yemen, or other groups elsewhere.

Warner called National Security Adviser Jake Sullivan to express his concerns.

Sullivan passed on Warner's thoughts to Biden, who followed up. But Biden seemed oblivious to concerns that Warner thought were rather obvious. The president was clearly not up to speed on this.

Warner wondered how much of this was related to the president's aging issues, which he felt were becoming visibly apparent to anyone watching.

DAVID AXELROD, PART TWO

In early November 2023, *The New York Times* and Siena College published their joint poll of battleground states, and the news for Biden was bad.

Trump was up ten in Nevada, six in Georgia, five in Arizona, five in Michigan, and four in Pennsylvania. Biden led by two percentage points in Wisconsin.

In 2020, 34 percent of voters had thought Biden too old to be president. In 2023, that figure shot up to 71 percent. In 2020, 45 percent of voters had thought that Biden lacked the mental sharpness to be president. In 2023, that percentage grew to 62 percent.

David Axelrod hoped someone in the White House would come to their senses and convince Biden and his family that this just wasn't tenable. There was still time for viable Democratic candidates to throw their hats into the ring, though practically speaking, only a few hopefuls could launch a race so quickly—Harris, Klobuchar, Pritzker, Whitmer, Newsom, and Buttigieg.

Biden wasn't just projecting as old—he was projecting as out of touch. In June 2023, the White House launched a campaign taking credit for how "Bidenomics" was working. At a time when Pew had the president with a 35 percent approval rating, 62 percent disapproval; in a month when 65 percent of those surveyed thought that inflation was a very big problem; in an era when seven out of ten Americans were worried that the economy was getting worse, Biden was taking a victory lap, branding with his name an economy that people hated.

Axelrod thought the strategy completely missed the fundamental point: Most people judge the economy through their own lived experience. And here was a guy whose empathy was supposedly his superpower, yet he was telling people that what they were feeling about the economy—based on what they were paying at the grocery store and the gas pump and so on—was wrong.

Biden was burnishing an image for himself as the voice of discredited Washington institutions, as someone who just didn't know what was going on. Trump was out there saying that the world had spun out of control and this guy was not in command, and Axelrod could see that to a lot of people, it was a very powerful argument.

Axelrod wondered if maybe the Biden family could be encouraged to have a serious chat with the president about what he was truly capable of doing as he prepared to turn eighty-one.

He copied a link to the battleground poll graphics and typed out on X: "It's very late to change horses; a lot will happen in the next year that no one can predict & Biden's team says his resolve to run is firm. He's defied CW before but this will send tremors of doubt thru the party—not 'bed-wetting,' but legitimate concern."

Axelrod continued: "Only @JoeBiden can make this decision. If he continues to run, he will be the nominee of the Democratic Party. What he needs to decide is whether that is wise; whether it's in HIS best interest or the country's?"

The response was fast and furious.

"Man who called Biden 'Mr Magoo' in Aug 2019 is still at it," Ron Klain remarked in a repost.

This was a reference to a comment that Axelrod had made after a 2019 debate, saying of Biden, "I wouldn't say he was a house of fire in any of the debates that we've been to. And yet he comes, kind of bumps along, kind of Mr. Magoo-ing his way through this. You keep worrying he's going to hit a wall, but he's moving forward."

Axelrod had gone on to note that Biden had a play to make in the 2020 contests "because of his strong support in the African American community and because he has a cultural kinship with working-class whites, non-college whites," but obviously, four years later, the reference to the clumsy, disaster-prone, and absent-minded elderly cartoon character still hit a nerve.

In response to Axelrod's 2023 post, Biden called Axelrod a "prick"—a private insult until someone leaked it to Jonathan Martin of *Politico*.

Axelrod received confidential messages of agreement from prominent Democrats who remained silent, they explained, because they were resigned to Biden's candidacy and did not want to weaken him as a looming rematch with Trump approached.

THE PENGUINS

David Morehouse was best known for his tenure as CEO of the Pittsburgh Penguins, a heralded era when the NHL team won three Stanley Cups, made the playoffs for sixteen consecutive years, and sold out every home game for fourteen seasons. But Morehouse had a career in politics before then, and he'd worked on four campaigns—both of Bill Clinton's, then Al Gore's in 2000 and John Kerry's in 2004.

On December 11, 2023, Morehouse flew to Philly for an afternoon

Biden fundraising luncheon at the Hilton at Penn's Landing. Well-heeled donors like Morehouse sat around a dozen round tables, ten to a table. Among the guests were Governor Josh Shapiro, former Governors Tom Wolf and Ed Rendell, Senator Chris Coons, Congresswoman Madeleine Dean, and Congresswoman Chrissy Houlahan.

Morehouse went up for his photo with the president and shook his hand. He was stunned by how frail Biden seemed.

"It was nothing but bones," Morehouse later recalled.

During their brief encounter, Biden told Morehouse a story involving him and Kerry that Morehouse knew had never happened. Morehouse worried about what he saw in Biden's eyes: It reminded him of his ailing mother. He remembered talking to his sister, telling her of his concerns about their mom. After sitting with their mother, his sister would say that Mom was fine. Morehouse would ask how long she'd sat with her. "Half an hour," his sister would say. "That's not long enough," Morehouse would reply. "It's on a loop. After an hour, the loop runs out and she begins repeating herself, because short-term memory is the first to go."

Looking at Biden, seeing how old he was, feeling his frail hand, and knowing firsthand from his past experiences what a non-COVID-era presidential campaign entails, Morehouse knew Biden couldn't do it. He immediately told a governor to whom he was close: "I know you can't respond, but just listen to what I'm saying. I've worked on four of these things. This guy cannot run for president of the United States."

Morehouse was so alarmed that he also called Anthony Bernal, who didn't have much to say in response. He called other alumni from the Clinton administration. One of them bluntly told him: "You can't talk about this stuff. We're backing Biden."

Having been a close adviser to Gore and Kerry, Morehouse began wondering about Biden's closest advisers. Okay, so neither the president nor the First Lady wanted to make the decision not to run again. Biden's close advisers had a responsibility to figure out how they could make him bow out. They had to do something. This was irresponsible.

CHRISTMAS PARTY

Washington Congressman Adam Smith was the top Democrat on the House Armed Services Committee, but he had had very little interaction with the president. In April 2022, he'd seen him at an Earth Day celebration at a public park in Seattle and thought Biden seemed about the same as he had been in 2020—long-winded, old, but fine. However, in December 2023, at the White House Christmas Party for members of Congress, Smith was stunned by what he encountered. Interacting with guests and standing in the photo line, Biden seemed completely out of it.

Other partygoers were similarly alarmed when they noticed that the First Lady was taking the lead in delivering remarks to the crowd, while Biden stayed wedded to a script.

He can't even do holiday party remarks?

At another Christmas party that week, standing in the East Room and speaking to the crowd, the president could barely be heard or understood, even though he had a microphone.

By the end of 2023, Biden seemed to have become significantly feebler. Some commentators spoke up—David Ignatius of *The Washington Post*, comedian Bill Maher who warned of "Ruth Bader Biden"—but very few Democrats were willing to say anything publicly about it. Minnesota Congressman Dean Phillips was a rare exception.

TEN

Dean Phillips

Congressman Dean Phillips's grandmother was Pauline Phillips, better known by her pen name, Abigail Van Buren—the famous advice columnist behind Dear Abby. The grandson had a tougher time getting people to take his advice, even though he was a member of the House Democratic leadership team.

Throughout 2023, as the president's speaking and walking skills seemed to visibly decline, it was clear to Phillips that Biden's communication problems likely indicated some cognitive issues. It was also clear that his fellow Democratic officials were in deep denial about this. "People will talk their way into beliefs," Phillips would later say. "Even O. J. believed he didn't do it at the end."

When Phillips pressed them, some Democrats would offer what the congressman called the "yes, but." As in: "Yes, Biden is in decline, but can you imagine Trump winning?"

Yes, Phillips could imagine Trump winning, especially if Biden were the Democratic nominee.

He tried to get other Democrats to talk about the president's decline, but no one was willing to say anything publicly. "The whale who spouts gets harpooned," Phillips later noted.

In July 2022, WCCO's Chad Hartman asked Phillips if he wanted Biden to run for reelection in 2024.

"No, I don't," Phillips told the radio host. "I think the country would be well served by a new generation of compelling, well-prepared, dynamic Democrats who step up."

He was going to push others to run against Biden in the Democratic primaries and caucuses. This was his new mission—to enlist competitors. He reached out directly to Governors JB Pritzker and Gretchen Whitmer, but both declined to take his call.

On August 5, 2023, a day before appearing on CBS's *Face the Nation*, Phillips called House Democratic Leader Hakeem Jeffries and the White House to give them a heads-up that he would be making a call for a competitive Democratic primary.

White House Chief of Staff Jeff Zients told him that what he was about to do was insane. Phillips wanted to talk to the president. Zients told him that wasn't going to happen.

Phillips had been planning on pushing the two Midwestern Democratic governors, but when asked about running himself, Phillips acknowledged that he was considering it if no one else stepped up.

On August 13, 2023, after meeting with some donors in New York City, Phillips went on NBC's *Meet the Press* and said he would like to see "Joe Biden, a wonderful and remarkable man, pass the torch, cement this extraordinary legacy." His preference for another Democratic presidential candidate, he said, would be "a moderate governor, hopefully from the heartland, from one of the four states that Democrats will need."

Moderator Chuck Todd threw some names at him: Whitmer, who had declined to take Phillips's call; Minnesota Governor Tim Walz; Wisconsin Governor Tony Evers.

Phillips agreed and added Pritzker, who'd also declined to take his call, and the new governor of Pennsylvania, Josh Shapiro. "Some people have asked me that I not use their names because of this institutional fear that it might impact you down the road," Phillips said.

He knew he was becoming a distraction, an irritant, a burr under the Democratic saddle. In September 2023, Phillips tried to resign from his leadership position; Jeffries wouldn't have it.

But a few weeks later, California Congresswoman Sydney Kamlager-Dove stood up at a meeting and asked: "How can one member of the leadership have a perspective that is so incongruent with the rest of us?" This time, when Phillips offered his resignation, Jeffries accepted it.

Soon, Phillips was huddling with advisers at the congressman's townhouse in Capitol Hill. They sat at his dining-room table and tried to envision and plan an insurgent campaign focusing on the New Hampshire primary, where other insurgent candidates—Eugene McCarthy in 1968, Gary Hart in 1984, Pat Buchanan in 1992, John McCain in 2000—had found friendly terrain. They were weeks away from the October 27 filing deadline.

Even after Biden's approval rating sank to a disastrous 37 percent by the end of October 2023, whatever argument Phillips was going to try to make would not be heard by most voters. Phillips announced his campaign on October 27. He was about to learn just how far the Democratic Party's commitment to democracy would reach.

Back in 2016, when Bernie Sanders would complain about the extent to which the process was rigged, with the DNC making it difficult to challenge Hillary Clinton, Phillips thought he was just being a sore loser. When Marianne Williamson, another outsider Democratic candidate, would complain about being shut out of the process in 2020, Phillips would deride her. But now he came to see what they had meant.

The previous year, in 2022, leaders of the Democratic Party hadn't even been sure that Biden was going to run for reelection. In the final months of 2022, the DNC started asking if it needed to prepare for a primary, which would mean setting up debates and figuring out the primary system. When the committee approached the White House, Jen O'Malley Dillon made clear that no further conversations were needed. Biden was running.

That was the end of the conversation—and the beginning of an effort by the Democratic establishment to exclude Phillips from the process as much as they could. Every White House pressures its party establishment to make things harder for potential challengers, but members of the Biden team acknowledged that they tested and pushed those boundaries.

They started with the primary calendar. In 2020, Biden had come in fourth in Iowa, fifth in New Hampshire, second in Nevada, and first in South Carolina, where he had deep appeal with older Black voters. Without looping in other Democratic Party leaders, Biden unilaterally called for making South Carolina the first state contest.

This move stunned party leaders. Not even Congressman Jim Clyburn or DNC Chair Jaime Harrison—both of South Carolina—had asked for their state to be first. Clyburn admitted later that the White House did it to protect Biden from "embarrassment."

Biden framed his decision as about lifting underrepresented Black voices and suggested that anyone who questioned it—including Phillips—was undermining Black voters, even racist. That claim was undercut by the fact that he called for the calendar change to be for only one presidential cycle—the one he was running in—and the calendar would be revisited in 2028. Internally at the White House and the DNC, aides privately admitted that the main motivation was helping Joe Biden, not uplifting Black voters. The DNC also made clear that there would be no party-sanctioned debates, challengers notwithstanding. It was machine-style politics to ensure that Biden would be the nominee, even as millions of Democratic voters were making plain their serious concerns about his ability to do the job. Most Democratic would-be rivals were deterred. Robert F. Kennedy Jr. and Marianne Williamson challenged Biden but struggled to gain traction.

The Democratic Party of Wisconsin and its chair, Ben Wikler, refused to recognize Phillips as a candidate. Phillips had to sue all the way up to the Wisconsin Supreme Court, which unanimously ruled that he should be included on the ballot.

Phillips would tell people that he ran to force a debate with the president. A debate, he maintained, would expose to the world that this man—while decent and a good president in the past—could not compete for the highest office in the land. He was not up for another term.

But Phillips could not get Biden on a stage to prove his point. And the entire Democratic Party apparatus went along with it.

Phillips suspended his campaign after a bad showing on Super Tuesday. He endorsed Joe Biden and watched his party sleepwalk toward disaster.

ELEVEN

2024

President Biden and the Politburo entered the election year feeling good about their accomplishments. In 2023, the House GOP majority had dragged them into a fight over raising the debt ceiling, and under the president's direction, White House officials had successfully negotiated a way for both sides to get something out of it. Four months later, they did so well at negotiating a government funding bill that it cost Speaker Kevin McCarthy his job. People pointing to how doddery Biden looked while stiffly walking to Marine One were missing the point, the Politburo argued. His gait had nothing to do with his presidential fitness.

Biden and his team were also spiking the ball on his inevitable win in the Democratic primary process. If the president were truly politically weak, Mike Donilon argued, some credible alternative candidate would have run against him. Politics abhors a vacuum. Ambitious politicians seize opportunities when they sense vulnerability—Ted Kennedy challenging Jimmy Carter in 1980, Pat Buchanan challenging George H. W. Bush in 1992. That didn't happen with Biden.

None of the possible credible candidates—neither Newsom nor Whitmer, Pritzker nor Klobuchar—challenged the president.

Carter was weak, so Kennedy challenged him, Donilon would say. H. W. was weak, so Buchanan challenged him. Biden was not weak.

That's what the president and the Politburo saw when they looked out the window at 2024.

They dismissed the ugly "right track/wrong track" polling numbers, noting how those had plummeted around the withdrawal from Afghanistan in August 2021 and emphasized instead how the numbers had never changed dramatically from that point in time. It was a lame horse to which they hitched their wagon, but it was their argument: *The polling numbers have always been weak; they're not much worse now.* They would circle back to this line of thinking after the debate in June.

Others in their orbit did not see it that way. They were worried.

Many Democratic senators were longtime personal friends of the president, holding him in high regard as a person and political ally.

They also viewed his aging from the skewed perspective of the Senate, a place that required, some would joke, a minor in geriatrics. As of January 2024, Iowa Senator Chuck Grassley was ninety; Vermont Senator Bernie Sanders, eighty-two; Kentucky Senator Mitch McConnell, eighty-one; Idaho Senator James "Jim" Risch, eighty; and Maryland Senator Ben Cardin, eighty. A year later, only Cardin had retired.

In early 2024, during private meetings with Biden, some Democratic senators would notice a considerable change, something more complicated than just aging. A marked decline in his ability to speak and move. It worried them. He was always expressing confidence to them that he would be able to handily beat Trump, and he had done so before, so they gave him the benefit of the doubt. But the alarming change in him did not go unnoticed.

Still, they kept silent.

As for White House staffers who had regular contact with the president, they seemed, at this point in his presidency, to split into three basic groups.

The Politburo made up the first group, its members having convinced themselves that the areas that caused people alarm were merely "performative" parts of the president's job. The decisions being made behind closed doors were all that truly mattered, they told themselves. They dismissed or ignored those who raised concerns.

It was a theology that bordered on zealotry: In January 2025, Donilon continued to hold the viewpoint that while Biden might forget and mix up names, when the president decided what the proposal should be for a peace deal between Hamas and Israel, he was pretty damn smart.

Not everyone so blithely ignored the need for a president who could communicate effectively.

There was a second group of staffers who believed that the president's decision-making was solid but also acknowledged that, yes, his communications were a problem. The president should be able to speak clearly and cohesively, off the cuff, to inspire confidence and convince others of the correctness of his views. Such "performative" parts of the job were neither superficial nor unimportant. They were, in this age, integral to presidential leadership. The second group took the concerns seriously.

There was also a third group: those who were concerned that the president was in serious decline. They were angry, feeling that the Politburo was doing the country and the president a deep disservice by pretending this wasn't happening.

THE UKRAINE MEETING

According to the official White House readout of the January 17, 2024, meeting between Biden, his top national security advisers, and House and Senate Republicans and Democrats, the president had convened the appropriate congressional leaders to "discuss the urgent need for Congress to continue supporting Ukraine as part of the global coalition we have built."

The White House comms shop wielded many action verbs: "President Biden underscored the importance of Congress ensuring Ukraine has the resources it needs. . . . He was clear: Congress's continued failure to act endangers the United States' national security, the NATO Alliance, and the rest of the free world."

Months later, when *Wall Street Journal* reporters began hearing that the official readout didn't reflect reality, the Biden White House circled the wagons and enlisted allies to push the narrative that in the meeting, Biden was "incredibly strong, forceful, and decisive," as Leader Hakeem Jeffries insisted.

After reading Jeffries's quote, a House Democrat who'd been at the meeting responded: "That's not true."

Said a second House Democrat who was also there: "It was a disaster. . . . It was a shitshow."

That Wednesday afternoon, they all sat around the table in the White House Cabinet Room. For the first twenty minutes of the meeting, the president listlessly read bullet points out of a binder. For many at the table, he was difficult to hear. He stumbled over words; he started sentences and then stopped abruptly; he trailed off.

When it was time to go around the table so that congressional leaders could ask questions, the president deferred to National Security Adviser Jake Sullivan and National Intelligence Director Avril Haines, asking them to weigh in with answers.

"He was clearly not capable of making a strong, forceful argument," said the first House Democrat. Biden would start talking and get going for a bit before he'd segue to another topic, and then all of a sudden, he would realize that he was drifting and abruptly stop, often hastily ending the digression by saying, "Anyway . . ."

The second House Democrat pointed to an interesting moment when Republican Leader Mitch McConnell, "who's hard to understand too, starts talking about something, and all of a sudden, the president gets interested. It's like the man has woken up! He was like, 'Oh, yeah, Mitch, you remember when we negotiated with that guy?' All of a sudden, he was a totally different person because he got engaged."

As the second House Democrat recalled, he left the meeting with "a flicker of hope where I thought, *The guy's not comatose.*"

The first House Democrat noted that Republicans took advantage of the president's limited communication abilities to slow-walk the vote on aid to Ukraine: "It's been one of the dodges that Republicans have used to excuse their lack of support for Ukraine. They say, 'President Biden just hasn't made a case to the American people.' And they weren't really wrong about that" in terms of Biden's "getting out there and making a strong case, though that was no excuse for abandoning Ukraine." (The aid bill would ultimately pass in April, after months of delay.)

This was yet another area where Biden's diminishment may have had a real impact.

For new House Speaker Mike Johnson, a Louisiana Republican, the Ukraine meeting marked the first time—other than a quick meet and greet after Johnson's election in October 2023—that he had been at a meeting with Biden. Though he was sitting directly across from the president, he found it difficult to hear him. It was disconcerting. But he also knew that anything he said about it would be discounted by Democrats as partisan sniping.

"WHAT THE FUCK are you guys doing?"

The senior administration official was direct with their White House colleague. In January, on the fifty-first anniversary of *Roe v. Wade*, the official had attended a meeting with the president and his task force on reproductive health-care access.

Biden had started the meeting, held in the State Dining Room, by reading remarks from a teleprompter. To the senior administration official, the high stakes of the subject matter—abortion bans and extreme restrictions—were undercut by the president's weak, slurry presentation.

He mixed up Homeland Security Secretary Alejandro Mayorkas, who was in the room, and Health and Human Services Secretary Xavier Becerra, who was participating via Zoom. Then when the cameras went away and the private meeting began with the roughly two dozen attendees around the table and more than a dozen more around the perimeter, it got worse. He confused Texas and Alabama even though they had just been talking about Alabama. He was barely audible and swallowing his words.

This is crazy, the official thought. *What's going on? I don't understand.*

The official left the meeting shaken and called the White House the next day.

"I don't get how this guy can do any campaigning to run for reelection," the official said.

A year later, that official told us, "I blame his inner circle, and I blame him. What utter and total hubris not to step aside and be a one-term president, as he said he would, and have an open primary when there was time to let the process play out. Even though he did so many good things for this country, I can never forgive him."

THE DEAL

In early 2024, Donilon and O'Malley Dillon left the White House for the campaign in Wilmington. Before he agreed to head north, Donilon negotiated with President Biden what he needed to be paid. His work would cost a significant amount.

Donilon had been paid a great deal in 2020 as well, making a commission on paid advertisements—with no caps. It was an arrangement that frustrated others in the campaign who thought it was malpractice for Biden to have agreed to that.

Biden agreed to a new arrangement for 2024. To leave the White House and advise the 2024 campaign, Donilon wanted approximately $4 million.

He wouldn't budge. The president told the campaign: Pay Mike what he wants.

Senior campaign staff were outraged when they heard about this arrangement. Four million dollars to work from February until November? The most highly paid person after him was the campaign chair, O'Malley Dillon, who was paid a fraction of that—$300,000, plus a $100,000 bonus after Biden won the nomination.

FUMBLE

Barack Obama set the tradition for the Super Bowl pregame interview, and it's a pretty smart one. A president gets a shot to talk football and a few pressing issues before one of the largest audiences in the world, and given that audience's general mood and disinclination toward buzzkills, matters tend not to get too intense. In addition to chatting with more traditional news anchors—Scott Pelley on CBS and Savannah Guthrie on NBC—Obama was even willing to mix it up twice with conservative Bill O'Reilly when the big game ran on Fox.

Biden had eschewed the opportunity to go on Fox for the 2023 Super Bowl—the network was in the midst of being sued by software company Dominion Voting Systems for platforming myriad lies about the 2020 election over months and months, casting Biden as illegitimate. But when it was CBS's turn again on February 11, 2024, with the Chiefs taking on the 49ers, Biden again opted out.

The opportunity being offered wasn't what it had been in the past. CBS Sports didn't want to air an interview with the president at all, preferring ratings-friendly content, and the offer to the White House was for a fifteen-minute taped interview, only three minutes of which would air during the pregame. The rest would go to *CBS Evening News* and *CBS Mornings*.

If one did not know all the machinations going on behind the scenes, it looked as though the White House was forgoing an opportunity for exposure because advisers knew that the president wasn't capable of an exchange. Without question, Biden's capacity to communicate was worrisomely diminished, and the White House was putting him out for serious news interviews less and less.

But there was another reason to refuse the opportunity.

The White House knew that Special Counsel Robert Hur's report on Biden's mishandling of classified information was going to drop any minute. It knew that the pregame offer would therefore turn into a fifteen-minute interview about the Hur report before a massive audience. And there was no way the White House was going to let that happen.

SPECIAL COUNSEL ROBERT HUR, PART THREE

In February 2024, the president and his loyalists took their denial of his deterioration to a new level. That was when the White House declared war on its own Justice Department over the issue.

Before submitting his report to the attorney general, Hur informed White House Counsel Ed Siskel that he and the president's personal lawyers could review the draft to correct factual errors and make sure it did not contain anything that they believed should be excluded on account of executive privilege claims. A secure room in a Justice Department facility near the White House was set up; Siskel could review the report on Saturday, February 3. He needed to sign a nondisclosure agreement before being allowed to see it.

The next day, the special counsel's team was annoyed but perhaps not all that surprised to read an *Axios* story by Alex titled "Biden's Team Bracing for Special Counsel's Report on Classified Docs." In it, Alex reported that "Biden aides don't expect criminal charges in the case, but they believe Hur's report will include embarrassing details—possibly with photos—on how Biden stored documents."

"Some in Biden's orbit have unflatteringly compared Garland to former FBI Director James Comey and his handling of the investigation into Hillary Clinton's email server," Alex continued. "Comey ultimately cleared Clinton of criminal wrongdoing but damaged her election campaign against Trump in July 2016 by making a public statement that she had been 'extremely careless' in her security protocols."

The White House war against Garland and Hur was just beginning.

The Hur report was officially delivered to Garland on February 5, 2024. It had three main points.

First, that Biden had almost certainly knowingly mishandled classified information. "Our investigation uncovered evidence that President Biden willfully retained and disclosed classified materials after his vice presidency when he was a private citizen."

Noting previous cases of what is sometimes called "spillage," especially with President Reagan and his diaries, Hur stated that "there is no record of the Department of Justice prosecuting a former president or vice president for mishandling classified documents from his own administration," with the one exception being former President Trump. Hur stressed several serious distinctions between Trump's case and Biden's, most notably the fact that "after being given multiple chances to return classified documents and avoid prosecution, Mr. Trump allegedly did the opposite."

However, Hur noted that when Biden was asked about his reaction to the image of the "top secret documents laid out on the floor at Mar-a-Lago," Biden said it was "totally irresponsible" and could "compromise sources and methods."

Biden's "emphatic and unqualified conclusion that keeping marked classified documents unsecured in one's home is 'totally irresponsible' because it 'may compromise sources and methods' applies equally to his own decision to keep his notebooks at home in unlocked and unauthorized containers," Hur wrote.

The second point was that Hur had concluded "that no criminal charges are warranted in this matter."

Points one and two would seem to be contradictory. The explanation could be found in point three: The prosecutors believed that a jury would see Biden "as a sympathetic, well-meaning, elderly man with a poor memory."

Prosecutors make calculations all the time about whether they can get a conviction. Some witnesses seem uncredible. Some victims might seem heartless. And some criminals might seem so addled that they're entirely sympathetic.

Painting a portrait of a man in decline, the report noted that Biden's memory in the Zwonitzer tapes, in the spring of 2017, had "significant limitations." Biden's recorded conversations from that time were described as "often painfully slow, with Mr. Biden struggling to remember events and straining at times to read and relay his own notebook entries."

Flash forward to the fall of 2023, when Biden had his interviews with the special counsel's office. Summing up their impressions, Hur concluded: "Biden's memory was worse."

Biden seemed to have difficulty grasping the fact that his vice presidency lasted from January 2009 until January 2017. Once, trying to understand a point in time in 2013, he asked, "Well, if it was 2013—when did I stop being vice president?"

"2017," a White House lawyer reminded him.

"So I was vice president," he said. "So it must've come from vice president stuff. That's all I can think of."

At another moment, asked about a "Facts First" file with documents "related to Afghanistan from 2009," Biden asked, "I'm, at this stage, in 2009, am I still vice president?"

Hur noted that Biden at one point "did not remember, even within several years, when his son Beau died." An uncomfortable but accurate assessment.

Hur noted these moments and explained that while he would have to prove at any potential trial that Biden kept these documents knowing he was breaking the law, he expected that the president's attorneys "would emphasize these limitations in his recall." The case just wasn't winnable, Hur concluded. "While he is and must be accountable for his actions—he is, after all, the president of the United States—based on our direct observations of him, Mr. Biden is someone for whom many jurors will want to search for reasonable doubt. It would be difficult to convince a jury they should convict him—by then a former president who will be at least well into his eighties—of a serious felony that requires a mental state of willfulness."

THERE WERE CAREER prosecutors who read the special counsel's report and thought to themselves, *Holy crap, the president clearly broke the law! The same law that Special Counsel Jack Smith is going after Donald Trump for breaking! There's even an audio tape of Biden talking about possessing classified information—much like the audio tape of Trump discussing the same thing!*

But this was not the part of the report that upset Team Biden.

Privately, in a February 5 letter to Hur from Bauer and Sauber, and then in a February 7 letter to Garland signed by Bauer and Siskel, Biden's lawyers said parts of the draft report—which had not yet been released to the public—"violate Department of Justice policy and practice by pejoratively characterizing uncharged conduct."

Primarily, Bauer and Siskel objected to the "multiple denigrating statements about President Biden's memory," which painted a picture of a president with "a failing memory in a general sense, an allegation that has no law enforcement purpose." The "pejorative judgment" that Biden had poor powers of recollection was "uncalled for and unfounded."

Many legal observers thought odd the decision by the two Biden lawyers to focus on the part of the report describing the president's memory and not the part that compares Trump's actions unfavorably with Biden's, or the essential exculpatory nature of their conclusion.

Siskel repeatedly called DOJ leadership to argue that Hur shouldn't have written those passages, implicitly arguing for them to be edited out. The White House team was furious, and word of their ire was spreading. They were mad at the recusal of Deputy Attorney General Lisa Monaco, who had worked with Biden when she worked for the Obama White House. They wanted her to protect Biden, but she didn't do it.

The implications of their objections were confounding. The White House wanted Garland to remove those passages before the report was released to Congress and the public.

Beyond the fact that such an action was not in Garland's makeup—he gave deference to his special counsels—Garland was arguably obligated by regulation to alert Congress anytime he directed the special counsel to take an action such as making a major edit. Did they somehow think that cutting comments about Biden's age wouldn't be scandalous? That this wouldn't leak? That a simple Freedom of Information Act filing might not reveal those words to the world?

Or were they more broadly pushing for the entire report to be quashed?

The previous August, when he had appointed Weiss to investigate Hunter Biden, Garland had made a pledge: "As with each special counsel who has served since I have taken office, I am committed to making as much of his report public as possible, consistent with legal requirements and Department policy."

Would the White House have preferred it if the special counsel had concluded that Biden would not present as sympathetically impaired to a jury—and had therefore proceeded with prosecution?

The task of responding to the Biden attorneys fell to the top career prosecutor, Associate Deputy Attorney General Bradley Weinsheimer, who said that the language they found objectionable was "neither gratuitous nor unduly prejudicial because it is not offered to criticize or demean the president; rather, it is offered to explain Special Counsel Hur's conclusions about the president's state of mind in possessing and retaining classified information."

Garland released the report to Congress, then to the public, on February 8.

THE PREVIOUS AFTERNOON, the president said that at the 2021 G7 summit, "Helmut Kohl said, 'Joe, what—what would you think if you picked up the phone—if you picked up the paper tomorrow and learned in the London *Times*, in the front page, that a thousand people stormed the Parliament, broke down the doors of the House of Commons, killed two bobbies, and, in the process, ended up trying to stop the—the election of a Prime Minister?'" Kohl, German chancellor from 1982 until 1998, died in 2017. Angela Merkel was the German chancellor who attended that G7 summit.

Just a few days before, Biden had said that during a different 2021 conversation, "Mitterrand, from Germany—I mean, from France—looked at me and said, said, 'You know, what—why—how long you back for?'" François Mitterrand, president of France from 1981 to 1995, died in 1996.

In the White House transcript of the 2024 remarks, the name of the current French president, Emmanuel Macron, was added, and Mitterrand was crossed off. The president made so many errors of name and fact—well beyond the normal here-and-there misstatements of anyone who talks a lot publicly—that White House transcribers quickly learned how to apply the "strikethrough" feature.

Throughout the day on February 8, the White House discussed how to respond to the Hur report. Earlier on, they were leaning toward releasing a simple written statement. But that idea was upended when Biden's family intervened.

Hunter and Val Biden were furious—at Biden's team. By this point, Hunter had been clashing with Anita Dunn and Bob Bauer for years and was frustrated that his father was now in this position. Incensed by Hur's assertion that his father couldn't place the year of Beau's death, Hunter argued for a more aggressive approach to prove the doubters wrong. He and the First Lady pushed for the president to fight back—in person.

The team chose the Diplomatic Reception Room, which meant that reporters would be close enough to Biden to shout questions. Top aides gathered in the Cabinet Room, which spoke to the gravity of the moment.

Just before 8:00 p.m., President Biden walked into the room. He leaned into the exoneration, yet then couldn't help but reveal his anger about "some language in the report about my recollection of events. There's even a reference that I don't remember when my son died. How in the hell dare he raise that. Frankly, when I was asked the question, I thought to myself, *It wasn't any of their damn business.*"

That, of course, was a complete misrepresentation of facts.

Hur had asked about the 2017–2018 period. He hadn't mentioned Beau. Biden had mistakenly thought Beau was deployed or dying during that time.

Asked about being described as someone who might seem to a jury like a "well-meaning, elderly man with a poor memory," Biden said, "I'm well-meaning, and I'm an elderly man, and I know what the hell I'm doing. I've been president. I put this country back on its feet. I don't need his recommendation."

"How bad is your memory?" asked a reporter from Fox.

"My memory is so bad, I let you speak," Biden snapped.

He denied being careless with classified material, saying that he took "responsibility for not having seen exactly what my staff was doing." He denied sharing classified material with his ghostwriter despite the evidence that he had.

"Mr. President, for months when you were asked about your age, you would respond with the words 'Watch me,'" CNN's MJ Lee said.

"Watch me," Biden repeated.

"Many American people have been watching, and they have expressed concerns about your age. They—"

"That is your judgment," Biden said. "That is your judgment."

"This is according to public polling," Lee countered.

"That is not the judgment of the press," Biden said, confusingly.

"They express concerns about your mental acuity," Lee said. "They say that you are too old."

Other reporters shouted out other questions. Asked to provide an update on negotiations to free the hostages seized by Hamas, Biden criticized the government of Israel, saying, "The conduct of the response in Gaza—in the Gaza Strip—has been over the top. I think that—as you know, initially, the president of Mexico, el-Sisi, did not want to open up the gate to allow humanitarian material to get in. I talked to him. I convinced him to open the gate."

El-Sisi is, of course, the president of Egypt, not Mexico.

The news conference ended after twelve minutes.

THE WHITE HOUSE communications strategy was to slime Hur as an unprofessional right-wing hack, and Garland as weak—and essentially fired.

On February 9, during an event on community violence prevention at the Eisenhower Executive Office Building, Vice President Harris purposely took a question so that she could weigh in on whether the special counsel report was fair.

"What I saw in that report last night I believe is—as a former prosecutor—the comments that were made by that prosecutor: gratuitous, inaccurate, and inappropriate," Harris said, then attacked Hur's integrity directly. "The way that the president's demeanor in that report was characterized could not be more wrong on the facts and clearly politically motivated—gratuitous," she averred. "And so I will say that when it comes to the role and responsibility of a prosecutor in a situation like that, we should expect that there would be a higher level of integrity than what we saw."

Gratuitous became the word of the day for partisan Democrats. "Special Counsel Hur report on Biden classified documents issues contains way too many gratuitous remarks and is flatly inconsistent with long standing DOJ traditions," tweeted Obama's Attorney General Eric Holder.

Garland disagreed and didn't even think this was a close call. Hur had examined whether the defense team would be more likely than not to convince a jury there was reasonable doubt as to whether Biden remembered he still had those documents, and had willfully done so—DOJ standards published in 1980, which Garland had a hand in writing. Hur's judgment about how Biden would present to a jury was not gratuitous—indeed, it was the essence of Hur's decision.

Biden's media allies didn't see it that way. MSNBC anchor Ari Melber devoted a segment to the question of whether Hur was succumbing to "ageism." One *New Republic* writer raised the stakes for fellow journalists, saying, "Any news org that puts Biden's memory in the headline is actively rewarding Hur's bad faith and giving the Trump campaign what they want."

Then the White House went after Garland.

On February 10, two people close to the president told *Politico* that Biden thought Garland hadn't done enough to rein in Hur's report, that "Hur went well beyond his purview and was gratuitous and misleading in his descriptions." The Biden sources said that most of the president's senior advisers "do not believe that the attorney general would remain in his post for a possible second term." They added that Garland "should have demanded edits to Hur's report, including around the descriptions of Biden's faltering memory."

To Garland allies, this was basically Biden publicly firing Garland, his exit date to come after the November election. The cause? He had behaved ethically.

Throughout the Justice Department, career attorneys saw this declaration as a sign that Biden was coming after Garland for behaving with allegiance to the law, not to a politician. Having lived through four years of Trump, four years of a president improperly meddling in investigations, they were distressed.

And now they were seeing the president who had pledged to restore the Justice Department's independence instead using the news media to put pressure on it.

The actions and carelessness of Biden and his son Hunter had tied Garland's hands. The upright choice was always to appoint a special counsel if the evidence so warranted—as it had with Trump's conduct. As for the notion of Garland making "edits," once Hur had written his report, his reasoning for declining to prosecute Biden was going to come out one way or another anyway.

Garland was disappointed in the White House attacks, which became widely known throughout the department. Hur was a straight arrow, never leaked, had treated the president with respect, and had come to a conclusion within the parameters of the law. The notion that Hur was a right-wing political actor was ridiculous; Hur could have announced that Biden violated the law and should be prosecuted after his presidency. Now that would have been a political blow!

To Garland allies, the White House criticisms were inconsistent with Biden's promise that the Justice Department would be independent. The promise had not been that Biden was going to be hands-off unless he or his son were being investigated.

Beyond that, the special counsel's assessments of Biden's mien were accurate. Kind, even. In fact, some senior White House officials who at first thought Hur was wrong to include such descriptions in his report acknowledged that what he said was true.

But this was an opportunity for the White House to flex some muscle when it came to judgments about Biden's demeanor. Everyone watched the fierceness, the ruthlessness, from the West Wing.

Hur had been stunned to hear the president falsely accuse him of bringing up Beau's death during his October 8 interview with Biden. The transcript would show that this wasn't the case. But even though allies of his offered to push back, even if only with factual assertions that contradicted the president's claims, Hur said no. That just wasn't how the Justice Department did things.

In March, to help drive a more sympathetic narrative, the White House gave embargoed copies of transcripts of Hur's interviews to journalists whom they perceived as friendlier. Right before Hur was called to testify to Congress about his conclusions, Democrats released the transcripts more broadly, hoping that the awfulness of Biden's answers would be subsumed by coverage of a partisan hearing at which Democrats hammered Hur for articulating the obvious about the president's acuity and Republicans attacked him for failing to prosecute.

Most news media coverage thus did not acknowledge the president's long, rambling answers; the troubling lapses of memory; and the disruptions in his thought process. Most did not point out that Biden's accusation about Hur bringing up Beau's death was false.

On the Hill, Hur got pummeled by both sides. "Unfortunately, you are part of the Praetorian Guard that guards the swamp out here in Washington, DC, protecting the elites," said Wisconsin Republican Congressman Tom Tiffany. "And Joe Biden is part of that company of the elites."

"You could have chosen just to comment on the president's particular recall vis-à-vis a document or a set of documents," observed California Democratic Congressman Adam Schiff. "But you decided to go further and make a generalized statement about his memory, didn't you?"

Hur argued that his "assessment in the report about the relevance of the president's memory was necessary and accurate and fair. Most importantly, what I wrote is what I believe the evidence shows, and what I expect jurors would perceive and believe. I did not sanitize my explanation. Nor did I disparage the president unfairly."

The special counsel was required to report to Garland and explain the reasons behind his decision not to charge the president. Hur's reasoning was based in reality, not in the lies and denial that ran rampant among Democratic officials in March 2024.

Hur had no doubt assumed that he would just go back to Gibson Dunn once he finished his stint investigating that "undersecretary of the Interior." But after the report came out, Hur had been roundly vilified by the Biden administration, Democratic officials, and Democratic allies in progressive media circles. It was not unlike how the political right had treated James Comey and Robert Mueller. Law firms and corporate legal teams got the message. Hur spent several months looking for work.

THE LAST MEDICAL EXAM

In the aftermath of the Hur report, Biden's final medical exam took on new importance. It would be the last one before the election in November, and political advisers involved themselves more than ever before.

Biden's physical deterioration—most apparent in his halting walk—had become so severe that there were internal discussions about putting the president in a wheelchair, but they couldn't do so until after the election. Given Biden's age, Doc O'Connor also privately said that if he had another bad fall, a wheelchair might be necessary for what could be a difficult recovery.

O'Connor had been consistent in his assertion that Biden's gait had changed largely because of "significant spinal arthritis" in addition to "mild post-fracture foot arthritis and a mild sensory peripheral neuropathy of the feet."

Biden's team was offering some new explanations that were more politically palatable. On February 10, *The New York Times* reported that "multiple people close to the White House" explained that the president's walk was "partly because of his refusal to wear an orthopedic boot after suffering a hairline fracture in his foot before taking office."

This contradicted what O'Connor had said at the time. After Biden wore a walking boot for ten weeks in late 2020 and early 2021, O'Connor noted that "both small fractures of his foot are completely healed" and that "this injury has healed as expected."

Biden's political advisers discussed whether he should finally undergo a cognitive exam to blunt questions about his mental fitness. O'Connor had long pushed back on political advisers interfering in his medical evaluations. He told others that he did not believe the science required him to do a cognitive test. He saw the president frequently, and if he had reason for concern, he would have performed one.

Ultimately, Biden's political advisers agreed. They had also boxed themselves in with their own public insistence that Biden had not lost a step and was as sharp as ever. Finally doing a test would be an admission that there were reasons for concern. And even if Biden did do a test, his aides believed that his critics would still not be satisfied. There was also the risk of the unknown, of what such a test might reveal.

On February 28, O'Connor released his final medical summary, which listed degeneration of Biden's spine and the new use of a nightly breathing machine for sleep apnea. But Doc declared Biden "fit to successfully execute the duties of the presidency."

Citing O'Connor, Press Secretary Karine Jean-Pierre said at the briefing that Biden had no need for a cognitive test.

"He passes a cognitive test every day."

A WEIRD PERIOD

Over 2023 and 2024, the circle of people with access to the president grew smaller and smaller. Even the majority of Biden's cabinet members weren't in it.

"Access dropped off considerably in 2024, and I didn't interact with him as much," said Cabinet Secretary Number One. "I didn't get an explanation." Instead, the secretary would brief other senior White House aides, who then briefed the president. Cabinet Secretary Number One thought it strange and asked if it was a way of filtering out particular information so that his closest aides could brief him in the way they preferred.

"Yes, the president is 'making the decisions,' but if the inner circle is shaping them in such a way, is it really a decision? Are they leading him to something?" Cabinet Secretary Number One wondered.

"I don't think he has dementia," said Cabinet Secretary Number Two. "But the thing is, he's an old man. The president can give you four to six good hours a day. When he got tired, *sloppy* isn't the right word, but his guard was down."

"I think the people around him had their own agenda, and they didn't want more people around him," Cabinet Secretary Number Two said. "Not because they were protecting him but because they didn't want people giving him contradictory information."

Cabinet Secretary Number Two added of the Politburo: "It's hard for an adviser to be honest with the principal. If he had asked me, I would have told him, 'Do one term and you're done to preserve your legacy.'"

A third cabinet secretary observed that—with the general exceptions of those in the national security portfolio, such as Secretary of State Antony Blinken and Defense Secretary Lloyd Austin—from October 2023 on, "the cabinet was kept at bay."

"That was a weird period," Cabinet Secretary Number Three told us of 2023–2024. "For months, we didn't have access to him. There was clearly a deliberate strategy by the White House to have him meet with as few people as necessary." At one rare meeting during that time, Cabinet Secretary Number Three was shocked by how the president was acting. He seemed "disoriented" and "out of it," his mouth agape.

Other senior and mid-level aides in the West Wing also noticed that access became more limited. Aides who had once seen the president regularly would now go months without seeing him. Others noticed that at some meetings, Biden would occasionally be mumbling and not making much sense.

Then there were preparations for events on his schedule. "They shielded him in every meeting," Cabinet Secretary Number Three recalled. "They always wanted to keep him happy. They would say, 'Don't say that. Don't tell him that.' They always wanted to shield him from bad news."

And now that bad news was about the president himself, about his deterioration. "The staff did him wrong," Cabinet Secretary Number Three said. "If you were with him every day and you knew this was a problem, why didn't you go to him and say something?"

It was a question that some in the White House, subordinate to the Politburo, would also voice. But only later. And only privately.

THE STATE OF THE UNION

The State of the Union address on March 7 had become politically important to Biden in ways that such speeches rarely are. It had become a de facto acuity test. What Biden said mattered less than how he said it.

Biden's team knew it and escaped to Camp David, where he could rest and rehearse as aides frequently brought him tea for his weak voice.

The prep worked, and Biden quieted his doubters with a fiery, energetic speech. His address was not only competent but also included a number of folksy ad-libs and one that could even be called agile.

"We have two ways to go," Biden said midway through the speech. "Republicans can cut Social Security and give more tax breaks to the wealthy. I will—"

Republicans in the House chamber began booing and razzing.

"That's the proposal!" Biden playfully protested, referring to a plan floated by a Republican senator that his GOP colleagues treated like nuclear waste. The hooting continued.

"Oh, no?" Biden added. "You guys don't want another $2 trillion tax cut?"

He smiled. He was having fun.

"I kind of thought that's what your plan was," Biden said, relishing the moment. "Well, that's good to hear! You're not going to cut another $2 trillion for the super-wealthy. That's good to hear!"

It was clever and nimble.

By 2024, aides likened the president's public appearances to holding a time bomb. Every time Biden was in front of the cameras, aides knew there was a chance that the bomb could go off.

But that night, as the president walked off the dais, he was swarmed by praiseful House Democrats.

"You were on fire!" said Texas Congressman Henry Cuellar.

"Nobody's gonna talk about cognitive impairment now!" chimed in New York Congressman Jerry Nadler.

"I kinda wish sometimes I was cognitively impaired," the president joked.

"Has anyone seen Sleepy Joe Biden?" wrote *USA Today*'s Rex Huppke. "I was told the current president is a dementia-addled fool incapable of completing a sentence, but there was a guy standing in his place giving Thursday night's State of the Union who was fiery, direct, sensible and a far cry from sleepy."

But in the scrum, Congressman Mike Quigley, who hadn't been this close to Biden since they were in Dublin almost a year before, put his hand on the president's back. He could feel his ribs, and his spine. It was like touching Mr. Burns from *The Simpsons*. The president's voice was soft and breathy. His eyes were darting from side to side. It again disconcertingly reminded Quigley of his late father.

In the hours following that address, White House aides noted the immediate return of Old Biden—the one Biden aides had been trying to obscure. The president gave a rambling rah-rah speech to senior aides that stood in stark contrast with the forceful one he had just given to the country. And they saw him continue to devolve from there.

In the East Room of the White House, high schoolers from the US Senate Youth Program were waiting to see the president. The First Lady came in first to briefly speak to the students, who were standing on risers at the back of the room. There was palpable excitement, with whoops and cheers from the students.

But the Biden who walked in wasn't the man many had just seen on TV. Standing alone in the middle of the room and addressing the students, Biden launched into a confusing story about getting into politics. Before he finished that yarn, he launched into another. And then another. Biden had been borderline yelling during his State of the Union, and now people just feet away were straining to hear him.

On one side of the room was Anthony Bernal, and on the other was one of Biden's granddaughters. As the president rambled, Bernal and Biden's granddaughter began inching closer and closer to him until they were finally right next to him. When his granddaughter attempted to coax him upstairs to go see the First Lady, Biden began telling another story, this one about his granddaughter. Bernal also made an attempt to usher him away. No luck.

One of the students later recounted that when Biden "spoke with us after his address, I felt a strange pang of surprise. He was strikingly human."

To some Biden aides, this was just another example of Biden rambling and spending extra time with people for what was supposed to be a photo-op.

But others who didn't regularly see Biden up close were disturbed. One White House aide left the East Room and strode back through the White House where other aides were still high-fiving and celebrating the positive reviews from Biden's energetic State of the Union speech. That White House aide couldn't help asking themselves what on earth they had just seen.

This isn't going to work, they thought. *He can't do it. This is crazy. Crazy. Crazy.*

BILL DALEY, PART TWO

In April, at the Chicago home of Michael and Cari Sacks, Bill Daley attended a small fundraiser for the Biden for President operation and the Democratic National Committee. Biden did a photo line and then, when it was time to speak to the crowd, read from a teleprompter. Daley had never seen such a thing for casual remarks in a room of roughly fifty people. (In fact, the hosts had balked, but the advance team told them that the teleprompter was nonnegotiable.) Immediately after the remarks, the president left the fundraiser. It was wild, Daley thought.

"Were you surprised at that?" a younger couple, in their thirties, asked the seasoned pol.

"At how he presented himself? What did you think?" Daley asked them.

They expressed shock at how feeble the president seemed, both physically and mentally.

Daley wasn't surprised.

Meanwhile, the Biden campaign was growing suspicious that other Democrats were quietly trying to sabotage the president. It wasn't paranoia. Lawmakers, donors, and strategists finally got an opportunity to see Biden up close, after many months of not seeing him in person. Quiet but urgent discussions were already beginning about what the party was going to do, including putting up another candidate like Whitmer.

In the spring, Campaign Chair Jen O'Malley Dillon started calling some governors' offices to get more information and tamp down any such plotting. She'd heard that Massachusetts Governor Maura Healey had previously talked up Whitmer as a possible candidate.

Whitmer swore she would never consider challenging the president but warned that the Biden campaign had a real political problem and needed a solution.

KATZENBERG

Hollywood mogul Jeffrey Katzenberg had been helping the Democratic Party with resources—money and connections—since the early '80s, back when he was an executive at Paramount Pictures and a student of the leadership of the legendary Lew Wasserman.

He'd backed candidates for state and local office, and some members of Congress, but Katzenberg's first real foray into the world of big-donor politics came in 1990 when he and David Geffen flew to Arkansas to meet a young governor named Bill Clinton. Since then, he had become one of the top, if not the top, fundraiser for Democratic presidential candidates.

Katzenberg had known Biden since the late 1980s and was on board with his presidential run as early as October 2018, when he hosted a meet and greet for the former vice president at his Wilshire Boulevard office, after which the two men dined at Madeo in West Hollywood. Katzenberg told Biden that he would support his campaign, that he thought him best positioned to beat Trump.

For the rematch in 2024, Katzenberg was even more dedicated.

He didn't want anything from him, he told the president. He might be the only one who didn't. He just wanted him to win.

Katzenberg had known other presidents and was well acquainted with their commonly held feeling that they were always correct. He also knew how to deal with talent, handling and stroking and cajoling some of the most popular movie stars in the history of the medium. He felt like he knew how to talk to Biden.

"I want Joe Biden back," he told the president, as was later relayed to top campaign staff.

"What do you mean by that?" the president asked.

As long as he and the voters had known Joe, Joe's flubbing was an essential characteristic of his, Katzenberg said. And, yes, he would get teased for it, but it was authentic, and it was him. And people liked him, flaws and all, and that's who they voted for. Since he had been elected, people only saw him as the president, in a suit and tie, behind a podium. Joe Biden had disappeared.

It was true that as president, Biden was less accessible, less able to talk to voters, less in his element of chatting with regular folks. The Secret Service was part of the reason why, but whatever the reason, Biden had drifted further and further away from his ability to be the great retail politician he was, Katzenberg explained.

Katzenberg saw Biden's communications struggles and thought he could fix them. He even enlisted the help of his show-biz friend Steven Spielberg. They worked on lighting, and a better microphone to amplify his voice when he would oddly speak in barely a whisper. Biden didn't always like getting notes on his delivery but would listen to someone like Spielberg. The famous director would also coach the president before speeches like the State of the Union. Katzenberg hoped that voters' age concerns about Biden could be assuaged with a little Hollywood magic.

THE POLLSTERS, PART ONE

For the three outside pollsters—Geoff Garin, Molly Murphy, and Jefrey Pollock—the campaign was generally a joyless, unpleasant experience. The fourth pollster, David Binder, who did focus groups for Biden, was less harsh in his assessment, though he also had lower expectations.

Garin and Murphy had been hired in 2023.

Their first poll was of the Blue Wall battleground states (Michigan, Pennsylvania, and Wisconsin) and the Sun Belt targets (Arizona, Georgia, and North Carolina). Biden was down but within the margin of error, anywhere from two to four points. Bad, but theoretically fixable.

It would prove, however, a remarkably static race. Bad news would come, and the numbers wouldn't change that much. Nor would they budge much when good news arrived. Whether hit with the damaging Hur report or the decent State of the Union performance, the numbers were immovable.

Voters knew a tremendous amount about both Trump and Biden, and everything seemed baked in.

The campaign's prevailing assumption was that the problem came down to Biden losing some of the voters who had pulled the lever for him in 2020 but were now supporting a third-party candidate or just not voting at all.

The campaign "assumed they would migrate back to Biden," said one of the pollsters. "There was no data supporting this."

"Even if we brought them all back, that wouldn't be enough," the pollster noted. "Because there would of course be new voters, and Trump generally did better with new voters."

The pollsters knew why those 2020 Biden voters were holding back. They had the actual data. Not hunches. Not gut instincts.

Those 2020 Biden voters were holding back because they had concerns about two issues: Biden's age and inflation.

The pollsters found themselves largely siloed off from the campaign, the top aides at the White House, and the president himself—and were rarely brought in to discuss strategy or weigh in on what the data suggested the campaign needed to do.

What the pollsters saw in their data was that the campaign's messaging, or lack thereof, was not working. "It was clear early on that President Biden needed to acknowledge that prices were too high and needed to come down," one pollster said. "But Donilon and others at the White House would refuse. They said if we acknowledged it, no one would remember anything else."

This instruction came from Biden himself, they were told. The pollsters thought this was cognitive dissonance. The president had to acknowledge the economic pain; not doing so was insulting to voters.

They're not hearing a fucking thing you're saying, one of the pollsters thought. *You're in Fantasyland. You're saying the economy's great, and voters are like, "On what planet?"*

But Mike Donilon's sense of mission, they felt, was twofold: One, make the case that Biden was a historically great president. Two, convincingly tell the story of how the country was much better off than it thought it was.

This was the exact opposite, the pollsters knew, of what Obama had done in 2012. When Obama ran for reelection, he didn't effusively praise the economy—and he certainly wouldn't have pushed anything as tone-deaf as "Bidenomics," as Biden was doing, following a period in which inflation had peaked at 9.1 percent. Obama's message had been that he understood why people remained unhappy with the economy, that it was getting better but much more work remained to be done, and he just needed more time. Voters bought it.

Then there was that other major concern: From the very beginning, voters were saying that Biden was too old, whether in open-ended poll questions or focus groups—smaller interviews and discussions with voters—run by Binder.

Binder worked for the DNC and then as a consultant to the campaign, and from late 2023 through 2024, he conducted focus groups. There hadn't been one where Biden's age didn't come up. Trump was only three and a half years younger, but voters just didn't see him the same way. The pollsters would read about or hear of voters regularly denigrating Biden—doddering, incoherent, unable to complete sentences—in ways that the pollsters felt, in early spring, were unfair.

Binder's job was to challenge these respondents, to see if there was anything that might convince them their opinions were wrong. He would play a video clip of the State of the Union or of a different public moment where Biden seemed energetic and engaging. Many of the respondents didn't buy it; they would say that Biden was reading from a teleprompter or note cards, and some would repeat the unproven theory that Biden had taken some sort of stimulant before the State of the Union address.

Many of them were worried. What if an international crisis unfolded in the middle of the night? They had seen what happened to their grandparents or parents; they were well aware of the tolls of aging.

Binder believed that Bidenland knew Biden's age was a huge problem but simply thought that it would end up secondary to the threat of four more years of Trump once the campaign played this out. The pollsters wanted better polling to glean more data on the issue, how to combat it, how to neutralize it. They wanted more ways to ask voters about his age and fitness, and whether Biden was up to the job. But the campaign wouldn't let them ask the questions they wanted to ask on the topic. They were allowed to approach only the outer circle of these issues.

In an early May poll of Michigan voters, the pollsters asked a question: "What is your biggest concern about Joe Biden?"

Their second-most-important concern was inflation. Twenty-three percent were worried about that.

Their number one issue, by far, was that Joe Biden did not seem mentally fit enough to be president.

Thirty-eight percent of Michigan voters said that was their number one concern about Biden.

It wasn't clear to the pollsters if any of their information was making its way to the president, but it was clear that the Politburo was hoping Biden could turn this around with a big moment: a debate.

TO DEBATE OR NOT TO DEBATE?

The campaign would internally discuss how to combat voters' concerns that Biden was too old to be president. They learned that being defensive was not persuasive. Nor was noting that Trump was only three years younger.

Some on the campaign would argue that they had only a select set of tools for showing that the president was up to the job. They wouldn't win unless they changed something. Which was why Biden, in the view of many on the campaign, had to debate. And the earlier the better. To put this age issue to rest.

"He has to debate," Ron Klain would argue.

Donilon thought highly of Biden's debate performances. Both of the 2020 debates had worked well for the president. And any notion that they could avoid a debate was unrealistic. Biden was going to have to get onstage with Trump; the pressure would build for him to do it.

Steve Ricchetti disagreed. The impact on polling was limited—Biden had destroyed Trump in both 2020 debates, he thought, and hadn't gotten much of a bump. Then there was the Trumpiness of it all. A candidate just didn't get a whole lot out of debating Trump, Ricchetti believed. Even if you were beating his ass, you would lose part of your soul in that debate. Trump was such a pathological liar that it was hard for anyone to maintain the nature of what they imagined themselves to be. Trump always took you down with him.

Anita Dunn also didn't think Biden had to do a debate. The Biden team was still mad at the Commission on Presidential Debates for not enforcing its own COVID rules at the height of the pandemic. Trump had made a mockery of the commission in 2020, then avoided all the GOP primary debates in 2024. Why should Biden risk getting onstage with him?

But then came the Hur report, which brought questions of Biden's age and acuity into the mainstream.

Okay, Dunn thought. *He has to debate now.*

O'Malley Dillon was pushing for an unprecedented early debate in June—months earlier than any other televised presidential debate. Grassroots fundraising was hurting, and they needed a moment to drive it, she believed.

That sounded fine to Dunn and Donilon, who were eager to see the presidential race become a choice between Biden and Trump, not a referendum on Biden.

A June debate also meant that if it wound up a disaster, the campaign would have time to recover.

The top aides who were able to acknowledge the president's declining ability to communicate knew that this was a high-risk scenario. They'd seen the shift. It was happening rapidly. Biden would be dramatically worse in 2024 debate prep than in his State of the Union prep earlier that year.

"It's true we were grading him on a curve every day," a top aide admitted. "Things that would have been considered a disaster in 2023—by 2024, we would have said, 'Okay, we got through that.'"

Donilon would assure colleagues: "He's going to get elected again with people thinking he's too old." After all, he had done it once before.

TWELVE

D-Day

At 9:00 p.m. on June 4, the White House went to war.

Against a newspaper.

The Wall Street Journal had just published an investigation with the headline BEHIND CLOSED DOORS, BIDEN SHOWS SIGNS OF SLIPPING.

Citing five sources, *The Journal* reported that in the meeting with congressional leaders about Ukraine in January 2024, Biden "read from notes to make obvious points, paused for extended periods and sometimes closed his eyes for so long that some in the room wondered whether he had tuned out." At another meeting, Speaker Mike Johnson left and told others that he was concerned about the president's memory, *The Journal* wrote, citing six sources.

The Journal interviewed more than forty-five people over several months, but the only ones who went on the record with their worries about Biden's age were Republicans. The reporters wrote that regarding meetings with the president, "most of those who said Biden performed poorly were Republicans, but some Democrats said that he showed his age in several of the exchanges."

The story was true. But the Biden team attacked the reporters for having relied on Republicans.

Ben LaBolt, the White House's communications director, insinuated with zero evidence that the piece was ordered by Rupert Murdoch—the founder of *The Journal*'s parent company, News Corp, and the Fox Corporation, which owns Fox News—to help Trump win the election.

The story's origins were actually much more mundane. After the Hur report came out, Washington Coverage Chief Damian Paletta and Washington Deputy Coverage Chief Janet Adamy called *The Journal*'s White House reporting team together to brainstorm ways to do more reporting on Biden's age. No reporter was even assigned.

White House reporter Annie Linskey decided to poke around and got some tips that Biden's lapses described by Hur may not have been isolated incidents. She looped in congressional reporter Siobhan Hughes, and Adamy told them to pursue the story.

The White House attacked the story relentlessly, with White House Deputy Press Secretary Andrew Bates going on the record to *The Journal* to deny its reporting. The deputy press secretary was loyal and a bulldog for the president. He would internally push colleagues to tell reporters that Biden was as sharp as ever—requests they feared turning down in case they could be labeled as disloyal.

Progressives and Biden supporters in the news media also openly bashed *The Journal*'s reporting. They were even more out there than some Biden aides, who internally started declining Bates's internal requests to vouch for the president's acuity. Access was so limited; how could they honestly say that Biden was fine when they hadn't seen him?

Some of Bates's colleagues believed that Biden's inner circle took advantage of his loyalty and told him to deny things they knew were true. He, along with most of the press team, rarely met with the president and didn't have firsthand knowledge of the president's wherewithal. They relied on senior staff for answers. Still, risking his own credibility, Bates willingly became the White House's tip of the spear when it came to fighting off any reporting on Biden's acuity.

Weeks before the *Wall Street Journal* story was published, a reporter with a different national news outlet had been hearing from White House aides that behind the scenes the president was having serious and disturbing moments, forgetting names and facts, sometimes seeming seriously confused at meetings.

The reporter reached out to members of the White House press office, which not only aggressively—and angrily—disputed her reporting but also took the unusual step of having Steve Ricchetti call her.

He talked to her off the record, so she couldn't use any of what he said or even attribute it to "a White House source." But he told her that what the others were saying was wrong, and that he was at the meetings as a counselor to the president.

The message from the White House was clear, this reporter believed: If she went forward with the story from anonymous aides, the White House would aggressively dispute it, on the record, and portray her as a liar. She chose not to publish.

NORMANDY

Biden's deterioration may never have been so obvious before a global audience as it was during the D-Day commemoration in June.

Members of Congress who'd flown to the event in Normandy were filled with pride as they watched the surviving D-Day veterans—some in wheelchairs, some walking—come out before the crowd.

The president followed.

One House Democrat was shocked. Biden looked frailer and was shuffling more than many of the World War II veterans who were nearing one hundred.

There was another odd moment where Biden, while in the midst of sitting, froze for a second while his secretary of defense was being introduced. It appeared he'd made the calculation that the physical difficulty of standing up and then sitting back down wasn't worth it—hence, he froze in place.

Watching the enfeebled US president next to the charismatic, energetic French leader, Congressman Seth Moulton, a US Marine Corps veteran and Massachusetts Democrat, felt "embarrassed as an American."

The president was supposed to meet the US Congressional Delegation about fifty to seventy-five yards away from the main stage for a photo. Moulton watched several D-Day veterans—well into their nineties—walk the distance. Biden was driven. Biden got out and spoke so quietly that it was tough to hear him.

He made eye contact with Moulton. The congressman's heart sank as he realized that this man with whom he thought he had a long-standing personal relationship didn't recognize him at all.

He wasn't the only one.

The president of France took it all in. Guests overheard Macron say that he was "gêné" on Biden's behalf. Embarrassed. (A French press aide reflexively denied to us that he said this.)

One aide to a European leader said his boss had been watching this happen for some time. At the United Nations General Assembly in

September 2022, the aide saw Biden before he went to speak. "He had to be guided and told where to go," the aide recalled. "'Go left, go right, watch out for your feet.'"

This wasn't a problem when Biden participated in phone conversations with his European counterparts, because those events were fairly scripted and Biden was decent when given what to say. But in the longer conversations that relied on a "thought process—that's when it was hard," the aide to the European leader told us.

During the Normandy trip, Biden sat down with ABC's *World News Tonight* for a rare interview. Some staffers who didn't regularly have access to him were alarmed as they helped with the preparations.

"I was shocked, but the other people around him didn't seem to be, so I didn't say anything," one said. Another grimaced while watching Biden's responses. His eyes were barely open, and he seemed older than ever.

Near the end of the interview, anchor David Muir asked Biden about Hunter's ongoing trial. "Have you ruled out a pardon for your son?" he asked.

"Yes," Biden said.

He hoped it would never come to that. What a guilty verdict might mean to Hunter's survival was too horrible to contemplate.

THIRTEEN

The Verdict

Some close to the president would tie his stages of deterioration to moments involving intense stress. They would point to two moments in particular: The first was when Hunter's plea deal fell apart in July 2023 and the risk that he could be sentenced to prison became very real. Then came the second in 2024, when Hunter was put on trial.

Throughout the first week of June, practically the entire Biden family sat front row at the Wilmington federal courthouse.

Jill, Val, Jimmy, and Ashley all watched as their family's darkest secrets were aired before the world.

Biden's own Justice Department compelled Beau's widow, Hallie Olivere Biden, and Hunter's ex-wife, Kathleen Buhle, to testify against a member of the president's family. Hunter's team called Biden's grand-daughter to the stand, only to see her humiliated. And a hometown jury in Delaware, where Biden had served as senator for thirty-six years, unanimously convicted his son after just three hours of deliberations.

Biden's top aides believed that the trial would exact a toll on the president and cause real psychic damage.

Biden felt guilty and believed that the case never would have been brought had he not run for president.

After Beau's death in 2015, Biden desperately and understandably clung to Hunter. He would privately refer to him as "my only living son." But Biden aides felt that Hunter manipulated his father's blind love for his own aims. The president struggled to say no to Hunter. Aides felt that he had tragically become Hunter's chief enabler—part of the reason why the family was now gathered in the courthouse.

The president had offered to testify at the trial. It would be an event without much, or perhaps any, precedent: a sitting president taking the witness stand in a case involving his own son. Biden repeatedly brought up the idea. Even the weekend before the trial began, Biden again offered to testify or come to court, despite his packed schedule.

Putting a sitting president on the stand carried risks, of course. Biden's presence in the courtroom could be read wrongly by the jury as a heavy-handed play for sympathy. Prosecutors—as evidenced by their pretrial filings and arguments—were not worried about sparing the Biden family from embarrassment. That wasn't their job.

The First Lady also offered to testify, but she had not witnessed as much of Hunter's downturn in 2018; her testimony would be less useful. To ensure that she could be in court for as many days as possible, the First Lady left the D-Day commemoration events early to fly to Wilmington and then back to Paris a day later—an exhausting round trip, mostly taxpayer-funded.

———

THE VERDICT

THE FACTS of the case were straightforward: In October 2018, Hunter bought a gun and, on the federal form, marked that he was not a drug user. He kept the gun for eleven days before Hallie discovered it, panicked, and threw it in a grocery store trash can, where it was discovered.

The prosecution had ample evidence that Hunter had been using drugs in the months before and after he purchased the gun. The defense conceded that Hunter had used drugs in the past, but argued that Hunter did not believe himself to be an addict when he bought the gun, given his time in rehab in August 2018. The trial would hinge on whether the mostly working-class Delaware jury related to Hunter and his addiction struggles or resented him as a scion of privilege who had squandered it. This meant delving into the Biden family melodrama of the past decade. No longer relegated to the tabloids, it was testimony under oath in a felony trial.

Biden's family members confessed it all.

After Beau's death, Hunter began having an affair with Beau's widow, Hallie, hiding it from Kathleen, to whom he was still married. Hunter introduced Hallie to crack; she, too, became addicted. Hunter also had a relationship with a young stripper and designer whom he would have shop for his daughters, since they were around the same age.

After years of denying or sidestepping questions about it, Hunter now watched prosecutors bring out a laptop with a serial number matching his Apple account that had been left behind at a repair shop. The FBI had confiscated the MacBook and now witnesses confirmed the authenticity of much of the content on it.

Hunter's ex-wife, Kathleen, told the jury she found a crack pipe at their home weeks after Beau's death. Hunter confessed he was using it.

167

Prosecutors played hours of the self-narrated audiobook version of Hunter's 2021 memoir, which they now framed as a partial confession to his drug use around the time he bought the gun. As his voice filled the courtroom, his sister Ashley—who had struggled with her own addiction—began to cry.

The gut punch for the family came when Hunter's eldest daughter, Naomi, took the stand. Hunter and his team had asked her to testify. She was eager and proud to help her dad, attesting that he was a reformed man.

She testified about visiting her dad while he was in rehab in August 2018. "He seemed like the clearest that I had seen him since my uncle died," she said. She also noted that when she saw him in October—soon after he had bought the gun—Hunter "seemed great, he seemed hopeful."

But during her cross-examination, the judge unexpectedly allowed the prosecutors to submit into evidence text messages between Hunter and Naomi that told a different story about that week in October. He was erratic and distant, firing off late-night texts and requests. After having trouble setting up a time to meet, Naomi texted Hunter: "so no c u!?"

Prosecutors read her next message aloud: "I'm really sorry, Dad, I can't take this. I don't know what to say, I just miss you so much, I just want to hang out with you."

Grilling her about the days she wanted to see her dad, prosecutors asked: "Did he tell you he was meeting with someone named Frankie?"

"I don't remember," she said, flustered.

"Did he tell you that he had Frankie come to his hotel room?" they pressed. A previous witness had referred to a dealer named Frankie.

"No. I don't remember," she said, her voice cracking.

"Did he tell you he had given someone named Frankie an access code to his Wells Fargo account?" they asked.

Naomi, holding back tears, managed to give a weak "No."

She left the courtroom and walked briskly to her holding room.

Afterward, Biden's family and many friends packed into Hunter's holding room, trying to come to grips with what had just happened.

Hunter's defense, such as it was, rested.

Hunter's closest friends and many in the family had been hopeful. Hunter's friend Kevin Morris—who had paid off Hunter's unpaid taxes—confidently told Alex in the courtroom that they were going to get a "not guilty" verdict. This was Delaware. Surely a local jury wouldn't convict a favorite son after he had cleaned up his act. Especially since the crimes carried a maximum sentence of twenty-five years.

Hunter's legal team was more clear-eyed. An acquittal was likely impossible. Beyond the facts of the case, the jury instructions were not in their favor, and the judge had barred them from calling certain witnesses, such as an addiction expert.

Their best hope was a hung jury.

The jury delivered a guilty verdict on all three felony counts.

It happened so fast that the First Lady and the president's sister, Val, weren't close enough to make it back for the reading of the verdict. Hunter took the news stoically and then tried to rally his stunned family.

After the verdict was handed down, the president made an impromptu trip to Wilmington and tightly embraced his son on the tarmac. He wanted to make sure Hunter knew that he was still proud of him.

They both knew it wasn't over.

A second trial was coming up in September. This one, a tax trial in California, centered on Hunter's failure to file and pay taxes during his addiction years. The special counsel's team was ready to subpoena all of Hunter's adult children and Lunden Roberts, as well as Kathleen and Hallie again. Hunter felt that the trial was designed to humiliate him and the president's family.

His supporters in the Democratic Party and in the media described the case as if it were merely about being late on his taxes, but it was much tawdrier than that, with Hunter at times earning money by cashing in on the family name and allegedly hiding this money from not only the government but also his ex-wife, to whom he owed alimony. He instead spent it "on drugs, escorts and girlfriends, luxury hotels and rental properties, exotic cars, clothing, and other items of a personal nature, in short, everything but his taxes," according to the indictment. One could only imagine the impact this would have on the already devastated president.

Handling the competing stresses of family scandals, presidential duties, and a troubled campaign would have been an extraordinary challenge for someone at the peak of their powers.

A fourth cabinet secretary with whom we spoke saw Hunter's June 2024 trial and conviction as akin to a five-hundred-pound weight dropping on the president's head.

Cabinet Secretary Number Four thought that the most precipitous moments of decline for the president came during the turmoil surrounding Hunter—the plea agreement blowing up the previous summer and now this.

Understandably, Biden had been intensely preoccupied with his son's fate. To anyone around the president, the impact was real. As were his fears he could lose a third child.

His duties still called. The day after Hunter's guilty verdict, Biden was on a plane to Italy for the G7. After that, he would head to Los Angeles for the biggest Democratic fundraiser in history.

GEORGE CLOONEY, PART ONE

George Clooney first met Biden when he was the top Democrat on the Senate Foreign Relations Committee. Starting in 2006, Clooney became a credible voice against the atrocities in Sudan, testifying before the UN, lobbying President Obama and Vice President Biden on the matter repeatedly. By 2024, the actor had known the president personally for almost twenty years.

Clooney had last seen Biden on December 4, 2022, when the megastar was with his wife, Amal, in DC to be celebrated at the Kennedy Center Honors. Biden seemed older, sure, but in the East Room of the White House, at the reception for the honorees, the president was playful and seemed cogent enough.

"We see Amal Clooney's husband," the president said, to laughter.

Yes, he was reading from prepared remarks, but far be it for an actor to take issue with someone reciting lines.

"Mentors—he mentors these—those historic kids from Parkland on their march and their lives—against gun violence," Biden said, stumbling a bit. "I met with every one of those kids, and they really appreciate what you did, George. Not a joke."

In February 2024, Clooney had thought the Hur report mean-spirited. And when Biden gave a rousing State of the Union address in March, he thought to himself, *Way to go, Mr. President.*

For the rematch in 2024, everyone involved with the campaign knew that beating Trump would be difficult—and would require a record-breaking amount of money. Jeffrey Katzenberg led the charge. He worked on a spectacularly successful March fundraiser, held at Radio City Music Hall and headlined by three Democratic presidents—Bill Clinton,

Barack Obama, and Joe Biden. It raised $26 million, the most ever at a single event for a Democratic presidential candidate.

In early April, they discussed when they could bring Biden out to California.

Katzenberg told the campaign that he wanted to try to hit another record number.

Katzenberg had learned over the years that there was a cadence in terms of how many times they could ask folks for money. He knew they could get a bite at the apple in the summer and then one last one on the other side of Labor Day.

Katzenberg and Clooney were pals, and they had a long, successful history of doing these events, breaking records for Obama with a nearly $15 million event at Clooney's Studio City home in May 2012, organizing two events for Hillary Clinton in 2016, and raking in more than $7 million with a July 2020 Zoom fundraiser in which Obama stumped for Biden..

In 2024, on a rainy Easter in France, Clooney heard from Katzenberg, who made the ask: a fundraiser in June.

But Clooney was going to be in London and Tuscany, acting in a big project for Netflix. Clooney looked at his calendar. There was one possible window. It would be brutal, though. He'd need to fly into Los Angeles from Tuscany, do the event, and leave that night for Rome before the fundraiser was even over.

"I can do one night," Clooney told Katzenberg.

"Great," Katzenberg said.

"Let's call Julia and see if she'll do it with me," Clooney said, referring to Julia Roberts. He texted her immediately. Katzenberg had been head of Disney when Roberts was cast in the role that made her a superstar, in *Pretty Woman*. He reached out to her too.

Coordinating it all was wildly complicated. Roberts was starting production on a film and also needed to get on a plane before the fundraiser was even over. Not to mention the president's schedule. He was going to be in Italy for the G7, right after honoring Allied veterans in France for the eightieth anniversary of D-Day, in between which he'd be in Wilmington with Hunter. They tried to figure out six different ways to move things around, but everyone ultimately agreed on June 15. Jimmy Kimmel would interview Biden and Barack Obama onstage. All Clooney and Roberts needed to do was pose for photos with the big donors before the event, then open the show. Afterward, they could fly to their sets, and God willing, another fundraising record would be set.

On Thursday, June 13, Clooney landed at a private airfield in the Los Angeles area. On Saturday, he rolled to the Peacock Theater, capacity 7,100, roughly four hours before the event was set to begin; he and Roberts had literally hundreds of photographs to take with the thousands of attendees whose perks depended upon their contributions, from $250 to $500,000. The event would once again set a record as the biggest fundraiser for a Democrat in American political history, raising more than $30 million.

Before Kimmel, Obama, and Biden hit the stage to toss bons mots back and forth in a cozy Q&A, a smaller series of private receptions was held, with photo lines and free-flowing booze and hors d'oeuvres. Clooney and Roberts were doing the work of charming the attendees and posing for pics when they heard the crowd starting to murmur. Clooney looked to the side and saw Obama walking in, grayer but still spry and electric.

A few minutes later, Secret Service agents entered the room and announced that President Biden had arrived.

Biden hobbled out from around the corner. Clooney knew the president had just arrived from the G7 Leaders' Summit in Apulia, Italy, that morning and might be tired, but hoooooooooooly shit, he wasn't expecting this.

The president appeared severely diminished, as if he'd aged a decade since Clooney last saw him in December 2022. He was taking tiny steps and had an aide guiding him by his arm.

"It was like watching someone who was not alive," a Hollywood VIP recalled. "It was startling. And we all looked at each other. It was so awful."

"Thank you for being here," the president said to guests as he walked past them. "Thank you for being here."

Clooney felt a knot form in his stomach as the president approached him.

Biden looked at him. "Thank you for being here," he said. "Thank you for being here."

"You know George," the assisting aide told the president, gently reminding him who was in front of him.

"Yeah, yeah," the president said to one of the most recognizable men in the world, the host of this lucrative fundraiser. "Thank you for being here."

"Hi, Mr. President," Clooney said.

"How are ya?" the president replied.

"How was your trip?" Clooney asked.

"It was fine," the president said.

It was obvious to many standing there that the president did not know who George Clooney was.

"It was not okay," recalled the Hollywood VIP who had witnessed this moment. "That thing, the moment where you recognize someone you know—especially a famous person who's doing a fucking fundraiser for you—it was delayed. It was uncomfortable."

"George *Clooney*," the aide clarified for the president.

"Oh, yeah!" Biden said. "Hi, George!"

Clooney was shaken to his core. The president hadn't recognized him. A man he had known for years. Clooney had expressed concern about Biden's health before—a White House aide had told him a few months before that they were working on getting the president to take longer steps when he walked—but obviously the problem went far beyond his gait. This was much graver.

This was the president of the United States?

Clooney was certainly not the only one concerned. Other high-dollar attendees who posed for photographs with Obama and Biden described Biden as slow and almost catatonic. Though they saw pockets of clarity while watching him on television, and onstage later that night, there were obvious brain freezes and clear signs of a mental slide. It was, to some of them, terrifying.

Obama was there for the fundraiser, and he didn't know what to make of how his former running mate was acting. At one point, in a small group of a few dozen top donors, Biden began speaking—barely audibly—and trailed off incoherently. Obama had to jump in and preside. At other moments during photos, Obama would hop in and finish sentences for him.

The former president decided that the fault lay with Biden's busy schedule. The man was eighty-one, and he had flown from Normandy, France, to Delaware, then back to Italy, and then to California in just ten days. The time zones were difficult enough, but this was a rough itinerary. Obama put it down to a bad scheduling decision by Biden and his staff.

It was a consistent theme in his conversations with Biden; he was a bit protective. "Why are you doing ten hours of a photo line at the holiday party?" Obama would ask him.

But Obama came to realize that scheduling was not the fundamental problem.

As HE AND his wife, Emily, pulled up to the event, Obama's former chief speechwriter, Jon Favreau, didn't know which Joe Biden was going to show up that night.

The official goal for the event was to raise $30 million for the president's reelection campaign, but there was a secondary goal of reassuring donors that Biden was fine and well and up for the presidential race.

Favreau had reason to wonder. He'd had two personal meetings with Biden in the previous two years, and two wildly divergent experiences.

The first was in December 2022, when he, Emily, their son Charlie, and Emily's parents, Marnie and Tim Black, visited the White House. Favreau took a moment to check in with Biden's chief speechwriter, Vinay Reddy, and when he rejoined his family in his old office, he was delighted to find Biden there engaging them all with stories infused by his stodgy Irish pol charm. Stunningly, Biden had recognized Marnie from an event in California years before, and said so as he regaled them.

The president invited everyone up to the Oval Office, where he was as sharp and garrulous as ever. To Emily's dad, a federal judge, he offered a detailed recounting of the failed confirmation hearings for Supreme Court nominee Judge Robert Bork—though his staff's willingness to indulge his windbaggy nature in the middle of a Wednesday afternoon disturbed Favreau a bit. It seemed a bit much. And his staff seemed a little too eager to let him waste the time in the midst of a crisis—a major railway strike.

The second encounter came a year and a half later, on Friday night, April 26, 2024, the evening before the White House Correspondents' Association Dinner. Favreau, one of the hosts of a wildly successful podcast called *Pod Save America*, was among the "influencers" invited to visit with the president at the White House, as were his cohosts Dan Pfeiffer and Jon Lovett.

That night, Joe Biden seemed to have aged fifty years in sixteen months. He was incoherent. His stories were meandering and confusing. Something about Iraq? What, exactly, was the point of this? He told one story twice.

After the president left the group, Favreau asked a staffer about his demeanor. Oh, no big deal, the staffer said. The president must have just been tired. It was nighttime at the end of a long week.

Lovett, Pfeiffer, Favreau, and Emily left the White House that night deeply disturbed. Biden seemed okay the next night at the dinner, capably reading from a teleprompter and projecting as aged but present.

And now here they were at the biggest fundraiser in the history of the Democratic Party. Yes, Biden would be helped by the presence of the younger, more charismatic Obama and Kimmel onstage with him. But they could only hide so much.

The Favreaus weren't ponying up $500,000 for the meet and greet; they would just sit in the audience and watch the show.

And hope. And pray.

AND THEN CAME the event: Jimmy Kimmel, fifty-six; Barack Obama, sixty-two; and Joe Biden, eighty-one, came onstage, all in dark suits, white shirts, no ties. Kimmel sat on the left, Biden in the middle, Obama on the right. The late-night comedian rattled off Biden's accomplishments and quipped, "Not bad for 'Sleepy Joe,'" reclaiming Trump's nickname for the president.

Some attendees later expressed concern about how Biden seemed onstage. The event was just half an hour or so, and the questions were friendly. Many in the audience were surprised by the president's apparent diminishment, his quiet and frail presentation, his inability to develop a strong, convincing sales pitch. Some of his answers were downright confusing.

When the event ended, the three men stood. Kimmel and Obama began to walk offstage, but Biden walked to the edge and stared blankly into the crowd. Obama walked back and grabbed Biden's arm, then guided him backstage. He later explained that he just wanted to get the hell out of there, but he didn't want to leave Biden alone up on the stage. Biden folks insisted that the president was just basking in the glow of a supportive audience, and they called clips of the very real moment "cheap fakes," a term for video content that has been deceptively edited or taken out of its full context. But even some supporters present in the arena wondered what was going on.

He doesn't look like he knows where he's supposed to go, thought New Hampshire Democratic Congresswoman Annie Kuster, sitting in the audience with California Congresswoman Julia Brownley.

They'd seen him backstage, and Kuster could tell it was a struggle for the president to engage. It reminded her of being with an aging grandparent, worryingly thinking, *Oh my gosh, what's going to happen next?*

In the audience, Emily couldn't believe how awful Biden seemed. "I want to make everyone stay in this theater and say, 'No one is going anywhere until we have a plan, because this can't be it,'" she said. To her, it had been a complete disaster. And she hadn't even seen what happened backstage.

Kuster had already reached the conclusion that there was no scenario in which Biden would make it through this campaign. She turned to Brownley.

"We can't go out there and campaign for 'four more years,'" she said. "That's just not tenable."

THAT SAME NIGHT, in New York City, Senate Majority Leader Chuck Schumer was at a wedding. He had jitters about the upcoming debate.

Sometimes the president would call him and forget why he'd called. Sometimes he rambled. Sometimes he forgot names. Schumer publicly insisted he wasn't concerned about Biden's acuity, but privately he conceded he was worried about the optics. Biden talked sluggishly—his voice was not just slower but oddly quieter, like that of Schumer's mother, who had Parkinson's. His gait was slower too. Schumer was concerned about the president's electability.

He talked about it with his staff, but he felt that he had to keep a close circle. If he talked about his worries with Obama or Jeffries or Pelosi and it got out that they were discussing whether Biden was too old to run, that would make it even harder for him to win.

At the wedding, Schumer was discussing his concerns and the fact that the debate was so early—just twelve days away.

"If things go south at the debate, it might change things," Schumer later recalled having said. The early date gave Democrats some time.

Another guest at the table recalled Schumer saying that "if things go south at the debate, me, Barack, Nancy, and Hakeem have a plan B," though Schumer later would deny it.

IMMIGRATION EVENT

The White House hosted an immigration-themed event on the afternoon of Tuesday, June 18.

At one point during the event, Biden spoke, reading from a teleprompter, and had some sort of glitch.

"Thanks to all the members of the Congress and Homeland Security Secretary—I . . ."

It was possible that Biden had forgotten the name of Homeland Security Secretary Alejandro Mayorkas, but it's difficult to specifically assess what was going on at that moment. For three seconds, he was mumbling incoherently, alarmingly.

To some expert physicians with whom we spoke, the moment looked neurological in nature, a lost train of thought and difficulty figuring out what to say next, an attempt to cover it up by mumbling and trying to retrieve the lost information.

"I'm not sure I'm going to introduce you all the way," he said, to nervous laughter, "but all kidding aside, Secretary Mayorkas, as well as Secretary Becerra and advocates and families for law enforcement, faith leaders, everybody who is here."

As he sat in the front row at the event, Colorado Democratic Senator Michael Bennet considered what Biden's age likely meant when it came to the issue of immigration. He'd never felt as if the White House had a coherent policy. It seemed like there were two competing sides of the debate within the administration—one pushing for tougher border regulations, another opening the country to new immigrants without any real process—but no one had publicly articulated the president's view on the matter.

In early June, Biden had instituted an effective ban on asylum requests from undocumented immigrants who crossed the US-Mexico border, putting them on a fast track to deportation.

But here they were two weeks later, Biden signing off on a policy to allow the undocumented family members of US citizens who'd lived in the United States for a decade or more to file paperwork for legal status.

Bennet had come to believe that Biden's inability to mediate between the people in his administration with different political viewpoints had led to an incoherent overall position on the issue.

It actually mattered, he felt, whether there was an elected official— elected by the American people—who could navigate and arbitrate disputes. It mattered if there was someone at the helm who could push back and say to policymakers, "Have you really thought this through?" Biden's advisers, however capable and intelligent, had never run for office, so they lacked a certain grasp of the politics of it all, Bennet thought. Was Biden able to play the role that Obama had played in these debates, play the role that Trump had played? Or was it just a bunch of senior staff capitulating to various advocacy groups, and capitulating to one another?

It was a fair question. After all, as one senior administration official recalled, there was a plan from day one of the administration to crack down on the southern border, to send US Border Patrol agents and immigration adjudicators to deal with undocumented immigrants, to build more facilities so that they could be processed and either deported or sent to the proper place as soon as possible.

But that plan disappeared, the official told us, and immigrants were instead released into the country immediately pending immigration hearings months or even years later.

What had happened?

One cabinet secretary believed that Biden's limitations had given his aides more power to steer the administration. "If you had a twenty-years-younger Joe Biden, I think he would have been more on top of the issues and what was going on," the cabinet secretary said.

When Bennet went back to his Senate office, he told his staffers: "We're in trouble."

DEBATE PREP

Biden's team knew the stakes. After weeks of travel and the emotionally draining Hunter trial, they blocked out substantial time to prep over several days at Camp David.

Once they began, Ron Klain was disappointed with the president. He'd been assured that Biden had been reviewing his prep materials before he arrived at Camp David, but he hadn't. He was rusty and exhausted when he arrived, essentially sleeping that whole first day. And even after that taking lots of naps.

Most of the more intense prep sessions occurred with just a few people. Klain, Steve Ricchetti, and Bruce Reed often conducted prep sessions with Biden at his cabin. Biden usually had open time in the afternoons, during which he often dozed off in his quarters in Aspen Lodge.

The mock debate sessions were alternately held in a small auditorium and in a more open area with a replica of the stage.

Biden's performance ranged from bad to passable. With Anita Dunn playing CNN's Dana Bash, Ben LaBolt playing Jake, and Bob Bauer playing Trump, the Biden team tried to prod and prick Biden on every topic. Katzenberg attended a few sessions to advise Biden on his optics. Spielberg video-called into a few of the prep sessions too.

Biden's answers were serviceable but not great. His voice was hard to hear, his delivery was halting, and his answers were all over the place. Advisers also told him his mouth was agape when he wasn't speaking and urged him to close it. His voice got raspier as the week went on, to the point that aides couldn't hear him during mock sessions. Biden kept asking for more cough drops.

The fundamental problem, Klain believed, was that in 2023, the president had been kind of locked down in the White House, not much engaged in domestic politics and focused on two things: trying to drum up funding for Ukraine and going around the country to talk about bridges. It had diminished his ability to talk fluidly about a broad range of domestic political issues.

"You have to decide if you're running for president of Europe or president of the United States," Klain had told him in early summer 2023.

The president shrugged. "I'm doing what I have to do on Ukraine," he said.

It was a year later, and Klain thought this focus on Ukraine—and since October 7, on the Middle East too—was a debacle for the president politically. He'd spent more time talking to European parliamentarians than American ones; he knew a lot more about what was going on in Europe than about what was going on in America.

His communications skills had also deteriorated, which Klain felt was due to lack of practice. He'd never fully embraced the performative aspects of the presidency, Klain thought. He'd always believed that if he delivered results, that's all that would ultimately matter.

Biden had the mindset that what Trump was saying was so outrageous and so stupid that if the American people saw them side by side, they would realize Trump was unfit—he just had to step aside and let Trump step on himself.

Debate prep was further undermined because the president was sick, having come down with a cold so bad that he was twice tested for COVID. His voice sounded awful, so Annie Tomasini pushed for him to rest it. The windows for prep time narrowed to make sure that he had a chance to recover.

But most of Biden's team left debate prep feeling good. Some even predicted that it would be boring. Time and again, aides had seen Biden be bad in prep and then better onstage.

As Katzenberg said when they left Camp David: "Okay, well, our guy is a game-day performer."

FOURTEEN

The Debate

He was late.

It was 8:00 p.m. and President Joe Biden had yet to arrive at CNN's Atlanta studios for the highly anticipated face-off between him and Donald Trump, which would begin at 9:00 p.m.

CNN had initially agreed with the campaigns that Trump and his team would be offered a walk-through at 3:00 p.m. in the Atlanta studios, while the Biden team would get one at 5:00 p.m. Both candidates arrived later.

Shortly after 6:00 p.m., Trump arrived with his campaign managers, Chris LaCivita and Susie Wiles, and a small entourage of top aides. They hung out in his greenroom before he was taken for a professional photo and then escorted into the studios for his walk-through at around 7:00 p.m.

Sir Mark Thompson, CNN's new president, gave him the tour.

Trump, a creature of television, had plenty of questions. Which one was his camera? What would CNN be showing when it was Biden's turn to speak? How could he get permission to speak if he wanted the opportunity beyond the question-answer-rebuttal-response rules?

An hour passed, and Biden still had not arrived. A CNN executive called Anita Dunn. Where was the president?

Dunn explained: Biden didn't feel as though he needed to be there; he had done plenty of debates.

He really should see the stage and setup, the CNN executive told her.

Biden finally arrived and did the walk-through between 8:32 and 8:50 p.m. Ten minutes before airtime.

JAKE MODERATED THE DEBATE, along with his CNN colleague Dana Bash. After the two moderators explained the rules, Jake said, "Please welcome the forty-sixth president of the United States, Joe Biden."

"How are you?" Biden said as he walked to his lectern.

For those who hadn't paid much attention during the previous few years, the president's gait was recognizably stiffer and more limited. In April, Alex and an *Axios* colleague had reported that Biden advisers were concerned that the images of the president "walking and shuffling alone—especially across the grass—have highlighted his age." Aides then started joining him on the broadcast walks to and from Marine One. This obscured Biden's rigid gait and allowed aides to be nearby in case Biden stumbled or needed help for balance.

"Great to be here," Biden said when he arrived at the lectern, his voice raspy and thin. "Thank you."

Then Trump was introduced, and he walked out to his lectern, from the left side of the television screen for the tens of millions watching at home.

By this point in his presidency, Biden's resting face could take on a frozen, slightly haunted expression, which may have been disconcerting to those who hadn't seen him in some time.

His first answer came three minutes and twenty-five seconds into the event. If one hadn't heard Biden speak in years, his voice was unquestionably reedier, weaker, softer, and less energetic. He was a far less effective communicator than he'd been in 2020. As even top Biden aides would admit, the split screen of Biden in 2024 and Biden in 2020—a man more assured, with a deeper voice, speaking extemporaneously with more confidence and alacrity—was shocking.

Still, for those not on YouTube comparing this presidential nominee with the one he'd been four years prior, the June 27 debate was fine for the first few minutes. Biden's first answer, and Trump's response about inflation and economic hardship, weren't particularly unusual. Biden sounded a little phlegmy and was coughing a bit. He had a few stumbles here and there but nothing out of the ordinary for Biden, let alone an eighty-one-year-old version of himself.

The first sign of trouble came with this Biden non sequitur: "When he was president, we still found ourselves in a position where you had a notion that we were this safe country." That was an odd sentence. Then came this one: "The truth is, I'm the only president this century that doesn't have any—this—this decade—doesn't have any troops dying anywhere in the world, like he did."

After the debate, much would be made about the number of audacious lies told by Trump, and rightly so. Trump falsely claimed he "had the greatest economy in the history of our country," continued to mislead the public about undocumented migrants being sent to the US from South American asylums and prisons, and lied about January 6, describing it as "a relatively small number of people that went to the Capitol and in many cases were ushered in by the police." But the notion that Biden had not had any troops die anywhere in the world was also jarringly false. Beyond the thirteen US servicemembers killed during the chaotic withdrawal from Afghanistan, three US servicemembers had been killed by Iranian-backed terrorists during a drone strike on a US outpost in Jordan in January. In a separate incident that same month, two Navy SEALS had died during a military operation in which they attempted to board an unflagged ship off the coast of Somalia.

The split screen of the debate didn't benefit Biden, who looked pale and considerably older than his three-years-younger opponent, and whose slack-jawed expressions and undetermined stare at the floor in front of him suggested that he wasn't even aware he was on camera for the entire ninety minutes of the debate. Critics can sniff at the superficialities of such matters, but television is a visual medium, and voters make decisions based on a host of factors. Presidents from Kennedy to Reagan to Clinton to Obama to Trump have taken such communications issues seriously.

Still, the debate up to that point had been standard, relatively, with both men taking shots at the other's economic records and more. Asked about Trump's record on the deficit and national debt, Biden had the facts and figures at hand: "He had the largest national debt of any president four-year period, number one. Number two, that $2 trillion tax cut, benefited the very wealthy."

It was just over eleven minutes into the debate.

After warding off a stammer, the president then started to wobble a touch on the data, though he was able to correct himself ("trillionaires— I mean billionaires," "twenty-four percent or twenty-five percent," "five hundred million—billion dollars").

This led to the first sign that things were going *really* wrong.

The transcript doesn't do justice to his difficulty finding the words, his facial expression as he closed his eyes to root around for what he was trying to say.

"We'd be able to right—wipe out his debt," Biden said. "We'd be able to help make sure that all those things we need to do"—this seemed a holding-pattern clause as he grasped for the list of priorities—"childcare, elder care, making sure that we continue to subtren-strengthen our health-care system"—his face betrayed a struggle here—"making sure that we're able to make every single solitary person, ay, ah, eligible for what I've been able to do with the, uh, with-with-with the COVID— excuse me—with, um . . . dealing with everything we have to do with . . . uh . . ." He made some guttural sounds. The moderators had iPads to communicate with the control room. Jake wrote: "Holy smokes."

The president was really having trouble accessing the right words he needed to communicate, relying on placeholders such as "all those things we need to do" and "eligible for what I've been able to do with."

"Look," he said, making the guttural sounds again, "if . . . we finally beat Medicare," he said.

Biden had reached his time limit, so Jake thanked him and threw it to Trump.

Dana wrote something down on a piece of paper and passed it to Jake: "He just lost the election."

"Well, he's right. He did beat Medicare," Trump said, opting not to raise the issue of Biden's difficulty communicating. "He beat it to death. And he's destroying Medicare, because all of these people are coming in. They're putting them on Medicare, they're putting them on Social Security."

This being the first presidential election since the US Supreme Court overturned *Roe v. Wade* with its *Dobbs* decision, Dana asked

Trump whether American women could have access to abortion pills, used in about two-thirds of all abortions. Would he block abortion medication?

Trump falsely asserted that the "Supreme Court just approved the abortion pill. And I agree with their decision to have done that, and I will not block it."

What had happened was that on June 13, the court unanimously ruled that plaintiffs suing to challenge the FDA's approval of the abortion pill mifepristone lacked legal standing to do so. The court did not rule on whether the FDA had the authority to approve the drug.

Trump falsely asserted that "everybody wanted" *Roe v. Wade* overturned so that states could make their own decisions about abortion rights. "Democrats, Republicans, liberals, conservatives—everybody wanted it back," Trump said.

This was a subject top of mind for millions of voters, one that had played a major role in the Democrats' better-than-expected showing in the 2022 midterms, and one that the Trump campaign hated discussing, since the GOP's underlying position—opposing legal abortion—was out of step with the majority of the country.

Biden campaign aides had been looking forward to this subject as much as they'd been dreading inflation. Trump bragged about appointing the three Supreme Court Justices who helped overturn *Roe v. Wade*. Rolling in apace were horror stories about the real-world results of strict antiabortion laws in states where, either by design or confusion, miscarrying women were denied lifesaving care. For any Democratic candidate, this should have been easy.

For Joe Biden, it was not.

"We're in a state where in six weeks you don't even know whether you're pregnant or not, but you cannot see a doctor, have your—and have him decide on what your circumstances are, whether you need help," he said confusingly.

Then, for an inexplicable reason, Biden brought up one of his weakest policy areas—the border crisis and the American victims of violence committed by undocumented immigrants. "Look, there's so many young women who have been—including a young woman who just was murdered, and he went to the funeral," Biden said. "The idea that she was murdered by a, by a, by an immigrant coming in, and they talk about that."

It was a cringe-inducing reference, at once tragic and bizarre, to the murder of Laken Riley.

"But here's the deal," Biden continued. "There's a lot of young women who are being raped by their, by their in-laws, by their, by-by their spouses, brothers and sisters, by—just—it's just, it's just ridiculous. And they can do nothing about it. And they try to arrest them when they cross state lines."

The horror of rape, the need for women and girls to be able to terminate pregnancies resulting from such acts of violence, was certainly one of the abortion rights movement's strongest arguments. That young women were being raped by their sisters was not.

Asked by Dana if he supported any legal limits on how late into a pregnancy a woman should be able to terminate it, Biden said, "I support *Roe v. Wade*, which had three trimesters. First time is between a woman and a doctor. Second time is between a doctor and an extreme situation. A third time is between the doctor—I mean, be-between the woman and the state."

On immigration and the border, Biden talked up a bipartisan border agreement that Trump had helped kill.

"Since I've changed the law, what's happened?" Biden asked. "I've changed it in a way that now you're in a situation where there are forty percent fewer people coming across the border illegally. It's better than when he left office."

He struggled to find the right words and here came another horrible moment: "And I'm going to continue to move until we get the total ban on"—here he lost his train of thought again—"the-the-the-the total initiative relative to what we're going to do with more border patrol and more asylum officers."

He seemed to be grabbing words in his arsenal, but it was difficult to discern an articulation of an actual idea.

It was President Trump's turn to respond.

"I really don't know what he said at the end of that sentence," Trump said. "I don't think he knows what he said either."

Biden turned to Trump, mouth agape, a painful moment of split screen.

It wasn't even twenty-two minutes into the ninety-minute debate.

EACH CANDIDATE HAD brought his top advisers to the CNN studios.

In the Biden campaign holding room, on Zoom with other Biden people sat Mike Donilon, Steve Ricchetti, Jen O'Malley Dillon, Jeffrey Katzenberg, Ben LaBolt, Bruce Reed, Ron Klain, and Jake Sullivan. In a holding room outside the spin room were Quentin Fulks, Rob Flaherty, and Michael Tyler. Others were Zooming in from Wilmington.

Some knew from the first answer that something was off. The question was on inflation—the topic they had rehearsed the most. But Biden's answer was completely different from what he had recited over and over.

Klain thought it was a disaster. They had a very serious problem on their hands. They had to figure out how to respond. What to say. What to do.

Donilon thought it was bad but nothing they couldn't handle.

At the first commercial break, the Zoom resumed, and O'Malley Dillon said the obvious: "Look, this isn't going well, but we'll obviously see how the rest of it goes."

Becca Siegel reported on the dials—a reference to the focus group testing the campaign was doing that night in which viewers registered their approval or disapproval on dials, recording the impact of key moments. The dials had already thought Biden was old, Siegel said, so these voters weren't learning anything new. The dials also indicated that they were remembering what they had disliked about Trump.

In the Trump holding room, Chris LaCivita turned to his co-manager, Susie Wiles, and pollster Tony Fabrizio.

"Oh, fuck," LaCivita said. "He's not going to last." Biden wouldn't make it to November.

The Trump campaign had been attacking Biden on his frailty, on his aging, on his missteps real and torqued and imagined. But they never thought it would be this bad.

"Guys, he's not going to make it," LaCivita said. "There's just no way."

Biden's two worst moments of the debate came up top, when viewership is traditionally highest.

Most of his performance was not as poor as those two moments. But as a matter of history, those were two of the worst moments—if not the absolute worst—for any major party candidate since televised American presidential debates began in 1960.

Yes, the viewpoint that policy matters more than style is perfectly legitimate, and yes, for those inclined to intensely dislike Trump on substantive and/or stylistic grounds, nothing in his performance was particularly convincing. He made an astounding number of exaggerations, told a historic number of lies.

On a general note, CNN executives had ruled that, consistent with sixty-four years of presidential debate history up until that point, Trump's lies would be for Biden to fact-check and dispute, as previous candidates had done with their rivals. (Ronald Reagan's most famous debate line—"There you go again"—came from his attack on President Jimmy Carter for an assertion about Medicare that Reagan took issue with.)

Biden attempted to fact-check numerous times but was largely incapable of doing so in an understandable way. And beyond that was the larger point of the debate catastrophe as it was unfolding.

The election was going to be decided by voters who were unsure if Biden was capable of being president, voters who were unhappy with the direction of the country and displeased with Biden's economic performance—but also unsure about Trump's stability. Biden needed to reassure those voters that he was indeed up to the task. And his debate performance, worse than all those other disconcerting moments caught on camera, achieved the exact opposite.

There was, of course, a political case to prosecute against Trump, but Biden proved unable to do it. Biden wanted to attack Trump for saying at a February 2024 rally in South Carolina that his message to any NATO member country not meeting the pact's commitment to military spending was that he would "encourage them"—the Russians—"to do whatever the hell they want. You got to pay. You got to pay your bills."

It came out like this: "We found ourselves in a situation where, if you take a look at what Trump did in Ukraine, he's—this guy told Ukraine, told Trump, 'Do whatever you want. Do whatever you want.'

And that's exactly what Trump did to . . . Putin, encouraged him. 'Do whatever you want.' And he went in."

After the second and final commercial break, each candidate was given two minutes for his closing argument. Not even a minute into his, Biden struggled to explain one of the biggest accomplishments of his administration: allowing Medicare to negotiate with pharmaceutical companies on drug prices.

"What I did when, for example, he wants to get away with—get rid of—the ability of Medicare to uh, uh, uh, for the ability to, for the . . . us to be able to negotiate drug prices with the Big Pharma companies. Well, guess what? We got it . . . we got it down to fifteen, uh, excuse me, thirty-five dollars for insulin instead of four hundred dollars. No more than two thousand dollars for every senior no matter what they—how much prescription they need."

The first half hour of the debate had those worst two moments, but Biden was weak throughout. Not necessarily on the substance but on his ability to communicate at all, and at times on his ability to follow what he himself was saying. A president's ability to communicate is a vital part of the job. Beyond that failure, Biden had projected such weakness it raised questions about his ability to even serve as president.

When it was over, the Bidens approached the table to say hello to the moderators. To Jake and Dana, it didn't seem as if Biden had any idea how bad his performance was, though he did say, "Sorry about my voice; I have a cold." He remarked on the wild claims Trump had made, then said he would go see what the commentators were saying. Jake didn't know what to say and attempted to make small talk with the First Lady by showing her that he was wearing Phillies cuff links.

Senior Democrats who had done work for Biden in 2024 later told us that they had watched the debate and wondered: *Just who the hell is running the country?*

FIFTEEN

The World Reacts

When the debate began, Jen Psaki couldn't believe what she was watching. Psaki had been Biden's White House press secretary until May 2022, when she left to become an anchor at MSNBC. During the debate, she was supposed to be participating in a TikTok live stream, talking about the stakes and the importance of the event.

Several minutes into the live stream, she remained speechless, and a staffer asked if she should turn it off. Psaki nodded.

"This is a fucking disaster," Psaki said.

She worried not only that Democrats would get wiped out in the November elections but also that Biden was seriously ill. His health seemed to be on a rapid downward spiral.

THE HOTTEST TICKET in Los Angeles was to the modernist Holmby Hills manse of James Costos, a former ambassador to Spain under Obama, and interior designer to the stars Michael Smith. Not only were Jane Fonda and Rob Reiner there, but so, too, were Second Gentleman Doug Emhoff and three Democratic governors—Beshear of Kentucky, Pritzker of Illinois, and Whitmer of Michigan.

The gathering had originally been planned as a fundraiser for the Biden Victory Fund, but then the debate was scheduled for the same night, so the hosts turned it into a fancy and hopefully fun debate watch party, with people sitting in three or four different rooms.

Until it became a debate watch horror show.

A few minutes into it, Reiner, in the main living room, stated plainly: "We are fucked!"

A few seats away, Fonda was equally distraught.

Reiner, an outspoken Democrat and fundraiser, was terrified of another Trump presidency. And Democrats needed someone who could go head-to-head with Trump. Not someone who just stood there fumbling around, he felt. The world had been watching Biden for many months, even a year, as his capacity dwindled. Reiner became angry. Soon he was venting, standing, full of fury.

He seemed to be looking at Emhoff. Daggers.

"We're going to lose our fucking democracy because of you!" Reiner yelled.

Because of me? Emhoff thought.

THE THREE HOUSE Democratic leaders—Leader Hakeem Jeffries of New York, Whip Katherine Clark of Massachusetts, and Caucus Chair

Pete Aguilar of California—were in Washington, DC, with roughly fifty of their fellow House Democrats at a debate watch party sponsored by Caucus Vice-Chair Ted Lieu of California in the rec room of an apartment building where many members of Congress live.

The House Democrats were, to say the least, taken aback by the president's performance.

Until it began, they had been chatting, sampling from the buffet. Many were now panicking.

Jeffries had been defending the president for months. Hadn't people seen him at the State of the Union? Did they understand the high-stakes nature of that address, delivered at 9:00 p.m. in a hostile work environment, with instigators like GOP Congresswoman Marjorie Taylor Greene trying to throw him off his game? Biden walked right into the lion's den an hour before the speech and stuck his head right into the mouths of the beasts, posing for selfies, taking his time walking down the aisle.

What was this?

Aguilar knew that many of his colleagues saw their fates as rising or falling depending on whomever was on top of the ticket. In a competitive race, a Democrat could outrun an unpopular president by a few points, but at a certain point, the laws of gravity would take over.

A few minutes into the debate, one House Democrat turned to Aguilar. "I just lost my job," he said.

After the debate, a number of Democrats surrounded Jeffries, worried.

"What just happened is not acceptable," one of them said. "Something has to be done."

They wondered, "Did he have a bad illness, or was there some sort of physiological thing that was temporary?" Some believed that there was no way Biden could stay in the race after what they'd just seen.

———

"Calm is an intentional decision," Jeffries told them, repeating one of his mantras. They would process it all and come up with a plan.

KAMALA HARRIS'S AIDES had already booked her for four post-debate television interviews on ABC, CNN, CBS, and MSNBC, and now they were scrambling to figure out what to say. What *could* they say?

The vice president was watching the debate with her closest aides in a conference room at the Fairmont Century Plaza in Los Angeles. She didn't say much as she watched but occasionally asked those with open laptops what people were saying. As the debate went on, one press aide told her it was so bad that serious people were calling on Biden to step aside.

Harris appeared surprised that the panic had reached this level so quickly. Some people on the Biden campaign suggested that she cancel her interviews. They argued that she didn't want to make it look like she was trying to upstage him.

Harris dismissed that idea. She and her team began brainstorming how they could at once address the poor performance and defend the president. They debated so long that they missed Harris's interview with CBS and were late for the next one.

Five minutes before going on CNN, Harris herself landed on the line she would use: Acknowledge the slow start but then point to the strong finish.

But CNN's Anderson Cooper kept pushing Harris to go beyond that talking point.

Cooper noted that Harris had debated Biden in 2019 "and he was a very different person on the stage four years ago when—when you debated him. You must—I mean, that—that's certainly true, is it not?"

In response to Cooper's follow-ups, Harris responded with a line she hadn't rehearsed beforehand.

"I got the point that you're making about a one-and-a-half-hour debate tonight. I'm talking about three and a half years of performance in work that has been historic." Many Biden aides cheered her defense.

After the interview, Harris was visibly angry with Cooper. He had been asking the questions the nation had been wondering, but she took it personally.

This motherfucker doesn't treat me like the damn vice president of the United States, she said to colleagues. I thought we were better than that.

"I SPEND a lot of time with him, and that's not who he is," Mike Donilon would tell Democrats who called him up in a panic. "He had a bad debate."

They would have to fight through it, Donilon thought. It was a tough problem, but he believed they could beat it. They still had the convention in front of them; they had not really started the advertising campaign in earnest; there would be another debate. It was June! People needed to calm down.

THE CAMPAIGN had also invited some of its biggest donors down to Atlanta for a watch party. DNC Chair Jaime Harrison, Campaign Manager Julie Chávez Rodríguez, and other top Democrats gathered the donors at a restaurant.

A few minutes into the debate, the Biden Victory Fund's finance chair, Chris Korge, was overheard saying: "We are totally fucked. This is over. It's all over." Donors were putting their heads in their hands.

Before the debate ended, donors across the country were texting and calling campaign leadership to insist that Biden needed to drop out or money would dry up.

The dazed campaign team tried to rally the donors, but no one knew what to say.

DURING AND AFTER the debate, friends and former colleagues of Robert Hur's texted him.

OMG, one said.

VINDICATION, another wrote.

Finally, the American people were watching what Hur had seen the previous October—what he had been vilified for saying. His friends wondered if he felt relieved.

Hur told them that all he felt was sad. How could anyone look at Joe Biden at that debate and not feel bad?

MINUTES INTO THE DEBATE, Biden was facing a crisis of confidence among his own staff.

Inside the White House and at campaign headquarters, some aides were defiant, others were panicking, and many were feeling fury.

"Is he okay?"

"Devastated."

"The realization of the worst-case scenario."

At the Biden campaign headquarters in Wilmington, in the eighth floor war room, senior-most staff watched and tried to not freak out. In a second watch space in a rented theater across the street, an audible gasp could be heard among the dozens of staffers watching when Biden started speaking "like we'd all been punched in the stomach," an attendee later recalled. In a third space, on the sixth floor, some Biden comms staffers and pro-Biden influencers had gathered, and several minutes into the debate one person dramatically lay down on the floor, despondent. When the debate's video feed was temporarily interrupted, a relieved campaign staffer blurted out, "Oh, thank God."

Some grew disillusioned as the debate went on. They had trusted White House and campaign leadership, who had insisted that Biden was fine. They had tried to convince their skeptical families and friends that Biden was in command. Now they felt foolish and betrayed by their own bosses.

AFTER THE DEBATE, at around 11:00 p.m., the president and the First Lady walked into a room at a debate watch party for a preplanned victory lap. With a DJ spinning tunes and silhouettes of aviators on the screens, the event was meant to show energy after a debate that had demonstrated the polar opposite.

The campaign staff had done an admirable job of keeping the crowd excited, shouting out "Four more years! Four more years!" as the Bidens entered the room. Jill walked ahead of her husband to the stage and immediately grabbed the microphone from the DJ so that she could speak first. With the campaign in crisis and her husband in deep trouble, she was putting her hands on the wheel.

"Joe, you did such a great job!" she said, sounding like a kindergarten teacher commending a student. "You answered every question! You knew all the facts!" she continued, piling on the infantile praise. ("This, to the guy who controls the nuclear codes," quipped columnist Maureen Dowd, who had covered Biden for decades, and whom the family read religiously.)

"And let me ask the crowd: What did Trump do?" the First Lady said.

"Lieeeeeeee!" she yelled along with the crowd. She was just trying to help her husband, but even she later confessed that the moment looked terrible.

She was right that Trump had told more than his share of lies during the debate.

But the primary reactions from even Democrats on progressive-friendly MSNBC were now focused on an issue that not only many had refused to publicly acknowledge—but some had aggressively disputed—for so long.

"It's kind of a DEFCON 1 moment," David Plouffe told MSNBC anchor Rachel Maddow. "And the way I think about it is, sadly, is it really pains me to say this: They're three years apart; they seemed about thirty years apart tonight."

"I am not going to put a fine sheen on it, or a spin on it, even though I am in the spin room," MSNBC's Alex Wagner said from CNN's post-debate spin room. "There has been a uniformly negative reaction to Biden's performance tonight." Wagner argued that the task before Biden that night was for him to fight "a caricature of himself as an enfeebled person . . . And he did nothing to disabuse, I think, the country of the notion that he is very old and was lost frequently in that debate."

Said then-MSNBC anchor Joy Reid: "The universal reaction was somewhere approaching panic."

Anchor Nicolle Wallace agreed: "I think conversations range from whether he should be in this race tomorrow morning to what was wrong with him."

Chris Hayes weighed in: "The job of the president is making decisions. The job of a presidential candidate is to communicate. It just is. That's the job. . . . I think Joe Biden has a very good record on making decisions. And I think he is a very poor communicator right now."

The fact that proudly progressive journalists on a proudly progressive network rooting for Biden were saying these things was unquestionably significant.

But Bidenland may as well have been on Mars.

"Look, folks," the president told the adoring crowd after his wife handed him the microphone, "you know, there, uh—I shouldn't say this, but my brother always uses lines from movies. There was a famous movie by John Wayne, and—and he's working for the, uh, the Northern military, trying to get the Apaches back on the reservation, and they were lying like hell to him. And they're all sitting on a bluff, and John Wayne was sitting with two Indian—they were, they were tr—Apaches. And one of them looked at John Wayne and said, 'These guys are nothing but lying, dog-faced pony soldiers.'"

The crowd roared and laughed.

"Except, he's just a liar," Biden added.

John Wayne never said any such thing in any movie. The fabricated quote—to attack Trump as a liar, no less—was a perfect encapsulation of the Biden campaign at that moment. However much Trump was a "lying, dog-faced pony soldier," there was at that moment in American history no lie more widely discussed than the one that millions of Americans now realized they'd been told for months, if not years: the lie that Joe Biden was perfectly fine and up to the task of being president for four more years.

"One of the great lessons from 2024," Plouffe would later tell us, is that "never again can we as a party suggest to people that what they're seeing is not true."

BIDEN'S TOP AIDES were largely dismissive of the concerns, but the campaign team was temporarily paralyzed.

After debates, each side sends dozens of surrogates to the spin room to try to convince reporters that their candidate won.

For the first twenty-five minutes after the debate, no Biden surrogates were in the room, as they were trying to figure out what to say. Meanwhile, Trump surrogates were everywhere.

Before the debate, the Biden team had decided that they were going to try to upend the spin-room model. Instead of spreading out across the room to give individual commentary, the surrogates would huddle together and essentially give a united press conference.

But after Biden's performance and the unusual delay, that approach made the campaign look even more defensive. The surrogates gave statements and then took a handful of questions. After a historically terrible debate performance, they only stayed for about fifteen minutes.

FIVE MINUTES into the debate, the pollsters were on texts and Signal chains acknowledging the reality: This was a fucking disaster.

Top campaign staff had huddled during the first commercial break—the pollsters, per usual, were not included in any strategy sessions—and the inner circle was soon firing off this message: "From campaign aide: President had a cold but he warmed up as he went and really had some very tough lines against Trump. Ultimately, substance over style is what matters to voters on the issues that affect their lives. On Roe, immigration, economy, democracy—we got off key contrast we needed. Our dials show the President [sic]"—the intended word was voters—"hated Trump—particularly his Jan 6 answer. MUST be noted. Trump refused to accept results of elect 3x."

This was an accurate description—David Binder's focus group respondents, forced to watch the entire debate, had not liked Trump's performance.

But there were two major caveats that Biden folks did not share when heralding the dials.

First, the group also disliked Biden's performance quite a bit: Any confidence they had in his ability to be president was depleted. The overall tenor was one of disgust with both nominees. After the debate was done, when the focus group moderator conversed with the voters, some pressed their hands to the sides of their heads, despondent that in a country of three hundred forty million people, voters had to choose between these two men.

Second, the dials did not reflect a cross section of average voters. They consisted of sixty-one voters in Phoenix, mostly independents, almost three-quarters of whom had not voted for Trump in 2020. Almost 60 percent of them had voted for Biden in 2020. These were the Biden voters he was failing to win back.

As one pollster put it later: "So, no shit they didn't like Trump—they had already voted against him. The troubling fact was that to hear them talk, their concerns about the two were fairly equal, and they were very concerned about voting for Biden again."

The campaign spin was thus misleading and in denial of how catastrophic the debate performance had been for Biden. Further, it did not consider the impact that coverage of the debate would have on the electorate. Though, truth be told, Biden was already behind, so polls immediately after the fact weren't all that much worse than beforehand, when he was also trailing.

The pollsters continued to sit outside the insular campaign circle, uninvited to weigh in, unwelcome to share their candid thoughts. The campaign was, however, asking the pollsters to talk to reporters and tell them that things were fine and looking fixable for the president, even though the campaign had no real data to back up that claim.

———

DAVID AXELROD WASN'T sitting there thinking, *I told you so.* He was worried. Sad for Biden. Angry at Biden. Absolutely convinced that Biden could not go forward. And Axelrod would be mad at the president and his family and his team for a long time.

Within a few minutes of the debate's shocking opening, Axelrod was getting texts from people he hadn't heard from in ten years. Democrats were in full-on panic mode. And a lot of it was "How could they?!"

He'd known Mike Donilon for thirty-five years and thought him very smart, but he also saw that Donilon was so blinded by his emotional attachment to Joe Biden—his fate and his life inextricably bound up with the president's—he just couldn't let go. He knew Steve Ricchetti had talent, especially legislatively, but compared him unflatteringly to the obsequious Ditto Boland in Edwin O'Connor's *The Last Hurrah*, an aide to the machine mayor who mimics him kind of sadly.

"They did such a disservice to Joe Biden and to the country," Axelrod later said. "The family as well. I don't understand how you could see him in the condition he's in and think, *Yeah, you oughta go* [run for president again]. To do that to someone you love?"

BILL DALEY SHOOK his head. He had always thought that would be what people saw when Biden finally hit the debate stage. It's why he wanted this exposed earlier in the process, on a debate stage with Gavin Newsom or Andy Beshear or JB Pritzker. It's why he thought the Biden team nuts for agreeing to debate Trump at all. But now it was too late. None of the Democratic officials now sounding the alarm had been willing to say anything when it counted.

———

SIXTEEN

The Bad Times

FRIDAY, JUNE 28, 2024

White House and Biden campaign staffers would come to refer to the period between the debate and July 21, when the president dropped out of the race, as "the Bad Times" or "the Dark Times." But the day after the debate, leaders in the White House essentially acted like it hadn't happened.

They acknowledged to their subordinates that it had been a bad debate but said nothing more. But Biden's aides felt like they were being gaslit by their own bosses. "Senior leadership has given us nothing. To act like it's business as usual is delusional," a White House official told Alex at the time.

People whom Alex had been reaching out to for years were suddenly talking. They were disillusioned and angry, but they feared speaking up.

If anything, the debate had made Biden aides more watchful for signs of disloyalty.

They saw the debate as just the latest instance of counting Biden out. A longtime Biden aide told Alex: "Davos Dems love to hedge their bets against us and get hysterical, like they did in 2019. And just like after 2020, they will come back with their DNC convention lanyards in their hands, begging for Christmas party invitations and then for a plus-one."

While Democrats across Washington, DC, were freaking out, the core Biden team retreated further into their bunker. On the plane ride from Atlanta to North Carolina after the debate, aides were dismissive of the anxiety: It was just a bad night.

At the Jim Graham Building in Raleigh, North Carolina, Biden spoke for twenty-one minutes to try to undo the damage of the previous night's ninety-minute debacle.

Mike Donilon had been up all night writing the remarks.

"I know I'm not a young man, to state the obvious," Biden read from a teleprompter. "Folks, I don't walk as easy as I used to. I don't speak as smoothly as I used to. I don't deba-debate as well as I used to. But I know what I do know: I know how to tell the truth. I know, I know, I know right from wrong. And I know how to do this job. I know how to get things done. And I know, like millions of Americans know, when you get knocked down, you get back up."

The crowd cheered him on and applauded.

"I give you my word as a Biden: I would not be running again if I didn't believe with all my heart and soul I can do this job. Because, quite frankly, the stakes are too high."

That may have been true—that he believed he could do the job. But an increasing number of Democratic officials didn't agree.

RON KLAIN CALLED Jeff Zients. He thought it was possible that Biden could repair the damage done at the debate. He would need to do press conferences and interviews and show he was able to answer questions— and he would need to get allies engaged. ASAP.

"You need to get the Progressive Caucus to the White House this weekend," Klain told Zients. "They need to meet with him face-to-face."

That Klain was focused on the progressives was not a surprise. Some of Biden's senior advisers saw that as Klain's go-to move—always running to the left, even if that meant running away from discussions about serious border security enforcement during his time as chief of staff.

"I agree that he's gotta get out there," Zients replied. "Progressives are important, but that's not our whole strategy. We're not going to bring progressives to the White House this weekend."

The president was headed to Camp David with his family. They were scheduled to do a photo shoot with Annie Leibovitz.

Klain was very disappointed to hear that. Hunkering down with the family was not what Biden needed to do at that moment. Klain thought he had an ability to talk to Biden in a way that Zients didn't. First, he was unafraid of offending the president, which he believed was part and parcel of being a good chief of staff. Second, he had a very long-standing relationship with Biden and a deep foundation of trust. Third, he had a strong political perspective, while Zients seemed to view himself more as a neutral broker of various political opinions.

Klain wanted Biden to do a press conference, to throw himself into interviews, to show he could handle tough questions. He urged Biden's staff to get people into the White House to meet with him. He watched. And waited.

AT A PREVIOUSLY scheduled meeting, Leader Hakeem Jeffries heard from members of the Blue Dog Coalition, a small group of more moderate Democrats, many of them from battleground districts who often broke from the party. Its members were not in a full-fledged panic, Jeffries thought, but then again, Biden had already been losing their districts. They were, however, concerned.

As were most of the House Democrats, constantly calling, texting, and approaching Jeffries. People were still processing what they had seen. If Biden stepped down, who would be next? Vice President Harris? What might that look like?

In his brief tenure as House Democratic leader, Jeffries had weathered a few challenges, through which he'd learned how to hold his caucus together—Ukraine funding, preventing the US government from defaulting on its debt, the House GOP leadership crisis. He'd learned what he called "maximum engagement" so that he could represent his caucus in as candid and clear-eyed a way as possible, talking and listening to everyone. He was going to keep his opinion to himself, at least for now.

CONGRESSWOMAN ANNIE KUSTER called Louisa Terrell, the White House's former legislative director, who remained in the Biden orbit.

"That was malpractice," Kuster said. "Who sent him out there? Did he have a stroke on the way out there?" She thought the campaign should have done everything it could have to avoid putting Biden on the debate stage. "How did you not find a positive COVID test?" she joked.

Kuster was relieved to hear that the Biden family was going to Camp

David for the weekend. She thought, *Phew, surely the family will arrive at the conclusion that it isn't possible for the president to continue.*

Instead, the Associated Press reported that Biden family members continued to think "he's the best person to beat the Republican presumptive nominee. They also believe he is capable of doing the job of president for another four years." Among the most vocal family members were Jill and Hunter. "The family questioned how he was prepared for the debate by staff and wondered if they could have done something better," sources told the AP.

Hunter privately talked about it as being the family against the world. People sensed a more manic quality in him post-debate. He was determined to save his dad.

It was journalist Tina Brown's good fortune that she was scheduled to interview Ari Emanuel at the Aspen Ideas Festival the next day, June 28.

"Democrats are jumping out of the window," Brown said. "What are you thinking?" She did not need to provide any further context.

"Well, I'm pissed off at the Founding Fathers," Emanuel said. "They had the start date of thirty-five; they just didn't give us the end date."

Emanuel had been obsessed with this train wreck he'd seen coming for a year or more and was ready to discuss it. "Here's what Biden did," Emanuel said. "He, uh, said he was gonna run for one term and he's doing it to restore democracy. . . . He now runs for a second term: first bit of malarkey, as he would say."

Emanuel noted that Biden's "cohorts have told us that he's healthy for over a year." Pointedly, he added, "I had a father who died at ninety-two, but at eighty-one I took away his car."

"I promised myself I wasn't going to swear," Emanuel said, struggling to contain himself. "We're in a—this is a pickle. . . . If this is, as Biden says, the fight for our democracy . . . he gave us a bunch of malarkey and I'm really pissed. We all should be really pissed," Emanuel continued. "I mean I cannot believe we're in this situation."

Finally, the famously profane Emanuel couldn't hold it in any longer: "We're in Fuck City."

EMANUEL'S BROTHER RAHM, the ambassador to Japan, put it differently in a call with National Security Adviser Jake Sullivan.

"This is not a recoverable moment," he said. "The president confirmed people's worst fears and made it the only issue that will be debated in the campaign from now on."

BARACK OBAMA THOUGHT his former vice president might need him to express some support publicly.

"Bad debate nights happen," Obama posted on X at 2:36 p.m. ET. "Trust me, I know. But this election is still a choice between someone who has fought for ordinary folks his entire life and someone who only cares about himself. Between someone who tells the truth; who knows right from wrong and will give it to the American people straight— and someone who lies through his teeth for his own benefit. Last night didn't change that, and it's why so much is at stake in November."

Obama's "bad debate night"—his first showdown with former Governor Mitt Romney in 2012—was nothing like Biden's, of course. Obama had seemed aloof and annoyed, not addled. Not unable to do the job.

A few hours after posting on X, Obama was scheduled to do a

fundraiser with Leader Jeffries at the New-York Historical Society (now the New York Historical) on Central Park West. At dinner before the event, Obama and Jeffries discussed whether they should raise the topic of the debate. "Let's just address it at the top, because it's what people are thinking about," Obama said. Jeffries did, and Obama gave an oratorial version of his tweet, downplaying the disaster that the world had witnessed.

"I hated debates," Obama said. "They're weird; they're artificial. I was never that comfortable with them, partly because I just talked too long. And I talk slow too. There's a clock. I would just be about to make my good point, and they'd be like, 'I'm sorry, your time is up.' And I'd be like, 'Oh, damn.'"

The crowd laughed.

HOUSE OF CARDS

Obama's phone was blowing up with texts and calls from panicked Democrats. So, too, were the phones of Democratic senators.

Senate Majority Leader Chuck Schumer heard from Mark Warner and many others, all of whom said they needed to talk about this. As a group. Schumer shared their concerns.

Warner reached out to maybe thirty of the fifty colleagues who caucused with the Democrats. He didn't bother with those who were running for reelection and had tough decisions to make that involved their political viability. He also didn't bother with the two independents who were retiring, Joe Manchin of West Virginia and Kyrsten Sinema of Arizona.

Warner wanted a group of senators to meet with Biden—to express their appreciation for him, yes, but also to make it clear that they didn't think he could win.

"I know this guy," Schumer said. "If we do something public, he'll get his back up."

He told Warner and any other Democrats: "Certainly, call the White House or the campaign if you're concerned, but don't go public right now." The air needed to clear, Schumer thought. The polling needed to come in. And the ugly reality of how bad it was had to set in for Biden. But it was going to take a little time. And if people called for Biden to step down, he'd get his Irish up, Schumer would say.

Schumer called Donilon and Ricchetti, who seemed in complete denial.

"Don't worry," they told him, "we're going to have this big speech at the end of the NATO Summit. He's going to set everything straight."

"That ain't good enough," Schumer said. "Even if he gives a good speech. People think he can give a set speech. He needs to go do everyday town halls, unscripted, town hall meetings unscripted, where he throws himself in and handles himself well. And that's the only way to do it."

Schumer would push them, but they seemed completely oblivious to the moment. They thought one speech would be the elixir.

The Biden folks called Schumer's office and asked if there were any senators in particular who needed reassuring. Who should they call? Schumer's team told them to go down the list of Democratic senators. To start at the top alphabetically and call every single one of them. It was that bad.

TEXAS DEMOCRATIC CONGRESSMAN Lloyd Doggett and his wife, Libby, had watched the debate at their residence off Capitol Hill and had been astounded. Doggett hadn't seen Biden in person in months. And what Doggett saw on the debate stage was evidence of a debilitating turn for the worse.

On the floor of the House the next morning, June 28, Doggett approached every fellow Democrat he could find—Nancy Pelosi, those in leadership, everyone.

"We need a new candidate," he told them. No one pushed back.

Washington Congressman Adam Smith agreed. While others were pointing fingers at Biden's staff for agreeing to the debate, Smith blamed Biden. He, after all, had made the decision to run. He should have seen where he was at; he should have known the moment.

The morning after the debate, Smith phoned Shuwanza Goff, Biden's head of legislative affairs.

"He's gotta step aside," Smith said. "He's gotta go."

Goff pushed back.

"Look, it's better if he makes the decision," Smith said. "I'm not going to push."

OTHERS SURE were pushing. In an op-ed titled "To Serve His Country, President Biden Should Leave the Race," the editorial board of *The New York Times* made their case that day: "The clearest path for Democrats to defeat a candidate defined by his lies is to deal truthfully with the American public: acknowledge that Mr. Biden can't continue his race, and create a process to select someone more capable to stand in his place to defeat Mr. Trump in November."

Writing from a hotel room in Portugal, *Times* columnist Thomas L. Friedman said the performance had made him weep. "I cannot remember a more heartbreaking moment in American presidential campaign politics in my lifetime," he wrote, "precisely because of what it revealed: Joe Biden, a good man and a good president, has no business running for re-election." He "clearly is not any longer" up to the job, Friedman concluded.

SATURDAY, JUNE 29

At the campaign HQ in Wilmington, Deputy Campaign Manager Rob Flaherty felt the need to push back against the news media and the Democratic officials. He wrote and issued a memo attacking the Democrats' "bedwetting brigade" and arguing that Biden was the strongest Democrat to take on Trump.

Top campaign staffers were eager for Biden to hit the campaign trail, to prove his get-up-and-go with town halls and public interactions. The only way to counter the "old" narrative was to show him performing as a younger man would. They waited for the plan—for Biden to make one hundred panic-quelling calls to Democratic officials, to do a bunch of interviews, to Zoom with his staff. But none of that was happening. Saturday came and went. They wondered: *Where's the plan? Why is he silent? We're getting killed!*

The plan never arrived.

SOME IN BIDEN'S circle tried to explain the night through the lens of Biden's stutter.

John Hendrickson, *The Atlantic* writer who lives with a stutter himself and who had written movingly in the past about Biden's struggles, found it disingenuous and offensive. What alarmed viewers, he thought, was everything else on display—his frailty, his freeze-ups, and his occasional vacant stare. Hendrickson would tell anyone who asked that stuttering is a stigmatized, misunderstood disability, but it's not a catch-all or a get-out-of-jail-free card. The Biden he interviewed up close for an hour in August 2019 was very different from the Biden who walked out onto the debate stage in June 2024.

THE BIDEN TEAM, convinced that they would prove their critics wrong once again, acted like it was just another bump in the road. Donilon retreated to Rhode Island the weekend after the debate. DNC Chair Jaime Harrison tried to reassure state party chairs and then jetted off for a Disney cruise with his family. Steve Ricchetti told a nervous aide that the debate wasn't a big deal.

When people on the campaign wanted Biden to get on the phone to reassure big donors, his inner circle said no—they didn't want to put the president in that position.

THAT SATURDAY, Biden attended a fundraiser at the home of New Jersey Governor Phil Murphy. Despite the meltdown around them, money was still coming in the door after the debate. That looked like loyalty, but donors also calculated most of the money was going to the Democratic Party and would be used against Trump even if Biden didn't make it. One donor arrived determined to go up to Biden and plead with him to drop out but was talked out of it at the last second.

Still, Biden did little to reassure attendees. Murphy and his wife got up to give their quick remarks to rally the crowd. They spoke without notes but then Biden appeared flanked by conspicuously large teleprompters that worried attendees. He rambled and his voice was barely audible. During a Q&A session, Biden would start answering the question but then lose the thread. He couldn't finish his thoughts. A Biden aide later said that the president just looked like he needed to go home.

DURING ONE of President Biden's post-debate trips, a campaign adviser discussed plans with him on Air Force One.

What are we doing here? the adviser thought as the president spoke. *This guy can't form a fucking sentence.* The president seemed so tired and weak.

What do you think we should do? the president asked the adviser.

The adviser and the president discussed tactics that would allow him to perform well in front of friendly audiences, maybe continuing to hold smaller, more intimate rallies. *I don't want to tell him we can't get more than two thousand people to show up,* the adviser thought. *This is so sad.*

They continued speaking.

Man, this is really rough, the adviser thought. *If I had a conversation like this with someone who wasn't the president, I would be worried about his health. And here he is, the sitting president of the United States.*

The adviser later brought this all up with others on the campaign.

"We can't live in this purgatory," the adviser said. "We can't stay in this situation where we're pretending everything is fine and it's not."

For one thing, the campaign was running out of money.

MONDAY, JULY 1

Then it got worse. On July 1, the US Supreme Court granted Donald Trump broad immunity from prosecution for official presidential acts, which raised the stakes even further, Doggett felt.

How do we stop Trump from ushering in a long, dark authoritarian era? Doggett wondered. He was convinced that if Biden stayed in the race, it would only open the door to such a calamity.

But despite an onslaught of public criticism from the media and a torrent of private panic among the Democrats, no one in elected office would say what needed to be said.

Someone needs to act, Doggett thought. *And it looks like that someone will be me.*

He phoned the White House. He wanted to talk to the president; he wanted to ask him to step aside.

The White House took the message. No one called back.

As BARACK OBAMA prepared to phone the president that day, he understood that his relationship with Biden had become so emotionally fraught, any advice he gave risked sparking the opposite reaction from Biden and his team.

Obama's North Star in these conversations was to preserve his ability to serve as a sounding board. He wanted to be a source of support and wisdom, someone Biden could call to discuss whatever tough decision he would make. Obama wouldn't suggest that Biden take one course of action or another; he knew that Biden still harbored resentment toward him over his nonsupport of Biden's plans to run for president against Hillary Clinton in 2016.

Long before the debate, whenever donors and pols had raised the question of whether Biden should run for reelection, Obama had demurred. "He's still pissed at me about Hillary," Obama would say.

MINNESOTA GOVERNOR TIM WALZ, chairman of the Democratic Governors Association, convened a Zoom where governors shared their thoughts.

Governor Maura Healey shared how she'd called Jeff Zients and told him, "Anyone who watched that debate, the images were irretrievable."

The consensus seemed to be that Biden was losing in states he'd won in 2020, and many wondered if the president knew that, if he had seen the real polls and heard about what was happening on the ground. There had been talk of the White House maybe putting the vice president on a call with them, but that wasn't going to be good enough. They needed to speak to the president.

FIRST LADY BIDEN appeared on the cover of *Vogue* alongside the quote "We will decide our future."

The August cover story had been in the works for months, though not only did her team not attempt to delay the article going up early online, the First Lady provided an updated post-debate note of defiance: that they "will not let those 90 minutes define the four years he's been president. We will continue to fight."

It struck many longtime Biden aides as tone-deaf.

It was her third *Vogue* cover in four years. It was a beautiful image but a terrible look, aides felt.

DELAWARE DEMOCRATIC SENATOR Chris Coons went on CNN's *The Lead* that Monday to defend the president and try to stanch the bleeding. Coons was Biden's most ardent supporter in the Senate.

After Jake ran a clip from the debate, Coons put up his defense: "You just took what was probably the most difficult moment to watch of the entire ninety-minute debate, but you didn't share what I found the hardest moments to watch, which was when Donald Trump was unleashing a torrent of lies, of invective, of vengeance."

Jake argued that Biden could settle the whole issue right then by doing a two-hour press conference. The fact that Biden hadn't done so, he added, was quite telling.

"That is what I am urging and recommending," Coons said. It didn't matter "whether it's a *60 Minutes* interview or something at the podium at the White House or a town hall. That's not up to me to decide, but that's what I've been encouraging our president to do."

The senator had, in fact, been pushing White House advisers and campaign staff on this point, and he had been assured that it would happen. But no major press conference or town hall had been added to the presidential schedule.

INTERNALLY, THE WHITE HOUSE, in a full defensive crouch, would hear Democrats say that the solution was for Biden to go out and do interviews and press conferences, to put on full display his ability to take tough questions and handle them with agility.

And over the next few weeks he did some of that, though not enough.

In an interview toward the end of Biden's presidency, one senior official acknowledged the reality: They could pull down the schedule and put up a press conference and ten interviews, but "I don't know they would have gone well."

And that was the whole of it. He couldn't *do* what folks were calling on him to do to prove his acuity.

TUESDAY, JULY 2

"He clearly has to understand, I think, what you're getting to here is that his decision not only impacts who's going to serve in the White

House the next four years but who's going to serve in the Senate, who's going to serve in the House, and it will have implications for decades to come," Congressman Mike Quigley told CNN anchor Kasie Hunt that morning. "We have to be honest with ourselves that it wasn't just a horrible night." Quigley was coming close to calling for Biden to drop out, but he wasn't there yet.

Congressman Lloyd Doggett wrote a statement calling for Biden to withdraw from the race, trying to make it as respectful and undamaging as possible, in case Biden ultimately remained the nominee. He pulled his punches, describing the debate as only a missed opportunity. Doggett's staffers reached out to their counterparts in the offices of Leader Hakeem Jeffries and Whip Katherine Clark.

And then they uploaded the statement and hit "Send."

"I represent the heart of a congressional district once represented by Lyndon Johnson," Doggett wrote. "Under very different circumstances, he made the painful decision to withdraw. President Biden should do the same."

The first domino had fallen.

HOUSE CONFERENCE CHAIR Pete Aguilar began getting texts from other House Democrats. The sentiment of many: *I share Lloyd's position but don't want to be the next one.*

As chair of the caucus, Aguilar's job was to talk to House Democrats and relay their concerns to Jeffries and Clark, not to mention Schumer and the White House.

It seemed to him that the overwhelming majority of House Democrats wanted Biden to step down, but most were keeping quiet out of respect.

WEDNESDAY, JULY 3

On the morning of Wednesday, July 3, First Lady Jill Biden visited YMCA Camp Manitou-Lin, near Middleville in western Michigan, to stand with Michigan Democratic Senator Debbie Stabenow and discuss programs that provided summer food assistance to low-income families.

Biden and Stabenow also visited with attendees at Camp Corral, an overnight camp for the children of wounded, ill, or fallen servicemembers.

Jill wouldn't take questions from the traveling press corps, so Stabenow did, offering a full-throated defense and endorsement of the president. She had known Biden since she came to the Senate in 2001. She found him gracious, welcoming, and generous with his time. And the sad reality was that, like so many senators, she barely recognized the man she'd seen on that debate stage.

After she'd gaggled with the reporters, Stabenow asked for a minute with the First Lady. She told Jill that she'd known Joe for a long, long time and supported him on every level. But, Stabenow said, she and her colleagues were concerned about what they'd seen at the debate. They cared about Joe. They were worried about him.

We don't know if this was a onetime thing or if there's something more going on with the president, Stabenow said to the First Lady. But *you* know.

The First Lady didn't answer the senator's implied question, but she later fumed about it to White House staffers.

FORMER CHIEF OF STAFF Ron Klain was calling congressional Democrats to help shore up support for the president. He was told over and over by members of Congress that they had not seen the president in more than a year, so they had no idea what was true or not.

Klain took this as evidence that the current White House team was isolating the president—to his detriment.

The White House would later explain away the dearth of 2023 and 2024 meetings with congressional Democrats as the result of three things: Republican control of the House, which meant no legislative agendas to craft; campaign busyness; and the need to limit Biden's schedule on account of his depleted energy.

Some also admitted that they were hiding what was happening to the president as much as they could.

THE WHITE HOUSE finally realized that it wasn't just the media and congressional Democrats who were second-guessing Biden's fitness— it was the White House's own staff.

On Wednesday, Jeff Zients held an all-staff call to try to rally his troops. By this point, some were so frustrated that they gave Alex the dial-in code so he could listen in on the call.

Zients argued that the debate was just "one night" and "that he is a great president."

He pushed staff to be "head down. We gotta keep doing what we've been doing to get things done."

Within the White House, those determined to slog through to November were the president and the First Lady, Anthony Bernal and Annie Tomasini, and the Politburo—Mike Donilon, Steve Ricchetti, and Bruce Reed. Anita Dunn was ferociously defending Biden's right to stay in the race, and Zients was doing the chief of staff role—making sure that whatever the president wanted was happening while also ensuring that all options were there for him. Others on the White House staff thought the continued campaign was a catastrophe.

There was one thing everyone at the White House seemed to agree upon: An open primary process would be a disaster.

That's not how two éminences grises in the party saw it. Privately, Barack Obama and Nancy Pelosi favored some sort of process. Pelosi in particular heard from voting-rights activists who insisted on such a thing. The Obama/Pelosi position would be viewed by the Harris camp as skepticism of Harris's political abilities.

DEMOCRATIC SENATORS SEEMED to fall into three groups. The first group wanted Biden to step down from the top of the ticket immediately. The second group was loyal and continued to argue that Biden was their best shot at keeping the White House. A third group understood that Biden was suboptimal, but they weren't sure what the process to replace him might look like.

Days had passed since the Politburo began assuring concerned Democrats that the president would be out there proving his alacrity by dazzling everyone in press conferences, one-on-one interviews, and town halls.

The onus was on the president to show that he could do this, Mark Warner told people. And he was not meeting the moment.

Donors had been furiously calling Warner with what the senator later joked were "fantasy football ideas" about the process: A mini six-week primary! Barack Obama and Bill Clinton mediating candidate forums! It had become evident, Warner believed, that Vice President Harris would have to be the nominee, not least because the most loyal Democratic voters were African Americans, particularly African American women. The senior Democratic African American constituency in Congress was making that very clear.

THAT SAME DAY, in Tucson, Arizona, Democratic Congressman Raúl Grijalva got on the phone with a reporter from *The New York Times* and became the second House Democrat to officially say that Biden needed to "get out of this race."

Massachusetts Congressman Seth Moulton was next. He had first really noticed the president's deterioration at a naturalization ceremony in Gloucester in September 2023. The welcoming video that was played showed Biden looking and sounding great. It took Moulton a second to realize that the video had been taped in 2021, and that what he was recognizing was, in fact, how much Biden had aged over the previous two years. Later in 2023, as he and his wife, Liz, left the White House Christmas party, they remarked on how frail the president looked and how unenergetic he seemed compared with the previous December. Moulton was not among those who thought that the 2024 State of the Union had been some sort of triumph; indeed, from where Moulton sat, the president appeared to be physically shaking.

And then came the D-Day anniversary commemoration at Normandy in June 2024.

So, no, the unmitigated disaster of the June 27 debate was not, as Moulton saw it, a surprise. And clearly, he thought, Biden needed to step down as the Democratic nominee.

But what to do?

After the debate, Moulton had approached an irreverent colleague on the floor of the House.

"What did you think of that performance?" he asked him.

"We need to sub in someone with more energy," the other congressman said sardonically. "Like Bill Pascrell."

Pascrell, an eighty-seven-year-old New Jersey Democrat, was sickly and just weeks away from death. It was a dark joke, but Democrats were in a dark place.

On July 3, Moulton worked with his staff on a carefully worded statement that didn't call for Biden to step down. Rather, Moulton said that beating Trump "will require prosecuting the case in the media, in town halls, and at campaign stops all over the country. President Biden needs to demonstrate that he can do that."

"What are you saying, Seth?" a US Marine friend of Moulton's asked him, angrily, during a phone call the night of July 3.

"That the president should step aside," Moulton said. "That's what I'm implying."

"Why don't you just say it, then? This is what's wrong with politicians—you guys can never just say the truth. If you don't think he should run, say he shouldn't run."

THE DEMOCRATIC GOVERNORS came to the White House by planes, trains, automobiles, and Zoom. The goal was to have a candid conversation with the president about what was going on in the different states and how they viewed the race. But any question about how open the president's mind was evaporated as he crossed the threshold into the room where the governors sat waiting, Vice President Harris trailing behind him.

"I'm not going anywhere," Biden said.

The president sat down at the head of the table, Vice President Harris to his right, followed by Delaware's John Carney, California's Gavin Newsom, Maryland's Wes Moore, New York's Kathy Hochul, and Kentucky's Andy Beshear. On his left sat Minnesota's Tim Walz, Michigan's Gretchen Whitmer, Illinois's JB Pritzker, Rhode Island's Dan McKee, Massachusetts's Maura Healey, and the mayor of DC, Muriel Bowser. Some aides, including Jen O'Malley Dillon and Steve Ricchetti, sat down at the table, while on the screen, governors stretching from Hawaii to Maine were present.

Folks, good to see you, governors, Biden said. I know I didn't have a good night, but I had a cold, and my team tells me I'm going to be cutting back on the travel and getting more sleep. I'm not going anywhere, but I want to win. I'm here to listen. Tell me how I can go win this thing. What do I need to do?

He began his refrain. The polls still say I am the best person to go up against Trump. The polls also say that people aren't concerned with my health, that folks are much more concerned with saving democracy. The polls actually haven't changed since the debate. Donald Trump should be way further ahead than he is. Tell me what I need to do to win.

Throughout the meeting, the president didn't really respond to questions. He leaned on familiar Biden tropes: He beat this guy once, and he was going to beat him again.

How are you doing, Mr. President? asked Hawaii Governor Josh Green, also a physician. Because the person I saw in that debate wasn't you. Are you okay?

The president insisted he was.

Newsom did some rah-rahing for Biden; Hochul and Moore praised him and said they were all in.

You need to talk about your health, Beshear said. That's a real issue in Kentucky and elsewhere. Voters are not believing, or they have real questions about that—so get out and speak to the voters; address that directly.

On Zoom, Connecticut's Ned Lamont affably said, Mr. President, since age is just such an issue right now, front and center, why not just take age off the table and just step aside and swap somebody else in?

Maine's Janet Mills spoke kindly about the president but noted that things get harder as we get older. Mills said she wasn't sure she could guarantee that Biden would win Maine, pointing to the tightening there as compared to four years ago.

New Mexico's Michelle Lujan Grisham was likewise polite but told the president that her reliably blue state was now "in play," and she believed that other states were moving rightward too.

Colorado's Jared Polis said he had been hearing from voters who were panicking about Biden—as was the donor class. People were mad; they felt they had been lied to about the president's health and condition.

Before everyone got a chance to speak, the vice president wrapped up the meeting. "We have to have the president's back," Harris said. "It's our fucking democracy at stake."

And with that, the meeting adjourned.

As governors and staffers milled about the room and greeted one another, Governor Healey approached the president. One of the first-ever lesbian governors in the nation's history, Healey had, as head of the Civil Rights Division of the Massachusetts Attorney General's office, successfully sued the Obama-Biden administration over the Defense of Marriage Act, which outlawed federal recognition of same-sex marriage.

It had been not only politically but legally significant when in May 2012, then–Vice President Biden told *Meet the Press* that he was "absolutely comfortable with the fact that men marrying men, women marrying women and heterosexual men and women marrying one another are entitled to the same exact rights, all the civil rights, all the civil liberties." Only the year before, the Obama–Biden administration had opted to not appeal the case, and not long after Biden's statement, the federal government began recognizing same-sex marriages. Healey grabbed Biden's hands in both of hers, looked him square in the eye, and said, "I have loved you as president. I loved you before you were president." She genuinely thanked him for his comments back in 2012, which had helped turn the tide on same-sex marriage. "You do not need to do this," she told him.

Then Healey left the room, bumping into Steve Ricchetti, whom she'd never met before. "The president's referencing polls where he's leading," she said to him. "What polls is he referencing? Because they're different from the polls that governors are seeing in our states."

Ricchetti looked at her. "I've been doing this for thirty years," he said. "I know polls."

THERE BEGAN to arise real concerns that the money was going to dry up. Behind the scenes, donors were sounding the alarm, venting, screaming. Many felt they had been lied to.

Hollywood producer and writer Damon Lindelof had attended the June fundraiser hosted by George Clooney, and he penned an op-ed for *Deadline*.

"I know what my eyes and my ears and my heart tell me," he wrote. "I've been asleep at the wheel and it's time to wake the fuck up. . . . Our president's debate performance has been characterized in many ways; disappointing, upsetting, terrifying . . . but for me it was simply game-changing."

Lindelof proposed a "DEMbargo"—no money to any elected Democratic official until Biden left the ticket.

In the following days, similar expressions of discontent with Biden at the top of the ticket came from other donors, including real estate billionaire Rick Caruso; former PayPal CEO Bill Harris, who called Biden's exit from the race "inevitable"; and Netflix's Reed Hastings, who told ABC News that "Biden is unfortunately in denial about his mental state."

The fundraising impact was real. Despite a good amount of cash on hand, Biden campaign aides told leadership that they couldn't guarantee making payroll in the coming weeks if this continued.

ALMOST AN ENTIRE week had passed since the debate, and Biden still hadn't called the Senate majority leader. But his fellow Senate Democrats sure were calling. They were all wondering why the president hadn't immediately gone out to prove he wasn't addled. Not by reading from a teleprompter but by demonstrating actual acuity.

The president finally called Chuck Schumer on July 3. Schumer doled out the same advice he'd been giving.

"Mr. President, you've gotta get out there," he said. "You've got to be in unscripted situations where people can see that you can respond just the way you did at the State of the Union. People need to see that the debate was a one-off, and the only way you can do that is getting out there and proving it to the public—not to me, not to senators, but to the whole public."

Schumer felt that he was offering Biden the chance to get out there and show he was okay, since no one was certain whether this debate was a one-off. Schumer was starting to worry, though; maybe the reason why Biden wasn't taking his advice was simply because he couldn't.

THAT EVENING, the House Democratic leadership held a virtual meeting. Many members expressed serious concern about Biden staying at the top of the ticket.

There was also serious confusion about the White House reaction. They were all acting as if House Democrats hadn't witnessed what had happened on that debate stage.

THURSDAY, JULY 4

In prerecorded interviews, President Biden appeared on a few radio shows with predominantly Black audiences. "I'm proud to be, as I said, the first vice president, first Black woman, to serve with a Black president, proud of the first Black woman in the Supreme Court," he told Philadelphia's WURD. "There's just so much that we can do because together we—there's nothing. Look, this is the United States of America."

Beyond the president saying he was proud to be the "first Black woman" in an interview designed to prove his abilities, the radio host later revealed that the Biden campaign had given her a list of eight questions to ask him. In the Biden campaign's efforts to demonstrate to the world that the president was sharp as a tack, it felt the need to feed questions to the hosts for a prerecorded call-in radio segment with a sympathetic interviewer.

THE NEXT MORNING, on the Boston NPR affiliate, Seth Moulton said of Biden, "Now is the time for him to follow in one of our Founding Father—George Washington's—footsteps and step aside to let new leaders rise up and run against Donald Trump."

Adam Smith was watching the White House and the Biden campaign dig in. He became convinced that the only way to get Biden to leave the ticket would be to aggressively and publicly force him out. He called White House Chief of Staff Jeff Zients and told him he was going to publicly call for Biden to step aside.

"Give us a few days," Zients said.

Smith gave him until Monday.

ON JULY 4, someone from the Bernie Sanders camp asked Washington Congresswoman Pramila Jayapal, chair of the Congressional Progressive Caucus, if the caucus could issue a statement of support for the president.

It was an awkward moment for Jayapal, one of Biden's fiercest defenders.

Jayapal initially estimated that about 60 percent of the ninety-seven-member CPC was "ridin' with Biden," including two of its most famous members, Sanders and New York Congresswoman Alexandria Ocasio-Cortez. But as the days went on without Biden putting to rest people's fears about him, that backing began to erode.

So when she was asked to get a statement of support from the caucus, Jayapal had to deliver some bad news.

"We don't have the numbers to do that as a caucus," she told the Bernie emissary.

GOVERNOR HEALEY was distraught by how everything had gone down. She felt deflated and despondent about the state of democracy and government. *This is what we work our asses off for,* she thought, *and it comes down to the decision of one person.* People thought there was some big Democratic Party apparatus making moves, putting people in, setting things up. But it wasn't a chessboard; it was just one old man and his enablers carrying out his every wish.

She issued a statement calling on Biden to "carefully evaluate whether he remains our best hope to defeat Donald Trump."

She was on a Fourth of July vacation with her family and trying not to get too depressed about the decline of the country and the inevitable reelection of Trump.

SECRETARY ANTONY BLINKEN arrived at the White House for lunch with the president.

Before the debate, he had witnessed moments of forgetfulness behind the scenes. Mostly, it was fine, nothing unusual for anyone over seventy, let alone eighty-one. And Blinken continually witnessed the president fully able to meet the moment, particularly when it came to the foreign policy and national security portfolio. He would be immersed in the details of an issue, asking good, hard questions and arriving at solid, well-considered judgments.

But whatever the reason behind it, the president's inability to project energy at this juncture meant that he was unable to convince the nation of the very real accomplishments of his administration—the uniting of NATO, the challenge to Putin.

And now here they were.

Specifically, in the small dining room right off the Oval Office.

Blinken began with the president's legacy.

"Anyone who's written about gets one sentence. That's the legacy," he said. So the president had a decision to make. "If it leads you to staying in and winning reelection, great. If it leads to you staying in and losing reelection, that's the sentence."

And, again, Blinken asked the president what he had asked him in March 2023: "Do you really want to be doing this for another four years?

As long as the election hinged on the question of Biden's ability, it would be hard to win, Blinken told Biden.

"This is not about today," Blinken said. "It's about when you're eighty-six."

Biden agreed that this was the right question.

And, at that moment, he didn't seem able to answer it to his own satisfaction.

Blinken left the lunch thinking that Biden was likely staying in the race.

He followed up on calls with Mike Donilon and Steve Ricchetti. "You guys know the data much better than I do," he told them, "but there are other analyses out there, and we need to make sure the president's getting the complete picture." Blinken believed that Biden was capable of dealing with advisers who poked and prodded and questioned the president's assumptions. He did this with Biden on the most serious and consequential national security decisions. He felt that they needed to do this with the president when it came to his own future.

FRIDAY, JULY 5

Mike Quigley talked to his pollster, John Anzalone, about it all. Anzalone had access to data from all over the country and was telling Quigley what a disaster this was for Democrats writ large. The president was pulling down everyone's numbers. But it wasn't clear if Ricchetti and Donilon were letting Biden know about the data.

"They're cloistering him," Anzalone said of the Politburo.

Quigley represented parts of northern Chicago, the city where the Democratic National Convention was scheduled to take place starting on August 19. He was terrified that they were all watching a disaster unfold and no one was doing anything about it.

That day, the president tried to stanch the bleeding by making an appearance on ABC News with anchor George Stephanopoulos, but the interview further underscored his issues.

"Did you ever watch the debate afterwards?" Stephanopoulos asked him.

"I don't think I did, no," Biden said.

You don't think you did? Quigley thought. *What?*

THE POLLSTERS WATCHED, HORRIFIED.

"You're still falling further behind," Stephanopoulos said.

"All the pollsters I talk to tell me it's a toss-up," Biden said.

That wasn't the perspective of the pollsters, but on the other hand, they never got to talk to the president. Colleagues started reaching out: *What polls are you showing the president?*

Jesus, one of the pollsters thought. *If people think this is true, I will have no credibility left.*

"AND IF YOU STAY in and Trump is elected and everything you're warning about comes to pass, how will you feel in January?" Stephanopoulos asked.

"I'll feel as long as I gave it my all and I did the good as [*sic*] job as I know I can do, that's what this is about," Biden said.

———

OH NO, Speaker Nancy Pelosi thought. *That's just not enough, "giving it your all."* The stakes were so much higher.

Since the debate, her phone had been blowing up with calls and texts from House Democrats. She didn't place calls to her colleagues, but they were constantly reaching out to her, and this Biden answer caused real distress. House Democrats in competitive districts were getting polling back that indicated Biden's campaign was going to drag dozens of them down with it.

This wasn't about Biden just giving it his all.

EARLIER THAT DAY, *The Washington Post* broke the story that Warner was "attempting to assemble a group of Democratic senators to ask President Biden to exit the presidential race."

Stephanopoulos asked the president about the report. "Well, Mark is a good man," Biden had said. "He also tried to get the nomination too."

Warner found this sadly telling. Yes, he had started building campaign infrastructure in anticipation of a possible presidential run, had visited Iowa and New Hampshire, had talked to precinct chairs, and had set up a political action committee. But then he talked to his family, surveyed the likely landscape, and opted not to run.

In 2006.

Eighteen years ago.

Biden ran in 2008, so maybe the idea that Warner, whom he didn't know that well, was a rival had locked itself in his brain, and that event, almost a generation before, was still how he thought of the senator from Virginia.

———

The ABC News interview was twenty-two minutes long. Stephanopoulos later told friends that "it was heartbreaking."

SUNDAY, JULY 7

President and First Lady Biden hit the campaign trail in Philly. Biden spoke at a service at the Mt. Airy Church of God in Christ, a church with many Black parishioners, then he popped by the Roxborough Democratic Coordinated Campaign office before he and Jill headed to AFSCME Council 13 headquarters outside Harrisburg. After that, Biden met up with Democratic Governor Josh Shapiro at Denim Coffee, across the street from the capitol building.

After ordering a coffee for the governor, a smoothie for the president, and a couple cookies in front of rolling cameras, the governor turned to the president.

"You want to hang out over here?" he asked. The president said he did.

So the governor and the president sidled up to the window bar and everyone else was ushered out. Jill joined them too.

"So how do you think it's going out there?" the president asked him.

Shapiro decided to give it to him straight. Frankly, the governor didn't know how much the president's senior advisers were telling him about how bad things really were for him.

"I'll be honest, Mr. President, I have some concerns," Shapiro said.

The polling Shapiro had seen suggested a rapid erosion of support for the president in must-win Pennsylvania within the previous few days. He didn't think the campaign sufficiently acknowledged the pain inflation was causing. And while the president needed to prove the debate had been an aberration, for some reason he hadn't yet done so.

The president addressed some of Shapiro's concerns by noting the plans they were making. But before he could fully respond, Shapiro got a clear signal that the conversation was over.

"Alright," said the First Lady, "we gotta go." She and her husband stood. Shapiro got up, too, and walked out with them. They headed to the Beast and drove off.

They didn't want to hear the facts on the ground, Shapiro thought.

POLLS CAME BACK to House Democrats indicating the impact of the debate. It was brutal. Democratic Leader Jeffries convened a Zoom meeting of the top Democrat on each House Committee.

"The purpose of the call is to see what the ranking members are hearing and thinking," Jeffries said before trying to set the tone. "Calm is an intentional decision. If you're calm, you can make the best possible decision."

Pennsylvania Congresswoman Susan Wild, of the House Ethics Committee, was the only person on the call in a competitive district. "I'm the only face on this Zoom that stands to be harmed by leaking from this meeting," she interjected. "So can I please beg people to keep this as a confidential meeting?"

Everyone agreed.

They spoke in order of seniority. New Jersey's Frank Pallone of the Energy and Commerce Committee said, "I have to be honest. I saw the president recently, and he was fine, but the reaction from my constituents has not been good." Virginia's Bobby Scott from the Committee on Education and the Workforce supported the president but added, "If you get rid of Biden and you think the person taking his place will be anyone other than Kamala, you are the senile one."

Adam Smith of the Armed Services Committee was the strongest opponent of Biden remaining in the race. "He should step aside," Smith said. "We got a good message. The president has shown he is not capable of delivering that message in an effective way."

Moreover, Smith said, they would all pay a price for pretending this was not the case. "Every day we're out there defending the indefensible, our own credibility on every other issue is taking a massive blow," Smith told his colleagues.

"He's clearly very, very fragile," said Virginia's Don Beyer of the Joint Economic Committee. "Fragile physically, although his handshake is very firm. He also really has trouble putting two sentences together. . . .

"In my perfect world, Joe—in deciding after talking to Leader Jeffries, Majority Leader Schumer, others—steps aside now, lets Kamala run as the incumbent, which I think makes her even stronger," Beyer added. "With that, I'm a team player. I'll do whatever the team wants."

"I was just with the president a little while ago," said Pennsylvania's Brendan Boyle of the Budget Committee, who'd greeted Biden on the tarmac in Philadelphia that morning. "He seemed in pretty good spirits. I'm sticking with him. I understand that people have made good arguments on both sides. I think that, ultimately, this is a decision he's going to make—he has won the Democratic nomination."

Wild had just received an alarming text from a staffer. "Don Beyer's comments just got leaked," she interrupted, to a reporter from *Punchbowl News*. "I don't know whether Don cares, but can I remind everyone that I need an assurance this stays among us?"

"We're at a precarious point," said Maryland's Jamie Raskin of the Oversight Committee. Raskin had been attending Fourth of July parades and barbecues, and by a ratio of twenty-five to one or fifty to one, voters were asking for Biden to bow out. "We need to make a decision soon!"

"If he wants to come to my district," Wild said, "and he needs to come to my district—it's the third-largest region in Pennsylvania; it's the biggest swing district and the fastest-growing—he needs to come here. But I have to tell you, I'm not going to be able to show up with him. I cannot campaign with Joe Biden. If I defend the president, I lose my integrity. How do we go after Trump for lying if people see us as liars?"

MONDAY, JULY 8

On Monday, Biden sent a letter to shut the skeptics up.

"The question of how to move forward has been well-aired for over a week now," Biden wrote. "And it's time for it to end. We have one job. And that is to beat Donald Trump. We have 42 days to the Democratic Convention and 119 days to the general election. Any weakening of resolve or lack of clarity about the task ahead only helps Trump and hurts us. It is time to come together, move forward as a unified party, and defeat Donald Trump."

His message was clear: He wasn't going anywhere.

Or, as Schumer interpreted it: "I'm running. Go fuck yourselves."

That defiance was to be expected, Jeffries thought. He was still going to try to get a sense of where all 213 House Democrats were. After all, they were all going to be on the ballot that November, not just the president.

"I'm going to talk to members of the caucus throughout the entirety of this week and get a clear sense of where the caucus stands moving forward," Jeffries told Ricchetti. "And on Thursday I'm going to come to the White House and tell the president where we are."

ADAM SMITH CALLED Jeff Zients that morning to tell him he was giving a public statement. He went on CNN to announce his decision with Jake.

It wasn't a particularly tough call. Smith thought that Biden never should have run in the first place.

"I think he should step aside," Smith said. "I think it's become clear that he's not the best person to carry the Democratic message." He conceded that this was not just about the debate, that there had been "concerns leading up to it in the terms of the president's ability to deliver a message, and it hasn't gotten better since the debate."

THE BIDEN FORCES hunkered down in their bunker and launched an aggressive campaign to thwart any possible attacks. About six Senate Democrats were preparing to call for Biden to step down, but the *Post* article prompted Schumer to tell them not to. The Biden team did a full-court press to stop any apostates.

That week was particularly tough for Mark Warner. Weighing on his mind was his anger, since 2015, with Republican senators who fumed about Donald Trump privately but dared not say a word publicly. It felt hypocritical for him to stay silent now, as if he were saying, *Oh, look, the emperor has perfect clothes on.*

And yet some argued they couldn't just abandon the president, that it was a matter of decency and respect. Warner felt horrible.

TUESDAY, JULY 9

A dark cloud hung over House Democrats as they huddled in the Wasserman Room of the Democratic National Committee Tuesday morning and worried about their future. "I lived through the 2010 bloodbath—we lost sixty-three seats," Illinois Congressman Bill Foster told his colleagues. "That could happen again."

Another House Democrat discussed the tragedy of his father's painful struggles with physical and cognitive decline. This wasn't a normal political issue, he said. Whenever he discussed his father's decline—everyone has a story like that in their family. When people discussed Biden's age, it got real personal, real quick.

The White House had been effectively lobbying members of the Congressional Black Caucus, and progressives, to stick with Biden. The night before, Biden had Zoomed with the CBC and told them: "You've had my back, and I'll continue to have yours."

Biden needs to stay in, one Black congresswoman argued before the entire caucus. If he gets out, this is going to fall on the shoulders of a Black woman. And Kamala Harris is going to lose, and everyone's going to blame Black people.

There was a real sense from Black members that a Harris candidacy—and a devastating loss that many seemed to anticipate as a foregone conclusion—would be horrible for people of color. And yet that argument often came with the caveat that the party could not pick any replacement nominee other than Harris.

"Everybody knows this is a problem," Seth Moulton said after describing his experience with the president in Normandy. He wanted other Democrats to know that it was safe for them to call for Biden's withdrawal too.

There was a lot of debate. Up at the front of the room, Hakeem Jeffries and Pete Aguilar were scribbling down what House Democrats were saying so that they could pass on the feelings to Steve Ricchetti.

"Are you going to the White House and telling them what we're saying?" Moulton asked.

"We're going to read the quotes to the White House but not tell them who said them," Jeffries said.

"I want to be quoted," Moulton said.

New Jersey Congresswoman Mikie Sherrill sat quietly. Before the June 27 debate was half over, she had decided there was no way Biden could continue as the nominee. She'd been hoping that the debate would be an inflection point to prove the opposite. It hadn't been. Whether it was aging or something worse, Biden had clearly revealed to the whole country that he wasn't up to the task

She was worried that the White House was successfully lobbying folks to keep quiet as the party marched to defeat. At a previous, smaller meeting of members in competitive congressional districts— so-called frontliners—she told Jeffries, "I'm going to have to say something because this seems like it's getting shut down."

At 4:47 p.m., Sherrill issued a statement asking Biden to "declare that he won't run for reelection and will help lead us through a process toward a new nominee." She argued that "the stakes are too high—and the threat is too real—to stay silent." She was the ninth House Democrat to do so.

For his part, Aguilar had had enough.

It had been two weeks. He felt that he needed to put more pressure on the White House, to reflect what House Democrats were thinking, to make plain the fear and anger so many of them felt.

"This is the first time I'm hearing that it's this bad in the caucus," Ricchetti told him. "He's staying in; it will get better."

He added: "Biden is an asset, not a liability."

———

Jeffries was coming to his own private conclusion. Something needed to change. Change was the most powerful force in politics. Certainly, if Vice President Harris became the nominee, she would represent change in a way that President Biden never could.

He said as much to Ricchetti, but generally kept this view to himself. His job as House leader required a more neutral public position.

Harris was trying to keep her head down. Her team didn't want to do anything that would rouse suspicion from Biden, his team, or other Democrats that she was trying to overthrow her boss. She felt it important to be seen as and to be loyal. That quiet posture created its own tensions with the Biden team, however. The Biden campaign had asked her to call members of Congress to help scare up support. Harris said she would call members she had long-standing relationships with but not people she barely knew. All it would take was one congressman misinterpreting Harris's call as an underhanded maneuver to poach support for herself, they argued. Harris dialing up a bunch of members could make the situation much worse. It was playing with fire.

Some on Biden's team fumed about Harris turning down a request at a time of crisis.

GEORGE CLOONEY, PART TWO

George Clooney had compartmentalized his encounter with the president at the LA fundraiser, chalking it up to the president's eighty-one spins around the sun and the long fucking trip from Italy, even if Biden had flown in on Air Force One.

But then the debate had confirmed all the fears he'd shoved aside. So many governors, senators, members of Congress, fundraisers, and activists were now reaching out to him—it was all anyone could talk about. What a disaster! Biden needed to take himself off the ticket.

Senator Joe Manchin reached out to Clooney, confiding that Biden, his old friend of decades, had lost the will to fight. He told Clooney that the Democratic senators were planning to confront Biden, to try to convince him to step aside. Manchin personally hoped they wouldn't do so until after the NATO Summit later that summer—"No need to show our ass to the world," he said. For whatever reason, no such meeting happened. Clooney held out hopes that Democratic governors would do so. But the readout he got on that confrontation suggested that no one had stepped up and told the president the truth. Then, on July 8, Biden released a last-ditch letter to try to end the crusade to push him out.

The letter shocked Clooney. Despite the Herculean efforts that the Democratic machine had made to shut down any sort of real contest, Biden cast his position as that of a true exercise in democracy, having "received over 14 million votes, 87% of the votes cast across the entire nominating process."

"This was a process open to anyone who wanted to run," he wrote, which was not true. "Only three people chose to challenge me." Of Robert F. Kennedy Jr., Biden wrote that he "fared so badly that he left the primaries to run as an independent." Of Dean Phillips, the president said that he "attacked me for being too old and was soundly defeated. The voters of the Democratic Party have voted. They have chosen me to be the nominee of the party."

This was too much for Clooney.

He reached out to Barack Obama to tell him that he was considering writing an op-ed to call for Biden to drop out. Obama advised that doing so would only make Biden dig in his heels deeper.

In his home office in the South of France, Clooney sat down at his laptop.

"I love Joe Biden," Clooney wrote. "As a senator. As a vice president and as president. I consider him a friend, and I believe in him. Believe in his character. Believe in his morals. In the last four years, he's won many of the battles he's faced."

But, Clooney added, "the one battle he cannot win is the fight against time. None of us can. It's devastating to say it, but the Joe Biden I was with three weeks ago at the fund-raiser was not the Joe 'big F-ing deal' Biden of 2010. He wasn't even the Joe Biden of 2020. He was the same man we all witnessed at the debate."

Clooney got down to the point: "We are not going to win in November with this president.... This is the opinion of every senator and Congress member and governor who I've spoken with in private. Every single one, irrespective of what he or she is saying publicly."

He wanted some sort of process for a new nominee. "Let's hear from Wes Moore and Kamala Harris and Gretchen Whitmer and Gavin Newsom and Andy Beshear and J.B. Pritzker and others. Let's agree that the candidates not attack one another but, in the short time we have, focus on what will make this country soar. Then we could go into the Democratic convention next month and figure it out."

And then he attempted to end the op-ed with a note that was both empathetic and firm: "Joe Biden is a hero; he saved democracy in 2020. We need him to do it again in 2024."

Clooney sent a copy to Jeffrey Katzenberg and told him to show Steve Ricchetti.

Ricchetti read it and was furious. Internally, he threatened to shut

Clooney down—some of his colleagues thought he sounded like a Mob boss.

Word came back that Ricchetti suggested it would be better if Clooney held it a week. Katzenberg told Clooney he was skeptical the op-ed would achieve its desired effect. He also thought it was kicking a good man when he was clearly down. He felt the op-ed was harsh and premature. "I was there for the fundraiser," Katzenberg told his friend. "You left early. You never saw him onstage."

"Yeah, but I saw him in the clutch," Clooney said, "and I was stunned by what I saw."

Katzenberg knew how difficult it is for a person of some achievement—Rupert Murdoch, Michael Eisner—to step down. He'd seen it close up. Hell, it had happened to him with the sale of Dream-Works Animation in 2016.

Your process is not the correct one to get the end you desire, he told Clooney. He really wanted Clooney to cut the line about the befogged Biden at the fundraiser being "the same man we all witnessed at the debate."

It's not fair, what you're saying, Katzenberg said.

You're right, it's not fair, Clooney agreed. Aging was awful. It really wasn't fair.

But, Clooney said, it's accurate.

Clooney's op-ed—"I Love Joe Biden. But We Need a New Nominee"—was published by *The New York Times* on July 10. The line Katzenberg had objected to stayed in.

KATZENBERG DID NOT agree with Clooney's assessment. Biden had been jet-lagged, and Katzenberg had been told that the president didn't sleep well on flights, even in the bedroom aboard Air Force One. So the president had gotten only four or five hours of sleep. Biden was one of those people who needed the full eight hours every night. Even just seven hours wouldn't cut it.

Yes, Biden had gone into that disconcerting whisper mode backstage at the fundraiser. Katzenberg still didn't understand why he had done that. But what he had said was perfectly fine. Yes, it paled in comparison with Obama's eloquence and elegance—but that had always been the case.

Katzenberg had been making huge efforts to boost Biden's performative abilities. Spielberg had helped with debate prep. Aides had credited the director's involvement with a significant improvement in Biden's performance in ads and videos. Biden hated doing video recordings and would snap at aides who asked him to try them again. But he was willing to take direction from the Academy Award–winning director of *Saving Private Ryan* in a way he never would from a campaign aide or ad maker. Multiple takes. It really helped—though not enough.

WEDNESDAY, JULY 10

Pelosi had never been in favor of Biden debating Trump, whose behavior she found grotesque, but after the debate, she couldn't wrap her head around the decision by Biden's staff—with all they knew and all they had seen—to let him get on the stage that day.

She heard from her fellow House Democrats, many of whom were terrified of what Biden's flailing candidacy would mean for them, for Democrats, for all the progress they had made as a party and a country. This wasn't about anything other than that. And the need for Democrats to win. The White House and the House and the Senate.

From July 9 to 11, President Biden was hosting the NATO Summit in DC. Weeks before, Pelosi had promised to go on *Morning Joe* with

Sviatlana Tsikhanouskaya, leader of the democratic opposition of Belarus, on July 10, to discuss a *Washington Post* op-ed they'd co-written on the importance of NATO. Asked on the air if the president had her support, Pelosi said, "It's up to the president to decide if he is going to run. We're all encouraging him to make that decision, because time is running short."

Some viewers may have felt a bit of disconnect, because of course Biden had been making it very clear that he was going to run—and that he had made his decision. And here was Pelosi talking as if that hadn't happened. Pelosi seemed to be urging him to reconsider.

"It's not for me to say—I'm not the head of the caucus anymore. But he's beloved, he is respected, and people want him to make that decision," Pelosi said. "I want him to do whatever he decides to do."

When Pelosi stepped down as the Speaker, she got such overwhelming praise and support, it was truly moving. Biden might get the same. She thought to herself, *You can't imagine what awaits you! You're just going to get overwhelmed with appreciation!*

She knew that she was not, right at that moment, making a wholehearted endorsement of the president. She saw the CBS News poll from that month suggesting that 72 percent of the American people did not think Biden should run or serve. That included a lot of Democrats, and to her, it was a staggering figure.

Pelosi thought she was serving her fellow House Democrats by being out there like that, in her oblique but effective way, providing them with the cover they needed to make the decisions they wanted to. She was in a unique position: unafraid, undeterred, and someone who genuinely loved Biden and had for decades. She had nothing to lose. But the party—and the country—had a lot to lose.

Inside the White House, the president and his aides were furious at Pelosi's comment. The Politburo felt that the momentum of this whole thing was finally shifting in Biden's favor. They thought they were rounding the corner until that moment.

House Democratic leaders were confused by the White House's reaction to Pelosi's comments on *Morning Joe*. The White House seemed to think that the tide had been turning, but Jeffries saw no evidence of that. He was still planning on meeting with the president on Thursday, and Chuck Schumer was planning to do the same shortly thereafter.

Caucus Chair Pete Aguilar thought Pelosi was creating a permission structure. With House Democratic leaders assuming a position of neutrality, House Democrats needed direction, and she was opening the door to Biden's exit.

Later that morning, Aguilar was at a House Appropriations Committee markup when Ricchetti reached back out to him. Aguilar ducked into a colleague's hideaway to take the call.

Things were bad, he told Ricchetti. Someone had to tell the president that the party was risking everything by proceeding as it was. Aguilar had scrawled down his thoughts to organize a fair and comprehensive take on where he and his fellow House Democrats were. He shared this with Ricchetti.

"Steve," Aguilar asked, "has anyone walked into the Oval and told him we could lose everything?"

"We know people feel that way," Ricchetti said.

"No, no, no, Steve," Aguilar continued, getting a bit frustrated. "Has anyone walked into the Oval and told him it could all go down?"

"No," Ricchetti conceded.

"I would have some big concerns about who he's talking to," Aguilar said.

Later that night, when Aguilar gave a readout of this call to Leader Jeffries and Whip Clark, they were floored.

No one had told the president that there were serious concerns about a Democratic wipeout?

Aguilar wondered if Biden was being told the truth about anything.

Discussing the insanity of the situation with a House Democrat, Aguilar remarked that "folks like Ricchetti and Donilon—they're living the first line of their obituaries right now. People don't give that up."

THOSE WHO REALLY knew politics understood that Nancy Pelosi was one of the most skilled tacticians of her era. Elected House Democratic leader in 2002, she had met with Apple's Steve Jobs, who imbued in her a respect for market research and data to achieve electoral victories.

So when Pelosi surreptitiously arrived at the White House residence later in the day on July 10, she had one question for Biden: What data were they looking at that made them think this race was winnable, as the president kept saying?

"I want you to listen to Mike Donilon and what he has to say about the polls," the president told her, then phoned him up and got him on the line.

Donilon thought the narrative about the debate was worse than the debate itself. Reagan had a bad debate, he would say. Obama too. It was just that people didn't lose their minds afterward. They were within the margin of error, maybe a little outside the margin in battlegrounds. They still had the convention ahead of them and more than a billion dollars in advertising to spend. It was only July.

Donilon's message to Pelosi was simple: According to the polls, the president could still win the election.

"That's interesting," Pelosi said. "And that may all be true, but it's not the complete truth now. Let's hear from other pollsters. Maybe they have different demographics, different methodologies. Whatever it is, pollsters are arriving at different results in my members' districts."

She encouraged them to seek the view of other pollsters and experts.

One of Pelosi's biggest concerns about the data was the lack of support for Biden among young voters who agreed with him on climate change, abortion rights, LGBTQIA+ rights, and more. Beyond the data, friends who were leaders of state parties would tell her, "I don't know that I can get my children to vote." She heard it over and over from friends and associates who had progressive adult children. The future belonged to them, and they had voted before, but they were sitting out the 2024 presidential election. It was happening across the country, and it was a phenomenon she had never seen before.

THAT EVENING, Senator Peter Welch became the first Democratic senator to publicly call for Biden to step down.

When one reporter noted that it didn't seem like Biden was getting the message, Welch said, "I hope he is listening."

But the Biden campaign was loudly sending the signal that it disagreed.

Senator Welch didn't get any public reactions from the Senate Democratic leaders. But one of them privately pulled him aside and walked him down the hall to a secluded spot. "What you did was significant," the senator told him, "and it will be very helpful."

THURSDAY, JULY 11

Chuck Schumer had gotten an earful from his fellow Democratic senators at their weekly lunch. Those up for reelection in competitive states—Jon Tester of Montana, Sherrod Brown of Ohio, Bob Casey of

Pennsylvania, Jacky Rosen of Nevada—were already being dragged down by the unpopular incumbent, and they feared the debate would be like an anvil. The White House had done nothing to assuage fears. In fact, Biden's refusal to engage in an active schedule for the sake of calming jitters was serving as proof of his inability to do so.

The Democratic leader called the White House and demanded that Mike Donilon, Steve Ricchetti, and Anita Dunn—he would privately call them the "Palace Guard"—come meet with the Democratic senators.

"You need to hear from them and answer their questions," Schumer said. "And if you don't do it, ten senators are going to send a letter to the president calling for him to drop out."

A meeting was put on the schedule.

On Thursday, Donilon, Ricchetti, and Jen O'Malley Dillon came to a conference room at the Democratic Senatorial Campaign Committee's headquarters. The senators packed into a crowded room, where they were offered box lunches. There was a weird, grim energy in the room.

Donilon presented to them the president's theory of the case: Getting rid of the president at the top of the ticket would be a mistake. He had won eighty-one million votes in 2020, more than anyone in history, and ran better with seniors and male voters than most Democrats. The problems they were facing were with voters who would likely come home to the Democrats.

Moreover, walking away from a completely known incumbent president would be a big mistake, giving the nomination to someone far less known. Basically, the race was between two incumbent presidents; if Biden got out, those seeking a comfort level would shift to Trump.

Donilon also made the case that the polling remained competitive—within the margin of error, or just outside it. They were down maybe three points nationally, five points in battlegrounds. If they looked back in history, polls in the summer were hardly predictive.

Washington's Patty Murray, the president pro tempore of the Senate, spoke first. She spoke of Biden's legacy, suggesting that he was ruining it. She didn't explicitly call for him to drop out, but she certainly implied it.

Rhode Island's Jack Reed, a sober and serious man, stood. "If the president wants to stay in the race after that debate performance," Reed said, "I would suggest he should submit to examination by two independent neurologists—ones willing to report their findings at a news conference." Even if Biden were okay today, voters might have legitimate concerns about how he would be in four years, Reed thought.

West Virginia's Joe Manchin said to the group that "there comes a time when you have to tell your dad, 'It's time for me to take away the car keys.'" It could be done in a humane and appreciative way, he argued. "'Hey, Dad, you've been great; now it's time for me to drive you places.'" But it needed to be done.

"As you know, I've been dissatisfied with the president's campaign, and I think this calls for a very significant course correction," said Rhode Island Senator Sheldon Whitehouse. "I think we should also think about who our best candidate would be going forward—and I think that would be the vice president. Please don't take back to the president the fact that almost nobody in the Senate is speaking up publicly as meaning that nobody's worried, because, in fact, a lot of us are worried. If this isn't corrected fairly soon, we'll be lying to the public. And that's not right."

By "lying to the public," Whitehouse was signaling to the campaign that the debate performance had made it painfully clear that the president was not okay. And that senators shouldn't be relied upon to continue vouching for the president's acuity.

Soon, Chris Coons spoke, first giving a forceful defense of all that Democrats had accomplished with Biden and of why he deserved a chance to continue as the candidate. Then he turned to the main topic. "I never saw before that night what we all saw at the debate," he said. Coons knew that his colleagues thought he saw Biden far more than he did; the president phoned him regularly to talk about the Senate or foreign relations, but it was always on his own timeline.

"I think I've earned a reputation here for two things—loyalty and honesty," Coons said. "And I intend to keep both of those intact. Right now, those two things seem like they're at odds. I intend to keep supporting Biden strongly, but if any of you saw anything like that before the debate, you should share it."

No one spoke up.

"You know the president," Coons continued. "You know he's a fighter, and he believes he can win. He has sent us all a letter saying he intends to stay in the race. If you think he's going to leave this race based on donors calling him, you're wrong. If you think he's going to leave based on what pundits or other national political figures are saying, you're wrong. But anybody here who is in a tough reelection, if your polls show that he is harming your chances, that he's dragging you down, that will mean something. If you have a direct conversation with him, as a senator, he will respect you for it."

Pennsylvania Senator John Fetterman had been waiting to speak toward the end. He wanted to gauge the sentiment in the room. Fetterman had survived a stroke during his campaign and was one of the most outspoken Biden backers there.

"Hey," Fetterman said, "how many people in the room are with the president?"

Coons raised his hand and looked around the room. Fetterman's hand was up. Senator Tammy Duckworth of Illinois.

And that was it. Maybe Nevada Senator Catherine Cortez Masto? Senator Alex Padilla of California?

Fifty-one senators caucused with the Democrats, and maybe five were with Biden.

Fetterman was riled up.

"So, if you're willing to fuck over the president, who's been a great president after everything—and I'd like to remind every last one of you he is the only person who has ever beat Trump in an election," Fetterman said. "I mean, we all understand he had a bad debate, but if debates were definitive, I wouldn't be here talking to you here today. I understand there were probably some really scary conversations after I had my bad debate—and my debate was much worse."

Fetterman said he was "tired of hearing about Joe Biden's legacy. You all have legacies too. And your legacy is going to be fucking over a great president after a bad debate. And if you go ahead and set this in motion, you better own that."

Donilon was convinced the senators had already made their decision and weren't open to any conversation. Schumer approached him and Ricchetti at the end of the meeting.

"I want you to tell the president in detail about this meeting," Schumer instructed him. Biden was a creature of the Senate. It might make a difference to know how few colleagues supported him now.

BARACK OBAMA HAD arrived at the conclusion that Biden didn't have a path forward.

He had been continually talking to Schumer and Pelosi about the Biden dilemma, helping them navigate the minefield on which they trod. Each of them had their different roles to play.

When Schumer called him, Obama expressed concern about whether Biden was getting the unvarnished information he needed. Was he talking to the folks he needed to talk to? Was there a legitimate process being run—and run well—for Biden? Obama had never been a fan of some of Biden's top aides.

You should talk to him, Obama told Schumer. You should bring the data to him.

THAT NIGHT—A FULL two weeks after the debate—Biden finally held a press conference. The occasion was the end of the NATO Summit, during which he had accidentally introduced Ukrainian President Zelensky as "President Putin," though he corrected himself. Biden read ably, if softly, from the teleprompter—a robust defense of the NATO alliance and withering criticism, substantively, of Trump on the issue. These were issues that animated him, ones he cared about deeply. He knew the substance—and, for sure, he knew it better than his opponent.

Then he took questions.

"What concerns do you have about Vice President Harris's ability to beat Donald Trump if she were at the top of the ticket?" Reuters's Jeff Mason asked.

"Look, I wouldn't have picked Vice President Trump [sic] to be vice president did I think she was not qualified to be president," Biden said.

Vice President Trump.

Another reporter asked if Biden would take a cognitive exam before the election.

"I'm tested every single day on my neurological capacity," he said. He nodded at the fact that politics were also a factor and added, "No matter what I did, no one's going to be satisfied."

When another reporter asked if he would reconsider his decision to stay in the race if his team showed him data that Harris would fare better against Trump, Biden said, "No, unless they came back and said, 'There's no way you can win'—me."

Then, for emphasis, he whispered, "No one is saying that. No poll says that."

"This ends tonight's press conference," Biden's press secretary said.

"Sir," a reporter shouted. "Respectfully, earlier you misspoke in your opening answer. You referred to Vice President Harris as 'Vice President Trump.' Right now, Donald Trump is using that to mock your age and your memory. How do you combat that criticism from tonight?"

"Listen to him," Biden said.

The press conference ended at 8:26 p.m.

Deputy Press Secretary Andrew Bates had already posted on X at 8:10 p.m.: "To answer the question on everyone's minds: No, Joe Biden does not have a doctorate in foreign affairs. He's just that fucking good."

The remark reflected the views of the Politburo, but among professional Democrats, it became an instant legend for its sycophancy and tone-deafness.

Minutes after the press conference ended, Congressman Jim Himes, ranking Democrat on the House Select Committee on Intelligence, posted, in part: "I hope President Biden will step away from the presidential campaign."

What led Himes to come to this conclusion? The debate, combined with the realization that the Democrats had so lowered the bar that when Biden strung four sentences together in a cogent way, they all celebrated.

BIDEN CAMPAIGN LEADERS also had a problem with their own staff.

On Thursday, campaign leadership organized an all-staff call. In a sign of how aides had soured on campaign leadership, they immediately shared a recording with Alex.

Jen O'Malley Dillon urged staffers to tune out "crazy fucking gossipland world" about the president and continue the work.

"We had two very, very, very hard weeks, very bad weeks," she acknowledged. "I told you I'd level with you. They've been bad fucking weeks. . . . This two-week window has really sucked, and it is hard, there is no doubt about it."

She added that Donilon kept saying in meetings that "he's never seen a presidential candidate have more thrown at him than Joe Biden, and do you know what Joe Biden does every day? He gets up, and he keeps fighting."

THAT EVENING, JEFFRIES MET with President Biden at the White House residence, just the two of them.

Jeffries brought data with him—polling showing how difficult it would be for Democrats to recapture the House if Biden remained at the top of the ticket. The word that he, Clark, and Aguilar had agreed on was *irretrievable*.

Overall, he told the president, among most of my members, there is a lot of concern about your ability to continue at the top of the ticket. The consensus view is that you should step down.

The president said he would take it under advisement.

To Jeffries, it seemed sincere. The president seemed to be listening and trying to find the right path forward.

FRIDAY, JULY 12

Washington, DC, Democrats were turning on him, but when Biden traveled to Detroit on July 12, the crowd began chanting "We've got your back!" and "Don't you quit!"

That night, leaders on the Biden campaign noted a sad irony: Biden was better on the stump than they'd seen him be in years. He had found a fire in the belly that had been absent. The crowds felt it too.

Some of this was the influence of Anthony Bernal, who had taken on a bigger role in designing the rallies. Even his detractors acknowledged that he had a gift for staging events.

But some of it was just Biden fighting with his back against the wall. His defiance whipped up the crowd. His rallies began to give off counter-echoes of the angry energy that coursed through his rival's. Crowds booed the media—though Biden asked them to stop—and chanted that Trump should be sent to prison.

Biden framed his candidacy as a fight against the elites: "I'm the nominee of this party because fourteen million Democrats like you voted for me in the primaries. You made me the nominee, no one else. Not the press, not the pundits, not the insiders, not donors. You, the voters. You decided. No one else. And I'm not going anywhere."

Watching Biden and the crowd's response to him, campaign leaders thought to themselves that the president just might make it after all.

NANCY PELOSI SAT DOWN and wrote the president a letter on her stationery.

"A master class press conference showing mastery of foreign policy," she wrote of the NATO event. "A positive grassroots event in Detroit. Not a reason to stay, but a way to go out on top."

She signed the letter and sent it to the White House.

She never heard back from him.

She would later hear how angry he was. And she knew why: She was one of his best friends in Congress. She admired and cared about him and worked in so many ways to ensure that House Democrats were well disposed to the president.

She believed that he was mad because he knew how much she cared about him.

And she was right. President Biden saw her as a close friend and a professional partner with whom he had accomplished a great deal. Her opposition to his continuance in the race stung so sharply because of their closeness. And, to him, Pelosi's position seemed like a quick conversion to the side of the chattering class by someone who had once been an ally.

ON FRIDAY, Chuck Schumer was told that Donilon and Ricchetti had not, in fact, shared a detailed accounting of their meeting with the Democratic senators. (Ricchetti often would dull some of the edges from what folks told him, figuring that it would be better for everyone involved if their concerns came across more politely.)

Schumer phoned Jeff Zients.

"I want to see the president," Schumer told the White House chief of staff. "And if you don't put something on the calendar, I will make the request publicly. And then you'll have to give me the meeting, and it will be public."

Schumer was invited to visit the president the next day in Delaware.

IN THE LATE HOURS of July 12, sliding into the next day, South Carolina Congressman Jim Clyburn found himself at a Manhattan meeting with big Democratic donors. They didn't just want Biden out of the race—they wanted his running mate out too.

"They were telling us why they thought he could not win—how bad his polling was, and her polling was just as bad," Clyburn later recounted. (Her polling was in fact far worse than his in many polls at the time.)

They presented him with data.

"I've heard all this information that you've shared, and I don't disagree with any of it," Clyburn told them. "I do, however, have one question that I need y'all to answer for me."

Clyburn wanted them to do some polling for him too.

"How long would it take you to go out in the field and get me the answer to a question?" he asked.

"About three days," they said.

"If Joe Biden were to get out of the race and Democrats were to then bypass Kamala Harris, what would be the impact on Black turnout? Y'all think you can come up with a polling question to get me that answer?"

"Yes," they said.

"Okay," Clyburn said. "When y'all come back with that answer, I'll be able to complete that conversation."

They never got back to him.

SATURDAY, JULY 13

It was good that being Senate majority leader meant you had a driver, because Chuck Schumer hadn't slept a wink the night before.

Schumer had note cards with him. He was steeling himself for the toughest one-on-one meeting of his life. He went over what he was going to say as his car sped over the Verrazzano-Narrows Bridge and down the New Jersey Turnpike to Rehoboth.

Pramila Jayapal had reached out to the president's team to set up a Zoom call with the Congressional Progressive Caucus. The Biden team finally set it up for that day.

California Congressman Jared Huffman, a vice-chair of the caucus, told Jayapal he wanted to ask a question—a pointed one that the president would have to answer.

Jayapal and the CPC staff wrote the question for him, but Huffman thought theirs was a softball and decided just to ask his own question live. "There was a lot of pro-Biden steering going into that call and the lead-up to the call," Huffman later recalled.

It wasn't clear if any of the staffers were helping Biden as he sat in his Rehoboth Beach, Delaware, beach house before the Zoom screen, which had been set up at such a high angle that participants had a good view of the thinning hair atop his head. He often seemed to be looking down at note cards, and he hadn't been told where to look to make eye contact.

Jayapal began the virtual meeting by praising Biden as the most progressive president in her lifetime. But, she continued, "our members have real concerns about whether you can win this race."

Throughout the call, Biden was defensive and angry in a way that many members of the CPC had never seen before. He insisted that he was the real progressive in the room. He challenged Jayapal quite directly. He suggested that progressives on the call had not been sufficiently aggressive in their focus on how America's wealthy were gaming the system.

"It was insane," one CPC member later said.

Jayapal was texting Biden's team during the meeting, and she let them know that it wasn't going well; he was getting way too defensive. A staffer in the room with Biden got the message, wrote it out, and handed it to him. Biden read it aloud: "Stay positive. You are sounding defensive."

Later, Biden supporters improbably claimed that he was just attempting levity.

"He was in complete defensive mode," the CPC member later said.

Biden didn't seem to want to get off the call when it was scheduled to end. CPC members texted Jayapal, asking her to try to end it. He had another call to do, this one with the more moderate New Democrat Coalition, or New Dems.

NEW HAMPSHIRE CONGRESSWOMAN Annie Kuster, chair of the New Dems, spent three hours on a flight to Washington State preparing her opening remarks on the Biden Zoom call; the last time she'd prepared for a conversation this painful, it was to discuss with her parents the need for them to enter assisted living.

Kuster had spent time with Biden on Air Force One in March, and she had been shocked by the degree to which he seemed not up to the task of running for reelection. She concluded that Trump was going to win, so she opted not to run again—she did not want to be pulled down by the Biden anchor in a red wave, nor did she want to spend the next two years dealing with his presidency.

While she didn't have to worry about her job security, House Democrats were terrified that they might lose forty seats or more.

Earlier in the week, Colorado Congressman Jason Crow had approached her and told her he was going to call for Biden to step aside. Kuster had asked him to hold off; she was setting up the Zoom, and the White House had made it clear that no one who had already called for the president to withdraw would be permitted to speak.

"I'd like you to do this," Kuster told him. Crow, a former Army Ranger, was a good voice for the New Dems to speak on national security issues, a role she wanted filled on the call, along with someone who was also a member of the CBC, such as Texas Congressman Marc Veasey, and someone from a battleground state, such as Pennsylvania Congresswoman Chrissy Houlahan.

After Kuster and her husband landed in Seattle, they rushed to a local library so that she could lead the New Dems' Zoom meeting with the president.

Three different people had called Kuster that morning and told her to be brutally honest with him, because he was not hearing the truth. So Kuster told the president, with all due respect, "Our constituents and our party need more than 'Don't look at the polls' or 'Watch me.'" They needed "a concrete plan and well-orchestrated strategy to alleviate the fears of millions of Americans who are terrified of what appears increasingly likely to be a second Trump presidency that's even worse than the first."

Kuster said she would then turn the conversation over to the president "to discuss how you will make that decision, whether you are getting the honest assessment you need from your team, and what changes need to be made to right the ship."

Biden's tone was one of annoyance—Kuster later likened him to the irascible old man played by Clint Eastwood in *Gran Torino*.

"The polling data hasn't changed at all," Biden said, "In fact, it shows me up in some polls."

The comment made many on the call wonder how much information was being kept from the president. Trump had been leading Biden in the polls for ten months, almost without interruption, and that lead had expanded since the debate.

Veasey spoke next.

"Mr. President, twenty-five polls taken before the debate showed you down," he said. "Post-debate, they're even worse. What's going to be done to turn this around?"

In response to Veasey, Biden said, "Trump has been on the hunt for so long that he's been able to—he's just a flat liar, and we've not exposed it, and I think it's important to do that." He meandered on: "If the folks in tough districts show me their polling, and I know any way I can help in terms of money and/or getting out of the way, you know, I'll campaign for you or against, whatever helps you the most.

"But the point is, the polling data we're seeing nationally, and on the swing states, it's been essentially where it was before. You notice the last three polls nationally, they had me up four points, and, and I mean, and, but—I don't have much faith in the polls at all, either way, because they're so. They're so hard to read anymore.

"Tell me what you need and see if I can help. And I'm not going to get—you run your districts; I never go into a district and tell another member what they should be doing. But I'm not sure I'm answering your question, but we have to focus on a fair tax system. We have to focus on taking on corporate greed. And the biggest thing is, in my view, although we have the best economy in the world, that didn't trickle down to most kitchen tables, at least not in that neighborhood I was raised in. And so we gotta focus on corporate greed. That's why, for example, I'm gonna be, I'm gonna be—I think it will stick an issue with an executive order that corporate rentals can't raise more than five, excuse me, five percent a year, a year. That we're gonna make sure that we're in a situation where we change the way in which we build housing and make it available.

"That's why, for example, look what's happened in the Black community. Look what I've been able to do in the Black community. More home ownership, more debt forgiveness, more ability to buy, I mean, across the board, you know, you have . . . a whole range of things, but I think I have to focus on that cadre of people that I used to represent in Delaware, when it was a red state, that in fact demonstrate that I know what they're up against, and that we can work for them, but I'm not sure that answers your question. There's a lot more to talk about, but I'm talking too long already, I think."

To Veasey, it was all very strange. Biden had rejected his premise, insisting that he was doing fine in the polls, and then he'd gone on to tell Veasey about all these things he'd done for Black people—which Veasey hadn't asked him about. Yes, Veasey was Black, but this was a New Dems call, and his question was about polling. Biden's short temper was the biggest shocker. To Veasey, the president was very angry that day—personally offended—and he didn't mind showing it.

If this call was intended to reassure House Democrats that the president would be able to deliver a clear and crisp message to bring the case to the American people, it failed spectacularly. He was rambling, long-winded, and at times incoherent.

Jason Crow was next.

"National security is a major issue in this campaign," Crow said. "Americans want a commander in chief who can project strength, vigor, and inspire confidence at home and abroad. Despite your many successes and the danger of Donald Trump, many of us are seeing overwhelming evidence, not just in polling but in our districts, that voters are losing confidence that you can do this in the second term. It's not fair, but it's true."

New Dems had "run some of the toughest races in the country . . . and we know that without a major change, we are facing a loss in November. The status quo won't work. Focusing just on Trump won't work. Focusing on policy accomplishments the last four years won't work. We need a major shift. We need a major change. What change to your campaign do you propose?"

Biden was not happy.

"First of all, I think you're dead wrong about national security," the president said. "You saw what happened recently in terms of the meeting we had with NATO. I put NATO together."

Biden continued: "Name me a foreign leader who thinks I'm not the most effective leader in the world on foreign policy! Tell me! Tell me who the hell that is. Tell me who put NATO back together. Tell me who enlarged NATO. Tell me who did the Pacific Basin."

He then got personal with Crow, a veteran: "Tell me who did something that you've never done with your Bronze Star like my son—and I'm proud of your leadership, but guess what, what's happening, we've got Korea and Japan working together, I put AUKUS together, anyway!

"I put AUKUS together. I have a, look what's happened, look at what's happening around the world. Things are in chaos and I'm making, bringing some order to it. And again, name—find me a world leader who's an ally of ours who doesn't, I don't, think I'm the most effective person they've ever—"

Crow said, "It's not breaking through, Mr. President, to our voters."

"You ought to look at it!" Biden said. "You know it. Talk about it! Talk about how I built NATO! Talk about how I enlarged NATO. Talk about how I put together what's happening in Asia. Talk about what's going on in the Middle East. Talk about it. Talk about how I got . . . Anyway.

"You know, look, a lot of you guys know better. I don't blame you if you don't want it. If it hurts you to talk about it, don't talk about it. But let's get things straight. On national security, nobody has been a better president than I have been.

"Name me one," Biden said. "Name. Me. One. So I don't want to hear that crap."

"That was the moment that we all went, 'Oh fuck,'" one of the New Dems later said.

Crow was stunned. He interjected one last time: "And I do want to be for you, Mr. President, and that's why we're all on this Zoom, trying to figure out the path forward. I think that's why we asked the question in that spirit. Thank you very much."

Congresswoman Houlahan, another veteran, tried to articulate the same basic thought, the idea that "it is fundamental that the president needs to make the American public confident that he's—"

Biden cut her off. He was still angry and in denial that the polling wasn't fine.

"Please, sir," Houlahan said, "have a look at the Pennsylvania polls."

At that point, the president said his staff was making him end the call so he could go to Mass.

"We can't get out there and say, 'Four more years,'" Kuster remarked. "I don't know if we can say, 'Four more months.'"

SCHUMER COULD HEAR the president shouting as he walked into the president's Rehoboth home. Later, he would be told that Biden was yelling at the New Dems.

Ricchetti had escorted the senator to an enclosed porch with a lovely view of marshlands, and past them the ocean. Soon enough the president walked in and was friendly, gentle, and kind. Schumer hadn't publicly called for Biden to drop out. He wasn't sure if Pelosi's public posture was helpful or not; she'd gone a bit rogue, he thought. For his part, he'd been saying, "I'm with Joe," which wasn't a strong endorsement, he knew, but stronger than what so many other Democrats were saying.

They looked out at the marshlands together, Biden alluding to his effort, decades before, to secure for Cape Henlopen State Park hundreds of those acres.

"This is one of the great things about what we do," Schumer said. "I can go to any corner of New York State and find something I've done that made it better. It makes me proud. I know you must have done ten times more in a smaller state."

Schumer then steeled himself for the tougher conversation.

He told Biden about the DSCC meeting, about what the senators had said.

Biden seemed surprised. I hadn't heard it was that bad, Biden said.

"If we had a secret ballot of the Democrats on whether you should keep running, I think you would only get five votes," Schumer said. "And you know how good I am at counting votes."

Jumping back and forth between calling him "Mr. President" and calling him "Joe," Schumer took on a philosophical note, having prepared his remarks.

"All of us have big egos in politics, but we go into it for different motivations," he said. "Some motivations are bad. Some people want to make money out of it, some want power, some want to lord themselves over other people. But some go into it for good reasons. They want to make the world a better place and build a legacy. I know you're that kind of politician."

He went through all the projects they had worked on together, first when Schumer was in the House and Biden in the Senate, then the ambitious legislative agenda of 2021–2022.

"If I had to leave politics tomorrow for whatever reason," Schumer said, "I would say to myself, 'All the shit we take in this job was worth it for making the world a better place.' Well, you've done twenty times more than that, Mr. President, so you have an amazing legacy."

But that wasn't going to be his legacy, Schumer told him.

"If you stay in the race and you lose to Trump, and we lose the Senate and we don't get back the House, that whole fifty years of amazing, beautiful work goes out the window. But it's worse than that—you will go down in American history as one of the darkest figures."

And that was likely, Schumer said. "Mr. President, you're not getting the information as to what the chances are. Have you talked to your pollsters?"

"No," Biden said.

Schumer said to him, "If I had a fifty percent chance of winning, Mr. President, I'd run. It's worth it. But, Mr. President, your chances of winning are only five percent. I've talked to your pollsters; I know all three of them. I've talked to Garin and Pollock and Murphy. And they think it's a five percent chance. Five percent."

"Really?" Biden said.

"They're not telling you," Schumer said of Donilon and Ricchetti. "The pollsters told me, 'He's not seen our polls. It all goes to Donilon, and Donilon interprets it.' Okay? You have a five percent chance. The analytics guy who probably knows this best said it's one percent."

"If I were you, I wouldn't run," Schumer said. "I'm urging you not to run."

"Do you think Kamala can win?" Biden asked.

"I don't know if she can win," Schumer said. "I just know that you cannot."

Biden said that he needed a week.

They stood. On their way out, Biden put his hands on Schumer's shoulders. "You have bigger balls than anyone I've ever met," Biden told him.

On his drive back to Brooklyn, Schumer called his staff and teared up while relaying their conversation. But soon the subject changed. At 6:11 p.m., at a campaign rally near Butler, Pennsylvania, Trump was nearly assassinated. One audience member was killed, two others were seriously wounded, and the gunman was shot dead by Secret Service countersnipers. The image of Trump bloodied but standing defiant, fist in the air, after a bullet grazed his ear would be one of the most memorable of the year.

Looking at that photo, Biden campaign aides couldn't help but think of how this would help Trump politically. "Fuck!" more than a few said.

MONDAY, JULY 15

That weekend, there was a pause in the drumbeat of calls to Chris Coons from reporters, donors, and Democratic Party leaders who wanted to know more about Biden's condition and campaign.

Then, on Monday morning, the calls about whether Biden would drop out started up again.

Coons concluded that this pressure on the president—the steady cycle of negative polling and Democrats calling for him to step aside— was simply not going to end.

"IN YOUR LAST TV interview," NBC's Lester Holt said to the president, "you were asked if you had watched the debate, and your answer was 'I don't think so, no.' Have you since seen it?"

"I've seen pieces of it," the president said.

Holt explained that he was asking because the big question on everyone's mind was whether Biden had seen what the rest of the country had at the debate.

"Lester, look," Biden said, shifting into lecture mode, "why don't you guys ever talk about the eighteen—the twenty-eight lies he told? Where—where are you on this? Why doesn't the press ever talk about that? Twenty-eight times, it's confirmed, he lied in that debate. I had a bad, bad night. I wasn't feeling well at all. And—and I had been— without making—I screwed up."

Biden continued to push as if the news media hadn't spent much of the previous eight years fact-checking Donald Trump.

"Seriously, you won't answer the question," Biden said, "but why doesn't the press talk about all the lies he told?"

"We have reported many of the issues that came of that debate," Holt countered.

"No, you haven't," Biden said.

"Well, we'll provide you with them," Holt said.

"God love you," the president said.

It was the news media's fault for not sufficiently covering Trump's lies, it was the Progressive Caucus's fault for not going after oligarchs enough, it was the New Dems' fault for not talking up his achievements enough. It was everybody else's fault.

THE WHITE HOUSE had invited South Carolina Congressman Jim Clyburn to fly with the president on Monday to Las Vegas, where both men would attend the NAACP National Convention the next day. During the plane ride, the congressman noticed that the conversations taking place on board didn't have much to do with politics or the campaign or the dire reality of the president's situation. White House staff seemed more focused on policy and legacy issues.

Clyburn's sixth sense went off. *He's going to drop out.*

WEDNESDAY, JULY 17

On Wednesday morning, Jeffrey Katzenberg flew to Las Vegas from California and met White House Communications Director Ben LaBolt for breakfast, then headed up to the president's suite at the forty-seven-story Waldorf Astoria.

There, Katzenberg went to a small conference room where Annie Tomasini was also waiting. When Biden walked in, he hacked out a deep, phlegmy cough. His eyes were watering, his nose running. He looked awful.

Katzenberg made his pitch for the campaign to launch a high-risk, high-reward strategy that would get him out and about and vigorously answering questions. In the early afternoon, Biden went to do a Univision radio interview at the Original Lindo Michoacán restaurant downtown, LATINOS FOR BIDEN-HARRIS signs decorating one wall.

A pool reporter thought the president's shuffle was pronounced, and he looked exhausted.

"I'm standing there," the pool reporter said, "and I remember thinking, *I can't diagnose the guy. I don't know if he's sick, but he does look slower.*"

Journalists had seen that Congressman Adam Schiff, in the midst of his Senate race, had now called for Biden to drop out. "A second Trump presidency will undermine the very foundation of our democracy, and I have serious concerns about whether the president can defeat Donald Trump in November," Schiff had said. Those journalists tried to get Biden to respond but were escorted out of the restaurant.

Biden was supposed to travel to the MGM Grand to speak to Unidos-US, a Latino advocacy organization. But the motorcade remained in place. Then the chief executive of UnidosUS stepped to the microphone.

"I was just on the phone with the president, and he shared his deep disappointment at not being able to join us this afternoon," she told the crowd. "The president's been at many events, as we all know, and he just tested positive for COVID."

Local police prepared to rush the president to a hospital.

"For everybody on the radio, right now POTUS is 421," one officer said, using the code for someone who is "sick or injured."

Officers were then instructed to meet at the "Valley Hospital ER parking lot." They talked about shutting down roads and intersections in preparation for the president's arrival.

Ultimately, the president ended up being rushed instead to Air Force One. The plane zoomed to Delaware in three hours and forty minutes. At one point, a flight attendant fell over. "This is faster than this plane has ever gone," the attendant said.

"It was intense," the pool reporter recalled.

President Biden struggled to get off the plane—two steps, stop, two steps, stop, down the rest of the stairs—then labored to sit down in the car on his own, taking thirty seconds to do so, according to video captured by ABC News. Fatigued and frail, he needed help from the Secret Service to lift himself into the car. It was tough to watch.

He entered COVID isolation at his Rehoboth home late that night.

IN THE DAYS after the DSCC meeting where Chris Coons had asked his colleagues if they'd ever seen signs before the debate of the kind of confusion the president showed that night, a few senators had approached Coons with troubling stories about the president—times when he'd seemed unusually tired, moments when he'd trailed off or lost his train of thought at campaign events.

Coons became concerned and started pressing to meet with Biden in person. He called Steve Ricchetti to try to get through to the president. He called Jeff Zients. "I have to have a conversation with him," Coons implored.

The president finally called Coons back when the senator was in

Colorado for the July 16–19 Aspen Security Forum at the end of that week.

"I am as loyal to you as anyone will ever be," Coons told the president. "I was the first one on this plane, and I will be the last one off, even if the view through the windshield is the ground, but I cannot honestly say that it's in the best interest of our party and our country.

"So I'm not telling you I will ever abandon you or stop supporting you or stop believing in you," Coons continued. "I don't care what Axelrod says or Pelosi says or any of the folks who you're hearing don't believe in you. I'm trying to tell you, as someone who you know and someone who loves you, you need to think hard about this.

"I want you to hear two texts that I've gotten," Coons concluded.

First he shared a very positive message for Biden from a Delawarean, a lifelong supporter. The note was about how much they loved the president, how loyal they remained to him, and how he'd changed the world.

And then Coons turned to the important message he wanted to pass on. It was from Billy, a leader in the International Brotherhood of Electrical Workers whom both Biden and Coons knew from years of taking the Amtrak train from Wilmington to DC. Billy had texted Coons, who hadn't heard from him in a while.

"Tell the president: You know I don't want anything," Billy had written. "You know I've known Joe for years. I'm praying for him and I love all he's done for our country. It's important we win this election given all the craziness from the Republicans. I've been watching him closely and I think it's time. He doesn't owe us anything, he's worked so hard for so long, and I just pray that you will encourage him to do the right thing for the USA and step back and take a rest from it all. And tell him this is his old friend Billy from the IBEW."

Even after the call, Coons didn't know what Biden would decide to do.

———

JEFF ZIENTS KEPT it to himself, but after the debate, he thought that the president should drop out.

Still, he saw his job as ensuring that the president had every option on the table.

If Biden wanted to stay in, the chief of staff would make sure he could do what he wanted to do. But Zients also wanted to make sure that the president had all the information he needed to decide if it was the right call.

THE WHAT IF? COMMITTEE

Biden had tapped longtime Democratic operative Minyon Moore to be chair of the 2024 Democratic National Convention shortly after the midterms, though it wasn't officially announced until August 2023. Well aware of all the unknowns, Moore formed and convened what she called the What If? Committee. Consisting of eight smart insiders, they gamed out any possible unpredictable "black swan" disruptions.

What if there were protests in Chicago 2024 that were as heated as Chicago 1968? What if there were serious ramifications to changing the primary schedule to jump over Iowa and New Hampshire? What if Biden decided not to seek reelection? What if there really were an open primary? They discussed it all—logistics, backup plans, every possible contingency.

After the debate, the what-ifs involving Biden not being the nominee became more seriously discussed. If Biden were to decide he wasn't running again, what would they do? How would they turn on a dime?

Members of the What If? Committee were in touch with the

———

delegates. By mid-July, it was becoming clear Biden's support among them was eroding significantly.

They called Ricchetti.

"Biden can still win at the convention," Ricchetti was told, "but it's going to be ugly. It will be tight."

Preparing for what-ifs was part of the job. Moore had even made sure that the design scheme of the convention was generic enough so a different candidate could be swapped in at the last minute, just in case.

THE POLLSTERS, PART TWO

Geoff Garin conducted another poll, this one to see whether Biden could climb back: What could they say? What could they do?

The numbers were worse—and Biden had already been lagging *before* the debate.

The relentless coverage of the president's performance—compounded by his inability to do anything to change people's impressions—took a toll. State by state, congressional district by congressional district, voters were punishing the Democratic Party with their disapproval.

Jeff Zients thought it important that Biden get all the data. Mike Donilon was the only one who shared polling numbers with the president, but some advisers worried that this information was first filtered through a Donilon spin machine that churned out the rosiest views. Zients wanted the president to hear directly from the pollsters. He had previously talked to Jen O'Malley Dillon, who emailed them on Friday, July 5. "The president wants a full briefing on Monday, July 8," she said. "Can you be available?"

She cautioned them: "Prepare to be honest, but I advise you not to say prescriptively what the president should or shouldn't do."

Finally, the pollsters thought. They could at last tell him what they were seeing. All the numbers and the fundamental problems underlying the data—the disapproval of the president's job performance, the majority thinking that the country was on the wrong track, the grave concerns that Biden was too old to do the job. They had long suspected that the Politburo wasn't really sharing the facts, the truth, with the president.

But the meeting was canceled. Their attempt to put it back on the calendar ran into scheduling issues as well as Biden's contraction of COVID. So Zients decided to have them present it all to the senior staff.

On Thursday, July 18, 2024, the pollsters finally got their chance to speak truth to the Politburo. They Zoomed into a meeting at Zients's office, where he hosted the Politburo, Anita Dunn, and O'Malley Dillon.

"Here are the facts from our battleground polling," the pollsters began. "We are behind in the trial heats in the battleground states, including the Blue Wall states, with a four-point deficit across the battlegrounds."

Using the state averages of other polls from the website RealClearPolitics (which were found generally to be in line with the campaign's internal analytics) and the analytics from other campaign committees, such as the Democratic Congressional Campaign Committee, the pollsters had determined that Biden trailed in every battleground state. The July 16 data: in Michigan, he was down 1.3 points; in Wisconsin, 3 points; in Pennsylvania, 4.5 points; in Georgia, 3.9 points; in North Carolina, 5.4 points; in Arizona, 5.7 points; and in Nevada, 5 points.

Worse news: In three states that Biden had won fairly comfortably in 2020—Minnesota, New Mexico, and Virginia—the race was now close. One pollster had even seen a poll from the president's home state of Delaware that had Biden up by only six points, but he didn't share that.

"We've seen improvement with Black voters but still face significant challenges with younger voters," the pollsters said.

The basic arithmetic, they pointed out, was tough.

"Trump gets an eighty-seven-point margin out of his 2020 voters," the pollsters said. "Biden gets an eighty-one-point margin out of his 2020 voters. Trump has a nine-point advantage with everyone else— and a twelve-point advantage with new voters."

Turnout was still an unknown, though Trump voters were excited about voting for him, and the same wasn't true for Biden voters.

The structural problems underlying the situation were even tougher.

"President Biden is the incumbent at a time when voters overwhelmingly are dissatisfied with the direction of the nation. A majority of voters (fifty-four percent) have little or no confidence in President Biden on the economy, ten points higher than Trump."

And then there was the age issue, which was devastating.

"A large majority of voters do not believe that President Biden is mentally and physically capable of serving four more years, and the belief that he is too old to be president is a settled question in voters' minds," the pollsters said.

"None of our messages of reassurance on the age issue is as convincing as the other side's attack on the age issue, but the best thing we can say is that being president is not a one-person job and highlighting the chaos of Trump's administration/team," the pollsters concluded.

Molly Murphy delivered this message, then Jefrey Pollock, then Geoff Garin.

Ricchetti and Zients asked questions; Dunn chirped up here and there, as did Bruce Reed on Zoom. Donilon didn't engage with the pollsters at all.

The general sentiment from the trio was this: *We don't see a path, but it's your call.*

"I look forward to reviewing your data," Donilon said curtly, and the Zoom ended.

SATURDAY, JULY 20

The pollsters had no idea whether the data they'd just shared would have any impact. They doubted it, frankly. Either way, they were all convinced that if Biden stayed in, there would be a political bloodbath.

Ricchetti phoned Garin at around eleven on Saturday morning. The call was immediately contentious.

"You were out of line for what you did," he told Garin. "If I were campaign manager, I would fire the pollsters. You're supposed to tell us how to win, not that we can't. Donilon has been looking at the data and has come to a different conclusion."

"We would love to talk to Donilon about what he sees in the data," Garin said.

Garin told Murphy and Pollock about the call. There was no way Biden was dropping out, they all thought.

MIKE DONILON AND Steve Ricchetti entered the president's Rehoboth house, meeting Biden on the screened-in porch.

Donilon went over the latest polling information. It was eroding but not catastrophic; they weren't in the free fall some seemed to be suggesting, he said. Maybe outside the margin of error in some polls but nothing that made it hopeless. In decades of doing this, neither Donilon nor Ricchetti had known of any politician who thought that being behind by five points was an unbridgeable chasm. "We've lost maybe a couple or three points since the debate," Donilon said. "Maybe we're minus five; maybe we're minus three. We believe we can devise strategy that would result in us being in a dead heat again by Labor Day. We can still win."

But, Donilon said, none of their pollsters thought the president could win. He disagreed. They thought it was definitive; Donilon didn't. He talked about the opportunities they had in front of them: the convention, another debate, a major advertising campaign.

Ricchetti discussed what they were hearing and the political dynamic on the Hill: The Congressional Black Caucus was still with Biden, and progressives like Bernie Sanders and AOC were still on board. But by their estimates roughly two-thirds of the House and Senate Democrats were pushing him to drop out. The insider political momentum was spinning out of control.

They'd been here before, Biden believed. In June 2019, the naysayers had all said, "Oh my god, Biden's dead," with David Axelrod and others pronouncing Biden over, the chattering classes harping about his age—"He's old!"—and attacking his debate performances. "He's not able to respond to questions!" they'd said. "He's lost his fastball!" Everything was about the surface, not the substance. The arguments were almost identical and came from many of the same people. The president had always thought that he was in better shape with the country than with the pundits and the pols.

Another key part of the Biden calculus: This was only July, and he still had time to recoup his losses. The narrative was going to change with the Democratic convention—the delegates were still with him—and then he would have a billion and a half dollars spent on his behalf to present his theory of the case and the substance of his argument. He had been a successful president. He felt that in his bones.

Donilon and Ricchetti agreed: He could fight through this. He would, without question, secure the nomination, and then they could reshape the narrative. By Labor Day, they would be back within the margin of error.

But, they said, it was going to be a turbulent month until they got there. Because the momentum in the party had moved against them.

"We're going to face continuing disaffection from high-ranking Democrats," Donilon said. "The party will be split. Money will be hard to raise."

Biden, ailing with COVID, would not be able to defend himself or make his case. It was unstated, but their allies would need to do it. The Congressional Black Caucus. Progressives. Labor. They would need to go out there. And they would need to fight back. It would get personal. It would get nasty. And it might tear the Democratic Party apart.

The president thought about what they were telling him. The previous three weeks had been demoralizing and exhausting. And now he was sick, really sick. He felt awful. And Donilon and Ricchetti were telling him that he could win, but it would be scorched-earth.

Donilon would tell folks that Biden wanted to win and wanted to be beloved. And he could still win. But he wouldn't be beloved.

Biden was worried. He felt that the party was split. He worried that for the rest of the campaign, there would be no conversation except about his age. Nothing about Trump and the threat he posed.

"That's not who I am," Biden said. "We need a unified party."

He was going to bow out.

"Sleep on it," Donilon told him.

Donilon and Ricchetti went back to the hotel, where Donilon prepared a letter for Biden to send out the next day if his mind was made up.

SUNDAY, JULY 21

Jake was anchoring CNN's *State of the Union.* Senator Joe Manchin came on and, after three weeks of silence, called for his old friend to drop out. "I say this," Manchin said, "and I came to the decision with a heavy heart, that I think it's time to pass the torch to the new generation."

The Republican Speaker of the House, Mike Johnson of Louisiana, was the next guest. Asked if the president had ever seemed, in private interactions, cognitively impaired, Johnson said yes. "I didn't want to come out and talk about personal interactions with the president, because I have been concerned about . . . this projection of weakness on the world stage at a very dangerous time," Johnson explained. "But now that the cat is out of the bag, you can hear from the Republican Speaker to affirm what everyone else has known and seen. They—the Democrats have been involved in a big cover-up here. They have been trying to prevent the people from seeing what all of us in close proximity have seen."

Next came Congressman Jim Clyburn. Many Democrats, including in the top echelons of the White House and Biden campaign, were watching to see what he would say.

Days before, after Clyburn had returned to South Carolina, he told close confidants of his suspicions that Biden would drop out. He kept waiting for the announcement. He was convinced it was imminent. Surely a late-afternoon Friday news drop would be the way Biden did it, in typical DC form, he thought.

But that didn't happen.

Saturday, still nothing.

So he came on *State of the Union* that Sunday morning—his eighty-fourth birthday—sensing that something was about to happen but not knowing what.

"Is it in the best interest of the Democratic Party for President Biden to remain the Democratic presidential nominee, do you think?" Jake asked him.

Clyburn did not directly answer the question, choosing instead to diplomatically say, "I support Joe Biden. He is still in this race. He will be our nominee if he stays in the race. And I think all of us should look for ways to coalesce around that candidacy." He would change his mind if Biden changed his, Clyburn said.

"Is the best person the Democrats can put forward President Biden?"

"I believe he is as good as they get," Clyburn said. "Is he the only one? No, he's not the only one. And he is among the best that we can put forward. And I stand with him until he changes his mind, if he should change his mind. I think the record is very clear here. We have got great candidates out there."

JILL FUMED with resentment about all the Democrats who she considered friends now pushing Biden out. She knew she had blundered in the aftermath of the debate with her belittling praise. She was only trying to help her husband in his moment of need.

In the end, she told Biden: "This is your decision. This is for you to decide."

WHEN ANTHONY BERNAL and Annie Tomasini returned to the Bidens' Rehoboth house that morning, the president was ready to make the calls to announce his decision. There was nothing more to discuss.

The president had clearly made up his mind, they thought. This was what he was doing, and he was now focused on executing.

IN THE VICE PRESIDENT'S residence at the US Naval Observatory that morning, Kamala Harris was sitting down to do a puzzle with her grandnieces after a breakfast feast she'd made of pancakes and bacon.

The phone rang; it was her boss, the president. He told her he was going to suspend his campaign. He was dropping out.

"Are you sure?" she asked. "Are you sure you want to do this? Don't let them push you out, Joe."

"I'm doing it," he told her. "I feel like I have to do this." And then the president said: "I want you to do it. If you want to do it. Are you up for it, kid?"

"Yes," she said. "I'd be honored to."

Harris had been adamant in front of the cameras and behind the scenes: *He's the president. He's the nominee. We're all in with Joe.* Without seeking her permission, however, senior members of her team—including her chief of staff, Lorraine Voles, and her brother-in-law, Tony West—had been taking calls. Their message was clear: *We're all in with Joe, but if he should choose to make another decision, the vice president is ready to grab the baton.* Harris wouldn't have sanctioned it if they'd asked her. But the job of a vice president—and her staff—is to be prepared for the worst possible contingencies.

The president's team emailed over the statement he was about to issue. She and her team read it. There was no endorsement.

"The statement is great, Joe," she said. "But in order for my campaign to be on a footing to be successful, I was wondering—there's nothing in here about endorsing me."

"I am going to endorse you," Biden said. "I was thinking about endorsing you in a statement in the Oval Office that I'm going to make later this week."

Mike Donilon and Steve Ricchetti were on the phone, and they expressed reluctance to add anything to the statement. The president wanted it to stand on its own.

Harris wondered if that was wise. "That open airtime will be filled with speculation about why you're not endorsing your own vice president. It will cripple our ability to get off to a strong start."

Donilon and Ricchetti said they understood what she was saying. "Let's think this through," they told her. "We'll call you back."

Biden called back a few minutes later. The president would put out a separate statement endorsing Harris in the fifteen to twenty minutes after his first message went out.

Great, Harris and her team said. They prepared a statement in which she said that she would work hard to "earn" the nomination. Obviously, they didn't want any competition or any sort of challenge. The convention wasn't even a month away; there was no time for that.

THE REST of the vice president's team was instructed to get to the Naval Observatory at once and prepare for the moment when the president made his announcement.

Sitting with Harris were Voles, West, Campaign Chief of Staff Sheila Nix, Vice Presidential Communications Director Kirsten Allen, Campaign Communications Director Brian Fallon, and others.

The Second Gentleman was on the West Coast, having been stranded at a campaign stop in Las Vegas by the Delta Air Lines tech outage, after which he went to their home in Los Angeles. Harris and her team kept calling and calling him, but he didn't pick up his phone.

Biden posted his statement on X at 1:46 p.m. ET. The reaction was seismic. Then, at 2:13 p.m. ET, he followed up: "My fellow Democrats, I have decided not to accept the nomination and to focus all my energies on my duties as President for the remainder of my term. My very first decision as the party nominee in 2020 was to pick Kamala Harris as my Vice President. And it's been the best decision I've made. Today I want to offer my full support and endorsement for Kamala to be the nominee of our party this year. Democrats—it's time to come together and beat Trump. Let's do this."

Harris hit the phones. Her team had put together a call sheet. She would need to touch base with Bill and Hillary Clinton, Barack and Michelle Obama, Jim Clyburn, Nancy Pelosi, Chuck Schumer, and Hakeem Jeffries.

Clyburn was kind and enthusiastically supportive. The Clintons could not have been nicer or more effusive in their praise. They sent out their endorsement at 3:10 p.m.

Harris called her pastor, Amos Brown. She called Obama, who said he didn't want to put his finger on the scale, given the possibility of others running. He thought it important that this not look like a coronation. Obama hadn't endorsed during the primaries in 2016 or in 2020 either, wanting to remain neutral in case the party needed a unifying statesman at the end of a divisive contest. Obama also thought Harris would look stronger if there were some sort of process from which she emerged.

"Please call me," he told her. "I want to give you advice and counsel. I'm here."

Obama's statement went out at 3:44 p.m. He praised Biden and said he had "extraordinary confidence that the leaders of our party will be able to create a process from which an outstanding nominee emerges." He didn't mention Harris.

Some on the Harris team were annoyed, but they remembered that the only endorsement she really needed was that of the guy to whom thousands of Democratic delegates had pledged—Joe Biden. And he had already given it to her.

Harris raised the prospect that they call the other Democrats who might at that moment be contemplating running themselves. Phone each one, tell them she was running, tell them she intended to earn the nomination, and say she'd love to have their support. Put them on the spot.

They started with one of the most ambitious among the lot—the young governor of Pennsylvania, Josh Shapiro. For whatever reason, he was the one they viewed as most likely to throw his hat into the ring. But Shapiro was immediately on board. She called California Governor Gavin Newsom but didn't reach him. Michigan Governor Gretchen Whitmer was nice but demurred when it came to an endorsement; she needed a moment to digest it all.

They reached out and tried to talk to them all: Illinois's JB Pritzker, Kentucky's Andy Beshear, and Minnesota's Tim Walz, because he headed the Democratic Governors Association.

Clyburn endorsed at 4:22 p.m., Newsom at 7:34 p.m. Pete Buttigieg, who likely would have run if Biden hadn't, said at 7:41 p.m. that he would "do all that I can to help elect" her. By the end of the day, all the major would-be Democratic candidates were on board except Pritzker and Whitmer.

Pritzker made some calls to other possible candidates, just to feel it out. Was anyone going to challenge Harris? He certainly wasn't going to be the only one.

Nope, they told him, one after the other.

Pelosi told Harris she would endorse her the next day, and then she spent some time calling other potential candidates to inform them that people were lining up behind the vice president. Pritzker and Whitmer soon got in line too. Obama's camp told the Harris campaign that Barack was on board; they worked to coordinate and schedule a video endorsement by the end of the week that would be something of an event. By close of business Monday, Harris had locked up all the delegates, whom she'd been meeting and schmoozing with for years.

The shortest presidential primary in modern history was over.

SEVENTEEN

Joy

B arack Obama called David Plouffe.

After Biden's debate, Plouffe had been hoping for an immediate end to his candidacy and perhaps some nod to a mini primary system or an open convention. But Biden had held on for more than three weeks after that, making such ideas—however daunting or unrealistic—seemingly impossible. The Democratic Party appeared to know that, given how all the other plausible candidates had endorsed Kamala Harris within the twenty-four hours surrounding her announcement.

"She's probably going to call you," Obama told him.

"She" was the vice president. And she was going to call to ask him to temporarily end his embargo on working on campaigns to help her out. Harris was going to keep Biden's campaign chair, Jen O'Malley

Dillon, along with much of the Biden campaign infrastructure and staff. Frankly, there wasn't time to build a new campaign.

Plouffe didn't know her well, but he'd dealt with her through the years and liked her. He also thought that she'd been handed a terrible situation. Her prospects of winning, he felt, were remote. But they were at least not zero, so better than Biden's. He talked to his family. This was going to be a 107-day sprint to save the country from Trump. He would be gone from home for much of it.

When Harris called, Plouffe said yes. It was the only solid thing to do.

MIKE DONILON LEFT the campaign and returned to the White House. Bruce Reed had taken his old office, so he went to the second floor of the West Wing.

With new folks such as Plouffe coming on board, O'Malley Dillon convened a meeting of the Harris campaign team. During the Biden/Donilon era, all of the data was closely held. Now was a new day. Becca Siegel was sharing the campaign's internal information with everyone, including the previously iced-out pollsters: Garin, Murphy, Pollock, and Binder.

Everyone could now see where the race had stood when Biden dropped out.

It was gruesome.

They got the first look at the internal data on right track/wrong track, on Hispanic voters, on the split among men.

Plouffe, who had relocated to Wilmington, his hometown, had known it was bad, but it was worse than he'd anticipated. Biden was barreling toward a historic loss for the modern era. It would have been an electoral bloodbath. Not only was Biden on track to lose the Blue Wall states of Michigan, Pennsylvania, and Wisconsin, as well as the

Sun Belt battlegrounds of Arizona, Georgia, Nevada, and North Carolina, but he was in serious danger of losing New Hampshire, New Mexico, Maine, Minnesota, and Virginia.

Plouffe also suspected that those polls wouldn't have even been the low-water mark, because if one envisioned Biden continuing his candidacy, continuing to perform the way he had post-debate for the rest of the campaign, it would have gotten worse. He guessed that if Biden had kept at it, he would have fallen another three to four percentage points in the popular vote, ending at roughly 44 percent. The House would have fallen to the GOP by dozens of votes. Republicans would have wound up with maybe fifty-eight Senate seats.

But, frankly, they didn't have time to wallow in these ugly facts.

They had the Democratic convention kicking off on August 19—just four weeks away. Before that, Harris needed to pick a running mate. They had to start running TV ads.

The Biden campaign had refused to do any real polling on her beyond focus groups, so they were starting from scratch.

IN A SMALL WAY, the accelerated time frame was a gift. It made decision-making fast, and they couldn't sweat the small stuff. But those were the only positives.

What the Harris campaign was attempting was unprecedented in American politics and would be unfathomably difficult.

For instance, looking back to when then-Senator Obama officially launched his campaign for president in February 2007, Jake recalled him seeming annoyed and listless as he campaigned throughout that year. It took the candidate and the campaign until that fall to really get cooking and more than a year to work out all his policy positions, to air dirty laundry, and to distance himself from anyone unsavory—anyone or anything the campaign would rather not have to address in October 2008.

Then, of course, he had to introduce himself to the voters. Not just once but twice. Even after he emerged triumphant from the 2008 Democratic primaries and caucuses after a high-pitched battle with Senator Hillary Clinton that captured the attention of millions of Americans, he then had to do it all over again for the lower-information voters who hadn't been watching, who didn't know that he'd been a community organizer in Chicago or that he'd been partly raised in Hawaii by his white Kansan grandparents.

Harris had three months.

The good news was that in the weeks after she announced her presidential campaign, many straying Democratic voters returned to the fold and expressed increased enthusiasm for her candidacy. She brought the race to within striking distance.

There were headwinds. Anti-incumbent headwinds blowing ferociously all over the world, anti-Biden administration gusts that would have been tough for any Democrat to withstand, let alone Biden's vice president.

She had a solid run from the time of her announcement up through her one debate with Trump, which she handily won. She had limitations as a candidate, though. She had not spent the previous four years doing the reps, engaging in tough interviews, and mixing it up with voters who might be inclined to view a fancy San Franciscan skeptically. She never did the work of erasing the far-left positions she'd taken to win the nomination in 2020.

That said, though she was decidedly not fully prepared for this moment, she rose to meet it.

But.

From the beginning of her campaign in July to the August weeks of picking a running mate, presiding over the convention, rolling out wave after wave of ads, and on through September debate prep, it was clear that Biden was a liability. And it was never clear to the campaign what she could do, or was willing to do, about it.

Top strategists would discuss it with her, but beyond Harris's loyalty to Biden, there were questions about what she could say to appeal to those up-for-grab voters—Never Trump Republicans, independents, disaffected Democrats—without alienating the essential Democratic base.

She talked it all over with her top strategists, gaming it all out.

First off, the issue that she truly and most strongly disagreed with the president on behind closed doors was Israel's war against Hamas in Gaza. And that was too politically fraught to bring to the fore.

Should she have said that the Biden-Harris administration handled the post-pandemic stimulus wrong, pumping too much money into the economy and exacerbating inflation? That would have prompted a rash of questions about why she hadn't said anything at the time. It was a no-win.

As would have been an admission that the administration should have firmed up security at the border, an issue where she had some purchase, having been given the portfolio of pushing officials in Central American countries to do more to address the root causes of immigration. The next logical question would be: *Okay, at which meetings did you urge Secretary Mayorkas to send more agents?* Nope.

Could she have said that Biden never should have run for reelection? It was obvious that was the reality of the Democratic Party's circumstances, but what would it get her to say this now, especially given that she had vouched for his mental fitness after Hur's report dropped? It would make her look hypocritical, and it would alienate the president and his die-hard supporters.

"I don't want you to go any farther than you're comfortable," Plouffe said to her, "but at the very least, you need to say, 'Look, these are new ideas; these are different ideas. I look at the world a little differently than Joe Biden.'"

But she wouldn't go as far as her campaign team wanted her to go. It wasn't her nature.

"If I were to really distinguish myself, how would that make me look?" Harris asked.

She answered the question herself: "Disloyal."

Left unsaid were the added complications that pollsters couldn't even measure. She wouldn't just be a vice president perceived as disloyal to her president; she would be a woman vice president disloyal to a man president. A Black woman vice president disloyal to a white man president.

The campaign was trying to introduce her to the nation as a breath of fresh air, not a backstabber negotiating a minefield of gender and racial politics that the campaign couldn't even fathom.

Harris was truly appreciative of the opportunity Biden had given her. Moreover, she had a close personal relationship with, and great affection for, Joe.

No, she wouldn't do that.

On October 8, Harris went on *The View*.

"What do you think would be the biggest specific difference between your presidency and a Biden presidency?" Sunny Hostin asked.

"Well, we're obviously two different people," Harris said, "and I will bring those sensibilities to how I lead." She started talking about home health care, violence against women and children, small businesses.

"Well, if anything, would you have done something differently than President Biden during the past four years?" Hostin followed up.

"There is not a thing that comes to mind," Harris said, in perhaps the worst moment of her short campaign.

Most of the public thought that the country was on the wrong track, and she was presenting herself quite literally as "more of the same." She tried to recover, but it was too late: She'd just provided new footage for a brand-new Trump TV ad.

HARRIS HAD AN even tougher time acknowledging the reason why Biden wasn't the nominee anymore.

"You were a very staunch defender of President Biden's capacity to serve another four years right after the debate," said CNN's Dana Bash on August 29, during a joint interview with Harris and her vice presidential pick, Tim Walz. "You insisted that President Biden is extraordinarily strong. Given where we are now, do you have any regrets about what you told the American people?"

"No, not at all," Harris said. "I have spent hours upon hours with him, be it in the Oval Office or the Situation Room. He has the intelligence, the commitment, and the judgment and disposition that I think the American people rightly deserve in their president."

This was basically what she told her strategists behind the scenes as well. "The times I saw him were mainly in the Oval Office or the Situation Room, and there was never a moment in those situations where I worried about his ability to be president."

It could well have been an honest statement, given any vice president's relatively limited interaction with a president on a regular basis, given that Biden was certainly still able to lead meetings, and given that—certainly in those discrete situations requiring the vice president's presence—he could rise to the occasion, especially when it came to national security moments that the president cared so much about.

She wasn't saying that she'd never seen him as an old man, growing weaker and frailer. But even in private, she would maintain with friends and colleagues that he was always in command.

Harris, like so many others around Biden, saw the fundamentals of the presidency as being about making sound decisions, and there she thought him solid.

As for the energy needed to wage a competitive presidential campaign, or even Biden's ability to communicate his sound decisions, those closest to Biden, who graded him on a curve, saw these abilities, or lack thereof, as separate from his core capacity.

The other fundamental truth is that Vice President Harris didn't see the president on a day-to-day basis. But telling voters, "Look, as vice president, I'm not one of the president's closest advisers on a regular basis, and he doesn't really lean on me the way he does Mike"—well, that wouldn't cut it either.

In an interview with NBC, Harris was pressed by Hallie Jackson on whether she'd been honest about the matter, and she insisted she had been. "It was a bad debate," Harris said.

But, obviously, if that's all it had been, she wouldn't have been sitting in that very seat.

On September 11, after an event in New York City honoring victims of the 9/11 terrorist attacks, President Biden and Vice President Harris visited the Shanksville Volunteer Fire Department in Pennsylvania. Given a hat for Station 627, Biden offered his presidential baseball cap to an elderly man wearing a red TRUMP 2024 hat.

"You gonna autograph it?" the man asked.

"Sure, I'll autograph it," the president said.

"You remember your name?" the man asked.

"I don't remember my name," Biden said. "I'm slow."

"You're an old fart!" the man said.

"Yeah, I know, man," Biden said. "I'm an old guy."

"And you're an old fart, right?"

"I know you would know about that," Biden said playfully.

"About what?"

"About being old," Biden said.

"Oh, I know," the man said.

After Biden autographed the presidential baseball cap that he was gifting to the old guy, he told him, "I need that hat," referring to the TRUMP 2024 cap.

"You want my autograph?" the man asked.

"Hell no," Biden said.

Biden took the TRUMP 2024 cap, and someone in the crowd said, "Put it on!" Biden shot back, "I ain't going that far." But then he plopped it on his head, right atop the Station 627 hat.

The crowd clapped and the image of Biden wearing a TRUMP 2024 baseball cap went viral instantly.

"Thanks for the support, Joe!" wrote the Trump campaign on social media, with a photograph of Harris's boss wearing a hat that honored Harris's opponent. It was unimaginable that Harris would ever have done such a thing.

"What is he doing?" Harris asked her team. "This is completely un-helpful. And so unnecessary."

That would be, the Harris campaign decided, the last time she would do a public event with the president before the election.

But it was not the last time that Biden did something unhelpful.

On October 22, at the New Hampshire Democratic Coordinated Campaign Office in Concord, New Hampshire, Biden said that Trump "thinks he has a right under the Supreme Court ruling on immunity to be able, if need be—if he—if it was the case, to actually eliminate, physically eliminate—shoot, kill—someone who is—he believes to be a threat to him."

Biden said, "If I said this five years ago, you'd lock me up." The Democrats laughed.

"We got to lock him up," Biden said to applause. He realized that he had just given ammo to Republicans who were accusing the Biden Justice Department of carrying out the president's wishes to arrest Trump. "Politically lock him up," Biden said.

Harris, in general, tried to focus on how the campaign would respond. Others on the campaign adopted a gallows humor about it. What in the hell was Biden doing? You couldn't make it up.

Meanwhile, the White House passed along messages saying that the president had seen Clinton and Obama and others out on the campaign trail and wanted to be out there too. He didn't seem to understand what a liability he had become.

The worst of it came on Tuesday night, October 29, one week before the election.

The week had started out great for the Harris campaign. On Sunday night, the Trump campaign hosted a rally at Madison Square Garden. Among the many speakers was comedian Tony Hinchcliffe, who made crude jokes about Blacks, Jews, and Palestinians. But, most controversially, Hinchcliffe said, "There's literally a floating island of garbage in the middle of the ocean right now. I think it's called Puerto Rico."

Many Republicans immediately condemned the joke, and Trump himself became aggravated at the self-inflicted wound. Negative media coverage filled the airwaves, newspapers, and internet on Monday. The Trump campaign had already issued—uncharacteristically—a statement denouncing the joke. Senior Trump officials grew concerned. If this was going to be a margin-of-error race, there was no room for the campaign to be providing the error.

The nastiness was a perfect setup for Harris, who on Tuesday was scheduled to deliver a big speech on national unity.

Enter Joe Biden.

Relegated to Zoom calls, Biden spoke on a Voto Latino Get-Out-the-Vote call scheduled for less than an hour before Harris's speech and commented on the controversy. "Just the other day, a speaker at his rally called Puerto Rico 'a floating island of garbage.' Well, let me tell you something . . . I don't, I-I don't know the Puerto Rican that I know . . . or Puerto Rico where I'm—in my home state of Delaware—they're good, decent, honorable people. The only garbage I see floating out there is his supporters."

Leaning on staffers in the transcript office, as they had been doing all year, the White House Communications Office—not without some internal pushback—insisted that a possessive apostrophe was needed to understand what the president had said. The only garbage he saw was "his supporter's," the White House said. Hinchcliffe.

It was preposterous.

That evening, Trump cited the new controversy while speaking in Allentown, Pennsylvania. "That's terrible," Trump said. "Remember Hillary? She said 'deplorable.' And then she said 'irredeemable,' right? . . . That didn't work out. 'Garbage' I think is worse, right?" The next day, he appeared in a Trump-branded garbage truck in Wisconsin, donning an orange-and-yellow safety vest. "This is in honor of Kamala and Joe Biden," he told reporters with satisfaction.

"What are we going to do about this?" Harris asked her team. Biden had stepped all over her speech and saved Trump from a spiraling news cycle.

By the end of the campaign, she had helped the Democratic Party but her own candidacy was barely treading water. And the albatross that was Joe Biden kept getting heavier.

EIGHTEEN

Out the Door

At the farewell party for Anita Dunn, before the election, after praising the communications shop as the best team she'd ever worked with, Dunn took out some notes to educate some of the young staffers there on lessons learned.

Among them, ones gleaned from *The Godfather*, the Hollywood offering she believed crystallized how power is best wielded. She quoted Vito Corleone: "Revenge is a dish best served cold." And his son, Michael Corleone: "Never hate your enemies. It clouds your judgment." (Neither of those quotes appears in either *The Godfather* or *The Godfather Part II*. Vito in the novel says "Revenge is a dish that tastes best when it's cold," while the other quote is from *The Godfather Part III*.)

After *Politico* broke news of her speech, Dunn would say she was only trying to educate younger staffers who had never seen one of the best films ever made, not to mention give them advice on being patient and clear-minded during challenges.

But her quoting fictional mobsters about "revenge" and "enemies" after Biden was chased off the ticket struck some attendees as odd. Some found them revealing about Dunn's attitude toward anyone who got on her bad side while the White House asserted to the nation that the president was fine and totally up for four more years as president.

As THE BIDEN PRESIDENCY came to its close, the president continued to work, but it was clear he was resentful. On January 5, after signing labor union–backed legislation to expand the Social Security benefits of large numbers of teachers, firefighters, and other groups, Biden responded to a reporter's question about his age, saying, "My being the oldest president, I know more world leaders than any one of you ever met in your whole goddamn life!"

It was that kind of final chapter—a moment of accomplishment marred by a lashing out. Or by a reminder of Hunter Biden sleaze. A month earlier, on December 1, despite repeated public promises that he wouldn't, the president gave his son Hunter a full and unconditional pardon—not only for his tax and gun convictions but also for any crime he committed over an eleven-year period, from January 1, 2014, to December 1, 2024.

It came after the annual Biden family Thanksgiving retreat to Nantucket. On the Saturday of that weekend, Hunter's lawyer Abbe Lowell released a fifty-two-page report titled "The Political Prosecutions of Hunter Biden." In that report, Lowell falsely asserted that "Garland kept Trump-appointed U.S. Attorney David Weiss in place as U.S. Attorney specifically because there was an open investigation of Hunter in that office."

That was false. Garland wasn't confirmed as attorney general until March 10, 2021; the decision to keep Weiss on the job was President Biden's. Some at the DOJ wondered if Biden even remembered that he'd been the one who made that call.

"There is no disputing that Trump has said his enemies list includes Hunter," Lowell wrote. "With the election now decided, the threat against Hunter is real."

Biden's aides understood the fatherly impulse behind the pardon. The timing was not politically ideal, but they also understood why Biden didn't want his son to go through sentencing hearings in December.

What angered some Biden staffers, though, was that the president's explanation for the pardon echoed Trump's claims about political prosecutions. "The charges in his cases came about only after several of my political opponents in Congress instigated them to attack me and oppose my election," Biden said, adding that "raw politics has infected this process, and it led to a miscarriage of justice."

Once again Garland was tremendously disappointed, which became widely known throughout the department. Yes, Biden never crossed lines the way Trump did. But when push came to shove, an independent Justice Department is truly not what Biden wanted.

Special Counsel Weiss was upset as well. "I prosecuted the two cases against Mr. Biden because he broke the law," he wrote. "A unanimous jury—who found Mr. Biden guilty of gun charges—and Mr. Biden himself—who pleaded guilty to tax offenses—agreed. As I have done for twenty years, I applied the Principles of Federal Prosecution and determined that prosecution was warranted." He called the president's accusations "gratuitous and wrong."

"Other presidents have pardoned family members, but in doing so, none have taken the occasion as an opportunity to malign the public servants at the Department of Justice based solely on false accusations," Weiss wrote.

There were some in the White House who agreed. Many people worked for Biden because they believed he was committed to the judicial norms that Trump had broken. *Why didn't Biden focus solely on the pardon as a father?* they wondered. The pardon and Biden's behavior after the debate had some of the president's own aides making uncomfortable comparisons between Biden and Trump.

A Trump legal adviser soon commented to CNN legal correspondent Paula Reid that members of the Trump legal team felt the Hunter Biden pardon gave them a great deal of leeway on whether they could pardon and free from prison the hundreds of convicted January 6 insurrectionists.

THE PRESIDENT'S FRAILTIES became even more obvious on his last foreign trips, and aides became less concerned about hiding anything from the public. At a November appearance in the Amazon in Manaus, Brazil, he stuck strictly to the script in front of him for seven minutes' worth of remarks about the environment, taking no questions, turning then shuffling down a path that made it look as if he were disappearing into the jungle. In Angola in early December, at the arrival ceremony to greet Biden, Angolan President João Lourenço grabbed Biden's arm to help him maneuver a step. At the country's National Museum of Slavery, exhibits were brought out to Biden, presumably because the museum's stairs were potentially difficult for him to navigate.

Democrats and longtime Biden aides watched in disbelief. How did we ever think he could do this for another four years? How did he think he could? Several claimed they had experienced a version of Stockholm syndrome. Others blamed themselves. Many pointed fingers.

One person from Biden's orbit asked, "I feel anger at Jill. How do you not recognize that the person you live with is in decline?"

One former Biden campaign senior aide reflected that "there shouldn't be revisionist history—the entire party apparatus supported him running again. What pains many of us is wondering how anyone who was spending time with him could think he was capable of serving another four years. . . . It had to be obvious for quite a while that there was no chance he would be able to serve out a full term."

This official added: "It is scandalous in my mind that a small group of people who many of us like and respect allowed this to happen."

In January 2025, during one of his last interviews—and the first one of his presidency with a major US newspaper—Biden told *USA Today* that he thought he could have won. Mike Donilon was telling him that, Nancy Pelosi knew. Even as he prepared to leave the presidency, his closest advisers were still feeding him sugarcoated falsities. What made him think he could have won?

Naturally, the claim incensed Harris. The president apologized to her when he got word of her reaction, and in one of his last press availabilities, he tried to fix it by making the nonsensical claim that he—or Harris—either one could have beaten Trump.

In its last few minutes, the Biden administration revealed that Biden had preemptively pardoned his brothers, Jimmy and Frank; his sister, Valerie Biden Owens; and two of their spouses. He said he'd done it not because they had committed any crimes but because he feared that Trump would weaponize the Justice Department to prosecute his political enemies. Jimmy Biden's business activities, however, had come under investigative scrutiny.

To many Democrats, this was another ignominious act by a president who repeatedly put the interests of his family ahead of those of his party and the country.

Hours later—despite Trump advisers claiming that the new president was going to engage in a careful review process and consider clemency for January 6ers on a case-by-case basis—Trump went and offered a "full, complete and unconditional pardon" to approximately 1,250 people who had committed January 6–related crimes. Most of them had pleaded guilty, many had assaulted law enforcement.

After Trump's inauguration, Biden headed out to Santa Ynez, in California, and Bernal and Tomasini became the co-chiefs of staff for Biden's post-presidency transition. They said it was not just Biden's transition office, but Biden and Jill's transition office. Biden aides couldn't help but notice that many of Biden's post-presidential aides had worked for the First Lady.

They were already having some trouble with the presidential library. Some donors didn't want to give money.

The inner circle had shrunk to its last handful of believers.

NINETEEN

Conclusions

I n 1994, long after President Richard Nixon fired him as special prosecutor, emeritus Harvard law professor Archibald Cox was asked what lessons Americans should take from the Watergate scandal.

Cox wrote that "we should be reminded of the corrupt influence of great power, especially when the power is in the hands of someone who is willing to resort to any tactics, however wrong, to retain and increase his power. Perhaps it is inescapable that modern government vests extraordinary power in the President and puts around him a large circle of men and women whose personal status and satisfaction depends entirely upon pleasing that one man."

Joe Biden is not Richard Nixon, and the hiding and cover-up of his deterioration is not Watergate.

It is an entirely separate scandal.

America's Founding Fathers left many of the messy inner workings of the government to be determined. After the first president to die in office, William Henry Harrison, did so in 1841, Vice President John Tyler insisted that a judge administer the oath of office that would make him president, but it wasn't as if he had an instruction manual to follow. The so-called Tyler Precedent was then followed for other presidential death scenarios, but after the assassination of President John F. Kennedy, Congress pushed to establish an official process. That led to the Twenty-Fifth Amendment to the Constitution, which not only officially established a path of succession but also detailed the process for the vice president to serve as acting president when the president is unable to do so.

What if a president is unable to discharge their duties but doesn't recognize that fact? The Twenty-Fifth Amendment also provides an opportunity for the vice president and a majority of the cabinet to send a written declaration stating as much to the president pro tempore of the Senate and the Speaker of the House, paving the way for the VP to take charge. Such a move would require an inordinate amount of courage by politicians.

Few of Biden's critics within these pages, even those who only spoke to us on background or anonymously, would assert that the president was always unable to discharge his duties. And it is possible that many of his supporters genuinely believed that he was fit to run again. In an exchange with Donilon after the completion of this book he told us that he believed, then and now, that Biden was not only fully capable but would make the best president, that his experience and judgment were better than anyone's, and that the concerns about his age paled in comparison to the threat Donald Trump posed to America. It seems eminently likely that Ricchetti and other senior Biden aides felt the same; that they were lying to themselves more than knowingly deceiving the American public. The truth is more complicated than Biden consistently being unable to function as president. He had moments of incoherence, of a stark inability to communicate or recognize people or recall important facts. Yet those same critics continued to the end to attest to his ability to make sound decisions, if on his own schedule. There's no way that description reflects optimal presidential capacity, but the Constitution isn't necessarily about optimal requirements. It's about minimum requirements. The US Constitution does not require politicians to be self-aware, or brave, or selfless.

Dr. Jonathan Reiner—an internist and cardiologist at George Washington University Hospital who has served as a White House Medical Unit consultant for the last four administrations—has strong feelings on the matter.

"While we don't have a confirmed diagnosis, it's apparent that Biden has had a steep cognitive and, I also think, physical decline," Reiner tells us. "One thing bears mentioning: There actually may not be an established existing diagnosis. The president and his team physician, caring for a unique patient like the president, may have declined to do the kind of cognitive testing and imaging that could have established a formal diagnosis. That way, there wouldn't be data to be reported. If there's no diagnosis, there's nothing to disclose. Personally, I don't agree with this. The public should be informed of the whole truth. Not selective truth."

One of the nation's top cognitive neurologists tells us that he and many of his colleagues spent much of 2024 wondering what that truth was. Before the debate, he had been texting with specialist colleagues, all of them speculating about the president's condition.

"It was the consistency of the problems that we'd been seeing on public videos" that caused the alarm, he said, talking to us on background because he's never examined the president. "We were all pretty worried that we might be seeing the tip of the iceberg of a neurodegenerative or brain vascular disease manifesting itself."

Then came the debate, and "it was like, 'We're done here'—this looked like clear evidence of some kind of brain disorder, impeding his ability to carry forward with his train of thought."

They were all devastated when they saw the debate, he said. He couldn't diagnose it—they all had different theories, whether early Lewy body dementia or Alzheimer's or a combination or something else. Whatever it is, the neurologists said, sooner or later it would declare itself conclusively.

Some doctors still maintain that diagnosing the president from a distance is irresponsible. But the president's doctors are up close. Reiner feels strongly that "the White House has a responsibility to the public to tell the whole truth about the health of the president. Without that, there can be no trust. Omitting a material diagnosis (such as cognitive impairment or frank dementia) violates that responsibility."

So what do we as a country do to ensure that this will never happen again?

Congress could legally require the president's physician to certify to Congress that the commander in chief is physically and cognitively fit to serve. "Currently, the yearly letter from the president's doctor is basically a tradition," Reiner says, adding that some White House physicians have provided very detailed presidential health summaries for the public, while others, such as those in the first Trump administration, "provide very little granular detail."

As of now, Reiner notes, the information released to the public is only the data that the White House permits to be made public. "But a law could require the president's doctor to provide a fulsome report, potentially at the penalty of perjury."

Without that enshrined into law, no president can be counted on to be fully open.

"If you're elected, you would be the oldest president ever," Jake told Biden in September 2020. "The American people have been lied to before by presidents about the president's health—FDR, JFK, Ronald Reagan. We don't know, still, what happened with Donald Trump and his visit to Walter Reed last year. Will you pledge that, if you're elected, you will be transparent about your health—"

"Yes," Biden said.

"—all facets of your health, with urgency, so that we know—"

"Yes, when it occurs, when anything occurs. And anything can happen. Anything can happen. . . . I have become a great respecter of fate, a great respecter of fate. I have seen too much of it in my family related to accidents alone. And so I guarantee you, I guarantee you, I will be totally transparent in terms of my health and all aspects of my health."

He was not.

SOURCES AND ACKNOWLEDGMENTS

We could not have written this book without the steadfast support of Scott Moyers, president and publisher of Penguin Press, and our representatives, Matt Latimer of Javelin and Sloan Harris at CAA. Thank you to Matt Klam, Geoff Shandler, and Fergus McIntosh for your wise suggestions. We also need to thank our supportive bosses. At *Axios*, special thanks go to Jim VandeHei, Mike Allen, Aja Whitaker-Moore, and David Lindsey. And at CNN, sincere thanks go to David Zaslav, Sir Mark Thompson, Virginia Moseley, Eric Sherling, Amy Entelis, David Leavy, David Chalian, and Abigail Crutchfield.

This book is rooted in Jake's decades of covering Joe Biden, from senator to vice president to president, and draws from countless interviews with him over the years. It also relies heavily on Alex's intense four years covering the Biden presidency and reelection campaign. Most especially, since the November 2024 election, it has been built on our interviews with approximately two hundred people who have first-hand knowledge of the events, including top officials from the Biden White House and administration; leaders of the House and Senate and their members; and donors, activists, and others who were there.

The topic of the president's decline and attempts to hide it remains an extremely sensitive one, so even now, you will notice that some of those closest to the president preferred to share their most candid thoughts without their names attached. As a general rule, our reporting of events relies on eyewitnesses or participants in those events, with a small number of exceptions.

Most of the reporting in our book is original, conducted after the November 2024 election ended. We want to thank everyone who talked to us. Some exemplary journalists have covered parts of this story before us: The infrastructure versus Build Back Better debate is laid out by Jonathan Martin and Alexander Burns in *This Will Not Pass*. The post-2022 press conference scene was first reported by Katie Rogers in *American Woman*. Secretary Antony Blinken's July 2024 lunch conversation with the president is discussed by Bob Woodward in *War*. Congressional machinations are explored by Annie Karni and Luke Broadwater in *Mad House*. The Biden family dynamics are elaborated by Ben Schreckinger in *The Bidens*. And Biden's view of Kamala Harris is detailed by Chris Whipple in *The Fight of His Life*.

Memoirs by Joe Biden and his family provided valuable firsthand points of view. These included Biden's *Promises to Keep* and *Promise Me, Dad*; Hunter Biden's *Beautiful Things*; Kathleen Buhle's *If We Break*; Valerie Biden Owens's *Growing Up Biden*; and Jill Biden's *Where the Light Enters*.

In these pages, we also refer to and use information from:

- Adam Entous. "The Untold History of the Biden Family." *New Yorker*, August 15, 2022.

- Alex Thompson and Tina Sfondeles. "Biden Proves the Haters Wrong." *Politico*, November 15, 2021.

- Alzheimer's Association. "New Alzheimer's Association Report Shows Significant Disconnect Between Seniors, Physicians When It Comes to Cognitive Assessment." March 4, 2019.

- Annie Linskey and Siobhan Hughes. "Behind Closed Doors, Biden Shows Signs of Slipping." *Wall Street Journal*, June 4, 2024.

- Arlette Saenz and Elizabeth Stuart. "Jill Biden Says the Idea of a Competency Test for Elderly Politicians Is 'Ridiculous.'" *CNN Politics*, March 5, 2023.

- Ben Schreckinger. "Guns, Lies and Audiotape: How Biden's Family Ties Could Lead to Another Pardon." *Politico*, December 8, 2024.

- Carla Marinucci. "California Democrats Lead Attack over Trump's Mental Health." *Politico*, August 23, 2017.

- Carlos Lozada. "Is Trump Mentally Ill? Or Is America? Psychiatrists Weigh In." *Washington Post*, September 22, 2017.

- Clara Bingham. *Women on the Hill: Challenging the Culture of Congress.* Times Books, 1997.

- Cleveland Clinic. "Cognitive Test." Last reviewed January 14, 2025.

- Cris Barrish and Jonathan Starkey. "Questions Remain About Beau Biden's Health." *News Journal*, February 21, 2014.

- Edward-Isaac Dovere and Phil Mattingly. "Biden's Age Is a Hot Topic as He Looks to Extend His Time in the Oval Office Until He Is 86." *CNN Politics*, February 16, 2023.

- Esteban Parra. "Former President Barack Obama Surprises Attendees at a Beau Biden Foundation Fundraiser." *News Journal*, September 25, 2017.

- Ezra Klein. "Democrats Have a Better Option than Biden." *New York Times*, February 16, 2024.

- George Washington to James McHenry, July 3, 1789. In *The Papers of George Washington: Presidential Series*. Vol. 3, *June 1789– September 1789*, edited by Dorothy Twohig. University Press of Virginia, 1989.

- Jane Mayer. "Dianne Feinstein's Missteps Raise a Painful Age Question Among Senate Democrats." *New Yorker*, December 9, 2020.

- Jenna Johnson and Lenny Bernstein. "Trump Did Exceedingly Well on a Cognitive Test, Top White House Doctor Says." *Washington Post*, January 16, 2018.

- John Hendrickson. "What Joe Biden Can't Bring Himself to Say." *The Atlantic*, January/February 2020.

- Jonathan Starkey. "Biden Remains Mum on Health." *News Journal*, November 21, 2013.

- Jonathan Swan, Charlie Savage, and Maggie Haberman. "The Radical Strategy Behind Trump's Promise to 'Go After' Biden." *New York Times*, June 15, 2023.

- Josh Gerstein. "One of Hunter Biden's Jurors Says His Defense Team Made Mistakes." *Politico*, June 11, 2024.

- Kevin Sack. "Thurmond's Robust Legend Shields Him at 93." *New York Times*, October 24, 1996.

- Maureen Dowd. "Hey, Joe, Don't Give It a Go." *New York Times*, August 6, 2022.

- NIH National Institute on Aging. "Assessing Cognitive Impairment in Older Patients." Last reviewed April 16, 2023.

- Peter Baker, Michael D. Shear, Katie Rogers, and Zolan Kanno-Youngs. "Inside the Complicated Reality of Being America's Oldest President." *New York Times*, June 4, 2023.

- Phil McCausland. "Biden Calls Xi a 'Dictator,' Fueling Chinese Anger." *NBC News*, June 20, 2023.

- Rebecca Boggs Roberts. "How Edith Wilson Kept Herself—and Her Husband—in the White House." *Smithsonian*, March 7, 2023.

- Robert Dallek. "The Medical Ordeals of JFK." *Atlantic*, December 2002.

- Ryan Lizza. "Biden Signals to Aides That He Would Serve Only a Single Term." *Politico*, December 11, 2019.

- Sharon Begley. "Trump Wasn't Always So Linguistically Challenged. What Could Explain the Change?" *STAT News*, May 23, 2017.

- Stanford Health Care. "Cognitive and Neuropsychological Tests." Accessed February 9, 2025.

- Steve Holland. "Biden, McConnell Kentucky Event Is a Roadmap for White House Under New Congress." Reuters, January 4, 2023.

- Steve Peoples. "Despite Risks, Trump Invests Big in Attacks on Biden's Age." Associated Press, July 8, 2020.

- The Las Vegas police radio recordings came from a FOIA request made by Judicial Watch, published October 2024.

INDEX